6. Enter your class ID code to join a class.

IF YOU HAVE A CLASS CODE FROM YOUR TEACHER

a. Enter your class code and click Next

b. Once you have joined a class, you will be able to use the Discussion Board and Email tools.

c. To enter this code later, choose **Join a Class**.

IF YOU DO NOT HAVE A CLASS CODE

a. If you do not have a class ID code, click Skip

b. You do not need a class ID code to use *iQ Online*.

c. To enter this code later, choose **Join a Class**.

7. Review registration information and click Log In. Then choose your book. Click **Activities** to begin using *iQ Online*.

IMPORTANT

- After you register, the next time you want to use *iQ Online*, go to www.iQOnlinePractice.com and log in with your email address and password.
- The online content can be used for 12 months from the date you register.
- For help, please contact customer service: eltsupport@oup.com.

WHAT IS iQ ONLINE ?

All new activities provide essential skills **practice** and support.

Vocabulary and Grammar **games** immerse you in the language and provide even more practice.

Authentic, engaging **videos** generate new ideas and opinions on the Unit Question.

Go to the Media Center to download or stream all **student book audio**.

Use the **Discussion Board** to discuss the Unit Question and more.

Email encourages communication with your teacher and classmates.

Automatic grading gives immediate feedback and tracks progress.

Progress Reports show what you have mastered and where you still need more practice.

OXFORD
UNIVERSITY PRESS

198 Madison Avenue
New York, NY 10016 USA

Great Clarendon Street, Oxford, OX2 6DP, United Kingdom

Oxford University Press is a department of the University of Oxford.
It furthers the University's objective of excellence in research, scholarship,
and education by publishing worldwide. Oxford is a registered trade
mark of Oxford University Press in the UK and in certain other countries

Adult Content Director: Stephanie Karras
Publisher: Sharon Sargent
Managing Editor: Mariel DeKranis
Development Editor: Eric Zuarino
Head of Digital, Design, and Production: Bridget O'Lavin
Executive Art and Design Manager: Maj-Britt Hagsted
Design Project Manager: Debbie Lofaso
Content Production Manager: Julie Armstrong
Image Manager: Trisha Masterson
Image Editor: Liaht Ziskind
Production Coordinator: Brad Tucker

ISBN: 978 0 19 481926 8 Student Book 4 with iQ Online pack
ISBN: 978 0 19 481927 5 Student Book 4 as pack component
ISBN: 978 0 19 481802 5 iQ Online student website

Printed in China
This book is printed on paper from certified and well-managed sources.

ACKNOWLEDGEMENTS

*The authors and publisher are grateful to those who have given permission to
reproduce the following extracts and adaptations of copyright material:*
p. 13 Adaptation of "Search for 100 Real-Life Heroes" by Kate Hodal and
Tom Phillips, from *The Guardian*, December 23, 2011, http://www.
theguardian.com/world/2011/dec/23/100-real-heroes-search-tithiya-sharma.
Copyright Guardian News and Media Ltd 2011. Used by permission;
p. 36 From "So Much Dead Space" by Paco Underhill, *Conference Board Review*,
September/October 2006, Vol. 44, Issue 5. Used by permission of Paco
Underhill, www.pacounderhill.com; p. 73 Excerpt(s) from *Bird by Bird: Some
Instructions on Writing and Life* by Anne Lamott, copyright © 1994 by Anne
Lamott. Used by permission of Pantheon Books, an imprint of the Knopf
Doubleday Publishing Group, a division of Random House, LLC, and by
The Wylie Agency LLC. All rights reserved; p. 134 Reprinted from "Anatomy
of a Nutrition Trend," *Food Insight*, March/April 2002. Copyright © 2002
International Food Information Council Foundation. Used by permission
from the International Food Information Council Foundation;
p. 163 From "Making My First Post-College Decision," by Devin Reams, *Ready
or Not, Here Comes Life*, http://www.employeeevolution.com. Used by
permission of Devin Reams; p. 186 From "A tribe is discovered in a clearing
of the Brazilian rainforest: should we leave them alone or prepare them for

the 21st century" by Jeremy Watson, from *The Scotsman*, June 1, 2008,
Sunday edition, News.Scotsman.com. Copyright © The Scotsman
Publications Ltd. Used by permission; p. 194 "Is Alaska's Pebble Mine the
Next Keystone XL?" by Svati Kirsten Narula, from *The Atlantic*. Copyright
2014 The Atlantic Media Co. as published in *The Atlantic Magazine*, March 14,
2014. All rights reserved. Distributed by Tribune Content Agency, LLC.
Reprinted by permission; p. 214 "The Promise of Play" from *Play* by Stuart
Brown, with Christopher Vaughan, copyright © 2009 by Stuart Brown. Used
by permission of Avery Publishing, an imprint of Penguin Group (USA) LLC.

Illustrations by: p. 34 Stuart Bradford; p. 64 Stacy Merlin; p. 73 Barb Bastian;
p. 94 Stuart Bradford; p. 124 Stacy Merlin; p. 154 Stacy Merlin; p. 184 Stacy
Merlin; p. 194 5W Infographics; p. 212 Stacy Merlin.

*We would also like to thank the following for permission to reproduce the following
photographs:* Cover: Yongyut Kumsri/Shutterstock; Video Vocabulary (used
throughout the book): Oleksiy Mark/Shutterstock; p. 2 HO/Reuters/Corbis;
p. 3 William Whitehurst/Corbis, Adrian Sherratt/Alamy; p. 7 Blend Images/
Alamy (woodworking), Tetra Images/Alamy (injured child); p. 13 Duravitski/
Alamy; p. 14 Sonja Kruse The Ubuntu Girl; p. 33 Bizroug/Shutterstock;
p. 35 Satish Kaushik/The India Today Group/Getty Images; p. 36 imagebroker/
Alamy; p. 43 Stagedhomes.com/Staged Homes (all); p. 51 imageBROKER/
Superstock Ltd.; p. 53 Koksharov Dmitry/Shutterstock; p. 58 Image Source/
Alamy; p. 63 KidStock/Getty Images; p. 66 BananaStock/Thinkstock;
p. 72 Robert Manella/Getty Images; p. 83 beasty/Shutterstock; p. 88 Chris
Pancewicz/Alamy; p. 93 Kurita KAKU/Gamma-Rapho via Getty Images;
p. 96 allOver images/Alamy; p. 97 Ermolaev Alexander/Shutterstock;
pp. 103, 104 Marco Secchi/Alamy; p. 112 doglikehorse/Shutterstock;
p. 115 David Sacks/Getty Images; p. 122 View Stock/Getty Images; p. 123 Tim
Gainey/Alamy, 237/Adam Gault/Ocean/Corbis; p. 124 ajafoto/iStockphoto
(chocolate), Stockbyte/Oxford University Press (tomato), Ingram/Oxford
University Press (carrot); p. 126 Lou Veltri/Alamy; p. 127 Paula Solloway/
Alamy; p. 132 Chris Schmauch/Alamy; p. 136 Rudchenko Liliia/Shutterstock;
p. 141 Mikael Karlsson/Alamy; p. 144 Amy Walters/Shutterstock; p. 153
Patrick Forget/AGE Fotostock; p. 154 Izabela Habur/Getty Images (students),
gulfimages/Alamy (businessmen); p. 156 Tom Wang/Shutterstock; p. 163
Serp/Shutterstock; p. 169 Super RF/Alamy (hands), avatra images/Alamy
(board); p. 176 racorn/Shutterstock; p. 182 Richard Herrmann/Minden
Pictures/Newscom; p. 183 Triff/Shutterstock, Ilan Amihai/Alamy, Paul
Biddle/Science Photo Library; p. 184 Doug Allan/Science Photo Library
(iceberg), Andreas Meyer/Shutterstock (space station), Stocktrek Images/
Getty Images (remains), Ocean Image Photography/Shutterstock
(shipwreck); p. 186 Johnny Lye/Shutterstock; p. 188 David J Slater/Alamy;
p. 195 Alaska Stock/Alamy; p. 200 Image Source/Alamy; p. 202 Jeff Rotman/
Getty Images; p. 210 Ernest Doroszuk/ZUMA Press/Newscom, Pakawat
Suwannaket/Shutterstock; p. 211 Blend Images - JGI/Jamie Grill/Getty
Images, David Allan Brandt/Getty Images; p. 212 Juanmonino/iStockphoto
(tennis), Rido/Shutterstock (business clothes); p. 213 Frida Azari/Stuart
Brown MD; p. 214 Hero Images/Corbis UK Ltd.; p. 221 Studio Grand Ouest/
Shutterstock; p. 223 Digital Vision./Getty Images; p. 229 2014
ChinaFotoPress/Getty Images; p. 234 Martin Siepmann/Getty Images; Back
Cover: mozcann/istockphoto.

SHAPING learning TOGETHER

We would like to acknowledge the teachers from all over the world who participated in the development process and review of the Q series.

Special thanks to our _Q: Skills for Success_ Second Edition Topic Advisory Board

Shaker Ali Al-Mohammad, Buraimi University College, Oman; **Dr. Asmaa A. Ebrahim**, University of Sharjah, U.A.E.; **Rachel Batchilder**, College of the North Atlantic, Qatar; **Anil Bayir**, Izmir University, Turkey; **Flora Mcvay Bozkurt**, Maltepe University, Turkey; **Paul Bradley**, University of the Thai Chamber of Commerce Bangkok, Thailand; **Joan Birrell-Bertrand**, University of Manitoba, MB, Canada; **Karen E. Caldwell**, Zayed University, U.A.E.; **Nicole Hammond Carrasquel**, University of Central Florida, FL, U.S.; **Kevin Countryman**, Seneca College of Applied Arts & Technology, ON, Canada; **Julie Crocker**, Arcadia University, NS, Canada; **Marc L. Cummings**, Jefferson Community and Technical College, KY, U.S.; **Rachel DeSanto**, Hillsborough Community College Dale Mabry Campus, FL, U.S.; **Nilüfer Ertürkmen**, Ege University, Turkey; **Sue Fine**, Ras Al Khaimah Women's College (HCT), U.A.E.; **Amina Al Hashami**, Nizwa College of Applied Sciences, Oman; **Stephan Johnson**, Nagoya Shoka Daigaku, Japan; **Sean Kim**, Avalon, South Korea; **Gregory King**, Chubu Daigaku, Japan; **Seran Küçük**, Maltepe University, Turkey; **Jonee De Leon**, VUS, Vietnam; **Carol Lowther**, Palomar College, CA, U.S.; **Erin Harris-MacLead**, St. Mary's University, NS, Canada; **Angela Nagy**, Maltepe University, Turkey; **Huynh Thi Ai Nguyen**, Vietnam; **Daniel L. Paller**, Kinjo Gakuin University, Japan; **Jangyo Parsons**, Kookmin University, South Korea; **Laila Al Qadhi**, Kuwait University, Kuwait; **Josh Rosenberger**, English Language Institute University of Montana, MT, U.S.; **Nancy Schoenfeld**, Kuwait University, Kuwait; **Jenay Seymour**, Hongik University, South Korea; **Moon-young Son**, South Korea; **Matthew Taylor**, Kinjo Gakuin Daigaku, Japan; **Burcu Tezcan-Unal**, Zayed University, U.A.E.; **Troy Tucker**, Edison State College-Lee Campus, FL, U.S.; **Kris Vicca**, Feng Chia University, Taichung; **Jisook Woo**, Incheon University, South Korea; **Dunya Yenidunya**, Ege University, Turkey

UNITED STATES **Marcarena Aguilar**, North Harris College, TX; **Rebecca Andrade**, California State University North Ridge, CA; **Lesley Andrews**, Boston University, MA; **Deborah Anholt**, Lewis and Clark College, OR; **Robert Anzelde**, Oakton Community College, IL; **Arlys Arnold**, University of Minnesota, MN; **Marcia Arthur**, Renton Technical College, WA; **Renee Ashmeade**, Passaic County Community College, NJ; **Anne Bachmann**, Clackamas Community College, OR; **Lida Baker**, UCLA, CA; **Ron Balsamo**, Santa Rosa Junior College, CA; **Lori Barkley**, Portland State University, OR; **Eileen Barlow**, SUNY Albany, NY; **Sue Bartch**, Cuyahoga Community College, OH; **Lora Bates**, Oakton High School, VA; **Barbara Batra**, Nassau County Community College, NY; **Nancy Baum**, University of Texas at Arlington, TX; **Rebecca Beck**, Irvine Valley College, CA; **Linda Berendsen**, Oakton Community College, IL; **Jennifer Binckes Lee**, Howard Community College, MD; **Grace Bishop**, Houston Community College, TX; **Jean W. Bodman**, Union County College, NJ; **Virginia Bouchard**, George Mason University, VA; **Kimberley Briesch Sumner**, University of Southern California, CA; **Kevin Brown**, University of California, Irvine, CA; **Laura Brown**, Glendale Community College, CA; **Britta Burton**, Mission College, CA; **Allison L. Callahan**, Harold Washington College, IL; **Gabriela Cambiasso**, Harold Washington College, IL; **Jackie Campbell**, Capistrano Unified School District, CA; **Adele C. Camus**, George Mason University, VA; **Laura Chason**, Savannah College, GA; **Kerry Linder Catana**, Language Studies International, NY; **An Cheng**, Oklahoma State University, OK; **Carole Collins**, North Hampton Community College, PA; **Betty R. Compton**, Intercultural Communications College, HI; **Pamela Couch**, Boston University, MA; **Fernanda Crowe**, Intrax International Institute, CA; **Vicki Curtis**, Santa Cruz, CA; **Margo Czinski**, Washtenaw Community College, MI; **David Dahnke**, Lone Star College, TX; **Gillian M. Dale**, CA; **L. Dalgish**, Concordia College, MN; **Christopher Davis**, John Jay College, NY; **Sherry Davis**, Irvine University, CA; **Natalia de Cuba**, Nassau County Community College, NY; **Sonia Delgadillo**, Sierra College, CA; **Esmeralda Diriye**, Cypress College & Cal Poly, CA; **Marta O. Dmytrenko-Ahrabian**, Wayne State University, MI; **Javier Dominguez**, Central High School, SC; **Jo Ellen Downey-Greer**, Lansing Community College, MI; **Jennifer Duclos**, Boston University, MA; **Yvonne Duncan**, City College of San Francisco, CA; **Paul Dydman**, USC Language Academy, CA; **Anna Eddy**, University of Michigan-Flint, MI; **Zohan El-Gamal**, Glendale Community College, CA; **Jennie Farnell**, University of Connecticut, CT; **Susan Fedors**, Howard Community College, MD; **Valerie Fiechter**, Mission College, CA; **Ashley Fifer**, Nassau County Community College, NY; **Matthew Florence**, Intrax International Institute, CA; **Kathleen Flynn**, Glendale College, CA; **Elizabeth Fonsea**, Nassau County Community College, NY; **Eve Fonseca**, St. Louis Community College, MO; **Elizabeth Foss**, Washtenaw Community College, MI; **Duff C. Galda**, Pima Community College, AZ; **Christiane Galvani**, Houston Community College, TX; **Gretchen Gerber**, Howard Community College, MD; **Ray Gonzalez**, Montgomery College, MD; **Janet Goodwin**, University of California, Los Angeles, CA; **Alyona Gorokhova**, Grossmont College, CA; **John Graney**, Santa Fe College, FL; **Kathleen Green**, Central High School, AZ; **Nancy Hamadou**, Pima Community College-West Campus, AZ; **Webb Hamilton**, De Anza College, San Jose City College, CA; **Janet Harclerode**, Santa Monica Community College, CA; **Sandra Hartmann**, Language and Culture Center, TX; **Kathy Haven**, Mission College, CA; **Roberta Hendrick**, Cuyahoga Community College, OH; **Ginny Heringer**, Pasadena City College, CA; **Adam Henricksen**, University of Maryland, MD; **Carolyn Ho**, Lone Star College-CyFair, TX; **Peter Hoffman**, LaGuardia Community College, NY; **Linda Holden**, College of Lake County, IL; **Jana Holt**, Lake Washington Technical College, WA; **Antonio Iccarino**, Boston University, MA; **Gail Ibele**, University of Wisconsin, WI; **Nina Ito**, American Language Institute, CSU Long Beach, CA; **Linda Jensen**, UCLA, CA; **Lisa Jurkowitz**, Pima Community College, CA; **Mandy Kama**, Georgetown University, Washington, DC; **Stephanie Kasuboski**, Cuyahoga Community College, OH; **Chigusa Katoku**, Mission College, CA; **Sandra Kawamura**, Sacramento City College, CA; **Gail Kellersberger**, University of Houston-Downtown, TX; **Jane Kelly**, Durham Technical Community College, NC; **Maryanne Kildare**, Nassau County Community College, NY; **Julie Park Kim**, George Mason University, VA; **Kindra Kinyon**, Los Angeles Trade-Technical College, CA; **Matt Kline**, El Camino College, CA; **Lisa Kovacs-Morgan**, University of California, San Diego, CA; **Claudia Kupiec**, DePaul University, IL; **Renee La Rue**, Lone Star College-Montgomery, TX; **Janet Langon**, Glendale College, CA; **Lawrence Lawson**, Palomar College, CA; **Rachele Lawton**, The Community College of Baltimore County, MD; **Alice Lee**, Richland College, TX; **Esther S. Lee**, CSUF & Mt. SAC, CA; **Cherie Lenz-Hackett**, University of Washington, WA; **Joy Leventhal**, Cuyahoga Community College, OH; **Alice Lin**, UCI Extension, CA; **Monica Lopez**, Cerritos College, CA; **Dustin Lovell**, FLS International Marymount College, CA; **Carol Lowther**, Palomar College, CA; **Candace Lynch-Thompson**, North Orange County Community College District, CA; **Thi Thi Ma**, City College of San Francisco, CA; **Steve Mac Isaac**, USC Long Academy, CA; **Denise Maduli-Williams**, City College of San Francisco, CA; **Eileen Mahoney**, Camelback High School, AZ; **Naomi Mardock**, MCC-Omaha, NE; **Brigitte Maronde**, Harold Washington College, IL; **Marilyn Marquis**, Laposita College CA; **Doris Martin**, Glendale Community College; Pasadena City College, CA; **Keith Maurice**, University of Texas at Arlington, TX; **Nancy Mayer**, University of Missouri-St. Louis, MO; **Aziah McNamara**, Kansas State University, KS; **Billie McQuillan**, Education Heights, MN; **Karen Merritt**, Glendale Union High School District, AZ; **Holly Milkowart**, Johnson County Community College, KS; **Eric Moyer**, Intrax International Institute, CA; **Gino Muzzatti**, Santa Rosa Junior College, CA; **Sandra Navarro**, Glendale Community College, CA; **Than Nyeinkhin**, ELAC, PCC, CA; **William Nedrow**, Triton College, IL; **Eric Nelson**, University of Minnesota, MN; **Than Nyeinkhin**, ELAC, PCC, CA; **Fernanda Ortiz**, Center for English as a Second Language at the University of Arizona, AZ; **Rhony Ory**, Ygnacio Valley High School, CA; **Paul Parent**, Montgomery College, MD; **Dr. Sumeeta Patnaik**, Marshall University, WV; **Oscar Pedroso**, Miami Dade College, FL; **Robin Persiani**, Sierra College, CA; **Patricia Prenz-Belkin**, Hostos Community College, NY; **Suzanne Powell**, University of Louisville, KY; **Jim Ranalli**, Iowa State University, IA; **Toni R. Randall**, Santa Monica College, CA; **Vidya Rangachari**, Mission College, CA; **Elizabeth Rasmussen**, Northern Virginia Community College, VA; **Lara Ravitch**, Truman College, IL;

Deborah Repasz, San Jacinto College, TX; Marisa Recinos, English Language Center, Brigham Young University, UT; Andrey Reznikov, Black Hills State University, SD; Alison Rice, Hunter College, NY; Jennifer Robles, Ventura Unified School District, CA; Priscilla Rocha, Clark County School District, NV; Dzidra Rodins, DePaul University, IL; Maria Rodriguez, Central High School, AZ; Josh Rosenberger, English Language Institute University of Montana, MT; Alice Rosso, Bucks County Community College, PA; Rita Rozzi, Xavier University, OH; Maria Ruiz, Victor Valley College, CA; Kimberly Russell, Clark College, WA; Stacy Sabraw, Michigan State University, MI; Irene Sakk, Northwestern University, IL; Deborah Sandstrom, University of Illinois at Chicago, IL; Jenni Santamaria, ABC Adult, CA; Shaeley Santiago, Ames High School, IA; Peg Sarosy, San Francisco State University, CA; Alice Savage, North Harris College, TX; Donna Schaeffer, University of Washington, WA; Karen Marsh Schaeffer, University of Utah, UT; Carol Schinger, Northern Virginia Community College, VA; Robert Scott, Kansas State University, KS; Suell Scott, Sheridan Technical Center, FL; Shira Seaman, Global English Academy, NY; Richard Seltzer, Glendale Community College, CA; Harlan Sexton, CUNY Queensborough Community College, NY; Kathy Sherak, San Francisco State University, CA; German Silva, Miami Dade College, FL; Ray Smith, Maryland English Institute, University of Maryland, MD; Shira Smith, NICE Program University of Hawaii, HI; Tara Smith, Felician College, NJ; Monica Snow, California State University, Fullerton, CA; Elaine Soffer, Nassau County Community College, NY; Andrea Spector, Santa Monica Community College, CA; Jacqueline Sport, LBWCC Luverne Center, AL; Karen Stanely, Central Piedmont Community College, NC; Susan Stern, Irvine Valley College, CA; Ayse Stromsdorfer, Soldan I.S.H.S., MO; Yilin Sun, South Seattle Community College, WA; Thomas Swietlik, Intrax International Institute, IL; Nicholas Taggert, University of Dayton, OH; Judith Tanka, UCLA Extension–American Language Center, CA; Amy Taylor, The University of Alabama Tuscaloosa, AL; Andrea Taylor, San Francisco State, CA; Priscilla Taylor, University of Southern California, CA; Ilene Teixeira, Fairfax County Public Schools, VA; Shirl H. Terrell, Collin College, TX; Marya Teutsch-Dwyer, St. Cloud State University, MN; Stephen Thergesen, ELS Language Centers, CO; Christine Tierney, Houston Community College, TX; Arlene Turini, North Moore High School, NC; Cara Tuzzolino, Nassau County Community College, NY; Suzanne Van Der Valk, Iowa State University, IA; Nathan D. Vasarhely, Ygnacio Valley High School, CA; Naomi S. Verratti, Howard Community College, MD; Hollyahna Vettori, Santa Rosa Junior College, CA; Julie Vorholt, Lewis & Clark College, OR; Danielle Wagner, FLS International Marymount College, CA; Lynn Walker, Coastline College, CA; Laura Walsh, City College of San Francisco, CA; Andrew J. Watson, The English Bakery; Donald Weasenforth, Collin College, TX; Juliane Widner, Sheepshead Bay High School, NY; Lynne Wilkins, Mills College, CA; Pamela Williams, Ventura College, CA; Jeff Wilson, Irvine Valley College, CA; James Wilson, Consomnes River College, CA; Katie Windahl, Cuyahoga Community College, OH; Dolores "Lorrie" Winter, California State University at Fullerton, CA; Jody Yamamoto, Kapiʻolani Community College, HI; Ellen L. Yaniv, Boston University, MA; Norman Yoshida, Lewis & Clark College, OR; Joanna Zadra, American River College, CA; Florence Zysman, Santiago Canyon College, CA;

CANADA Patricia Birch, Brandon University, MB; Jolanta Caputa, College of New Caledonia, BC; Katherine Coburn, UBC's ELI, BC; Erin Harris-Macleod, St. Mary's University, NS; Tami Moffatt, English Language Institute, BC; Jim Papple, Brock University, ON; Robin Peace, Confederation College, BC;

ASIA Rabiatu Abubakar, Eton Language Centre, Malaysia; Wiwik Andreani, Bina Nusantara University, Indonesia; Frank Bailey, Baiko Gakuin University, Japan; Mike Baker, Kosei Junior High School, Japan; Leonard Barrow, Kanto Junior College, Japan; Herman Bartelen, Japan; Siren Betty, Fooyin University, Kaohsiung; Thomas E. Bieri, Nagoya College, Japan; Natalie Brezden, Global English House, Japan; MK Brooks, Mukogawa Women's University, Japan; Truong Ngoc Buu, The Youth Language School, Vietnam; Charles Cabell, Toyo University, Japan; Fred Carruth, Matsumoto University, Japan; Frances Causer, Seijo University, Japan; Jeffrey Chalk, SNU, South Korea; Deborah Chang, Wenzao Ursuline College of Languages, Kaohsiung; David Chatham, Ritsumeikan University, Japan; Andrew Chih Hong Chen, National Sun Yat-sen University, Kaohsiung; Christina Chen, Yu-Tsai Bilingual Elementary School, Taipei; Hui-chen Chen, Shi-Lin High School of Commerce, Taipei; Seungmoon Choe, K2M Language Institute, South Korea; Jason Jeffree Cole, Coto College, Japan; Le Minh Cong, Vungtau Tourism Vocational College, Vietnam; Todd Cooper, Toyama National College of Technology, Japan; Marie Cosgrove, Daito Bunka University, Japan; Randall Cotten, Gifu City Women's College, Japan; Tony Cripps, Ritsumeikan University, Japan; Andy Cubalit, CHS, Thailand; Daniel Cussen, Takushoku University, Japan; Le Dan, Ho Chi Minh City Electric Power College, Vietnam; Simon Daykin, Banghwa-dong Community Centre, South Korea; Aimee Denham, ILA, Vietnam; Bryan Dickson, David's English Center, Taipei; Nathan Ducker, Japan University, Japan; Ian Duncan, Simul International Corporate Training, Japan; Nguyen Thi Kieu Dung, Thang Long University, Vietnam; Truong Quang Dung, Tien Giang University, Vietnam; Nguyen Thi Thuy Duong, Vietnamese American Vocational Training College, Vietnam; Wong Tuck Ee, Raja Tun Azlan Science Secondary School, Malaysia; Emilia Effendy, International Islamic University Malaysia, Malaysia; Bettizza Escueta, KMUTT, Thailand; Robert Eva, Kaisei Girls High School, Japan; Jim George, Luna International Language School, Japan; Jurgen Germeys, Silk Road Language Center, South Korea; Wong Ai Gnoh, SMJK Chung Hwa Confucian, Malaysia; Sarah Go, Seoul Women's University, South Korea; Peter Goosselink, Hokkai High School, Japan; Robert Gorden, SNU, South Korea; Wendy M. Gough, St. Mary College/Nunoike Gaigo Senmon Gakko, Japan; Tim Grose, Sapporo Gakuin University, Japan; Pham Thu Ha, Le Van Tam Primary School, Vietnam; Ann-Marie Hadzima, Taipei; Troy Hammond, Tokyo Gakugei University International Secondary School, Japan; Robiatul 'Adawiah Binti Hamzah, SMK Putrajaya Precinct 8(1), Malaysia; Tran Thi Thuy Hang, Ho Chi Minh City Banking University, Vietnam; To Thi Hong Hanh, CEFALT, Vietnam; George Hays, Tokyo Kokusai Daigaku, Japan; Janis Hearn, Hongik University, South Korea; Chantel Hemmi, Jochi Daigaku, Japan; David Hindman, Sejong University, South Korea; Nahn Cam Hoa, Ho Chi Minh City University of Technology, Vietnam; Jana Holt, Korea University, South Korea; Jason Hollowell, Nihon University, Japan; F. N. (Zoe) Hsu, National Tainan University, Yong Kang; Kuei-ping Hsu, National Tsing Hua University, Hsinchu City; Wenhua Hsu, I-Shou University, Kaohsiung; Luu Nguyen Quoc Hung, Cantho University, Vietnam; Cecile Hwang, Changwon National University, South Korea; Ainol Haryati Ibrahim, Universiti Malaysia Pahang, Malaysia; Robert Jeens, Yonsei University, South Korea; Linda M. Joyce, Kyushu Sangyo University, Japan; Dr. Nisai Kaewsanchai, English Square Kanchanaburi, Thailand; Aniza Kamarulzaman, Sabah Science Secondary School, Malaysia; Ikuko Kashiwabara, Osaka Electro-Communication University, Japan; Gurmit Kaur, INTI College, Malaysia; Nick Keane, Japan; Ward Ketcheson, Aomori University, Japan; Nicholas Kemp, Kyushu International University, Japan; Montchatry Ketmuni, Rajamangala University of Technology, Thailand; Dinh Viet Khanh, Vietnam; Seonok Kim, Kangsu Jongro Language School, South Korea; Suyeon Kim, Anyang University, South Korea; Kelly P. Kimura, Soka University, Japan; Masakazu Kimura, Katoh Gakuen Gyoshu High School, Japan; Gregory King, Chubu Daigaku, Japan; Stan Kirk, Konan University, Japan; Donald Knight, Nan Hua/Fu Li Junior High Schools, Hsinchu; Kari J. Kostiainen, Nagoya City University, Japan; Pattri Kuanpulpol, Silpakorn University, Thailand; Ha Thi Lan, Thai Binh Teacher Training College, Vietnam; Eric Edwin Larson, Miyazaki Prefectural Nursing University, Japan; David Laurence, Chubu Daigaku, Japan; Richard S. Lavin, Prefectural University of Kumamoto, Japan; Shirley Leane, Chugoku Junior College, Japan; I-Hsiu Lee, Yunlin; Nari Lee, Park Jung PLS, South Korea; Tae Lee, Yonsei University, South Korea; Lys Yongsoon Lee, Reading Town Geumcheon, South Korea; Mallory Leece, Sun Moon University, South Korea; Dang Hong Lien, Tan Lam Upper Secondary School, Vietnam; Huang Li-Han, Rebecca Education Institute, Taipei; Sovannarith Lim, Royal University of Phnom Penh, Cambodia; Ginger Lin, National Kaohsiung Hospitality College, Kaohsiung; Noel Lineker, New Zealand/Japan; Tran Dang Khanh Linh, Nha Trang Teachers' Training College, Vietnam; Daphne Liu, Buliton English School, Taipei; S. F. Josephine Liu, Tien-Mu Elementary School, Taipei ; Caroline Luo, Tunghai University, Taichung; Jeng-Jia Luo, Tunghai University, Taichung; Laura MacGregor, Gakushuin University, Japan; Amir Madani, Visuttharangsi School, Thailand; Elena Maeda, Sacred Heart Professional Training College, Japan; Vu Thi Thanh Mai, Hoang Gia Education Center, Vietnam; Kimura Masakazu, Kato Gakuen Gyoshu High School, Japan; Susumu Matsuhashi, Net Link English School, Japan; James McCrostie, Daito Bunka University, Japan; Joel McKee, Inha University, South Korea; Colin McKenzie, Wachirawit Primary School, Thailand; Terumi Miyazoe, Tokyo Denki Daigaku, Japan; William K. Moore, Hiroshima Kokusai Gakuin University, Japan; Kevin Mueller, Tokyo Kokusai Daigaku, Japan; Hudson Murrell, Baiko Gakuin University, Japan; Frances Namba, Senri International School of Kwansei Gakuin, Japan; Keiichi Narita, Niigata University, Japan; Kim Chung Nguyen, Ho Chi Minh University of

Industry, Vietnam; **Do Thi Thanh Nhan**, Hanoi University, Vietnam; **Dale Kazuo Nishi**, Aoyama English Conversation School, Japan; **Huynh Thi Ai Nguyen**, Vietnam; **Dongshin Oh**, YBM PLS, South Korea; **Keiko Okada**, Dokkyo Daigaku, Japan; **Louise Ohashi**, Shukutoku University, Japan; **Yongjun Park**, Sangji University, South Korea; **Donald Patnaude**, Ajarn Donald's English Language Services, Thailand; **Virginia Peng**, Ritsumeikan University, Japan; **Suangkanok Piboonthamnont**, Rajamangala University of Technology, Thailand; **Simon Pitcher**, Business English Teaching Services, Japan; **John C. Probert**, New Education Worldwide, Thailand; **Do Thi Hoa Quyen**, Ton Duc Thang University, Vietnam; **John P. Racine**, Dokkyo University, Japan; **Kevin Ramsden**, Kyoto University of Foreign Studies, Japan; **Luis Rappaport**, Cung Thieu Nha Ha Noi, Vietnam; **Lisa Reshad**, Konan Daigaku Hyogo, Japan; **Peter Riley**, Taisho University, Japan; **Thomas N. Robb**, Kyoto Sangyo University, Japan; **Rory Rosszell**, Meiji Daigaku, Japan; **Maria Feti Rosyani**, Universitas Kristen Indonesia, Indonesia; **Greg Rouault**, Konan University, Japan; **Chris Ruddenklau**, Kindai University, Japan; **Hans-Gustav Schwartz**, Thailand; **Mary-Jane Scott**, Soongsil University, South Korea; **Dara Sheahan**, Seoul National University, South Korea; **James Sherlock**, A.P.W. Angthong, Thailand; **Prof. Shieh**, Minghsin University of Science & Technology, Xinfeng; **Yuko Shimizu**, Ritsumeikan University, Japan; **Suzila Mohd Shukor**, Universiti Sains Malaysia, Malaysia; **Stephen E. Smith**, Mahidol University, Thailand; **Moon-young Son**, South Korea; **Seunghee Son**, Anyang University, South Korea; **Mi-young Song**, Kyungwon University, South Korea; **Lisa Sood**, VUS, BIS, Vietnam; **Jason Stewart**, Taejon International Language School, South Korea; **Brian A. Stokes**, Korea University, South Korea; **Mulder Su**, Shih-Chien University, Kaohsiung; **Yoomi Suh**, English Plus, South Korea; **Yun-Fang Sun**, Wenzao Ursuline College of Languages, Kaohsiung; **Richard Swingle**, Kansai Gaidai University, Japan; **Sanford Taborn**, Kinjo Gakuin Daigaku, Japan; **Mamoru Takahashi**, Akita Prefectural University, Japan; **Tran Hoang Tan**, School of International Training, Vietnam; **Takako Tanaka**, Doshisha University, Japan; **Jeffrey Taschner**, American University Alumni Language Center, Thailand; **Matthew Taylor**, Kinjo Gakuin Daigaku, Japan; **Michael Taylor**, International Pioneers School, Thailand; **Kampanart Thammaphati**, Wattana Wittaya Academy, Thailand; **Tran Duong The**, Sao Mai Language Center, Vietnam; **Tran Dinh Tho**, Duc Tri Secondary School, Vietnam; **Huynh Thi Anh Thu**, Nhatrang College of Culture Arts and Tourism, Vietnam; **Peter Timmins**, Peter's English School, Japan; **Fumie Togano**, Hosei Daini High School, Japan; **F. Sigmund Topor**, Keio University Language School, Japan; **Tu Trieu**, Rise VN, Vietnam; **Yen-Cheng Tseng**, Chang-Jung Christian University, Tainan; **Pei-Hsuan Tu**, National Cheng Kung University, Tainan City; **Hajime Uematsu**, Hirosaki University, Japan; **Rachel Um**, Mok-dong Oedae English School, South Korea; **David Underhill**, EEExpress, Japan; **Ben Underwood**, Kugenuma High School, Japan; **Siriluck Usaha**, Sripatum University, Thailand; **Tyas Budi Utami**, Indonesia; **Nguyen Thi Van**, Far East International School, Vietnam; **Stephan Van Eycken**, Kosei Gakuen Girls High School, Japan; **Zisa Velasquez**, Taihu International School/Semarang International School, China/Indonesia; **Jeffery Walter**, Sangji University, South Korea; **Bill White**, Kinki University, Japan; **Yohanes De Deo Widyastoko**, Xaverius Senior High School, Indonesia; **Dylan Williams**, SNU, South Korea; **Jisuk Woo**, Ichean University, South Korea; **Greg Chung-Hsien Wu**, Providence University, Taichung; **Xun Xiaoming**, BLCU, China; **Hui-Lien Yeh**, Chai Nan University of Pharmacy and Science, Tainan; **Sittiporn Yodnil**, Huachiew Chalermprakiet University, Thailand; **Shamshul Helmy Zambahari**, Universiti Teknologi Malaysia, Malaysia; **Ming-Yuli**, Chang Jung Christian University, Tainan; **Aimin Fadhlee bin Mahmud Zuhodi**, Kuala Terengganu Science School, Malaysia;

TURKEY **Shirley F. Akis**, American Culture Association/Fomara; **Gül Akkoç**, Boğaziçi University; **Seval Akmeşe**, Haliç University; **Ayşenur Akyol**, Ege University; **Ayşe Umut Aribaş**, Beykent University; **Gökhan Asan**, Kapadokya Vocational College; **Hakan Asan**, Kapadokya Vocational College; **Julia Asan**, Kapadokya Vocational College; **Azarvan Atac**, Piri Reis University; **Nur Babat**, Kapadokya Vocational College; **Feyza Balakbabalar**, Kadir Has University; **Gözde Balikçi**, Beykent University; **Deniz Balım**, Haliç University; **Asli Başdoğan**, Kadir Has University; **Ayla Bayram**, Kapadokya Vocational College; **Pinar Bilgiç**, Kadir Has University; **Kenan Bozkurt**, Kapadokya Vocational College; **Yonca Bozkurt**, Ege University; **Frank Carr**, Piri Reis; **Mengü Noyan Çengel**, Ege University; **Elif Doğan**, Ege University; **Natalia Donmez**, 29 Mayis Üniversite; **Nalan Emirsoy**, Kadir Has University; **Ayşe Engin**, Kadir Has University; **Ayhan Gedikbaş**, Ege University; **Gülşah Gençer**, Beykent University; **Seyit Ömer Gök**, Gediz University; **Tuğba Gök**, Gediz University; **İlkay Gökçe**, Ege University; **Zeynep Birinci Guler**, Maltepe University; **Neslihan Güler**, Kadir Has University; **Sircan Gümüş**, Kadir Has University; **Nesrin Gündoğu**, T.C. Piri Reis University; **Tanju Gurpinar**, Piri Reis University; **Selin Gurturk**, Piri Reis University; **Neslihan Gurutku**, Piri Reis University; **Roger Hewitt**, Maltepe University; **Nilüfer İbrahimoğlu**, Beykent University; **Nevin Kaftelen**, Kadir Has University; **Sultan Kalin**, Kapadokya Vocational College; **Sema Kaplan Karabina**, Anadolu University; **Eray Kara**, Giresun University; **Beylü Karayazgan**, Ege University; **Darren Kelso**, Piri Reis University; **Trudy Kittle**, Kapadokya Vocational College; **Şaziye Konaç**, Kadir Has University; **Güneş Korkmaz**, Kapadokya Vocational College; **Robert Ledbury**, Izmir University of Economics; **Ashley Lucas**, Maltepe University; **Bülent Nedium Uça**, Dogus University; **Murat Nurlu**, Ege University; **Mollie Owens**, Kadir Has University; **Oya Özağaç**, Boğaziçi University; **Funda Özcan**, Ege University; **İlkay Özdemir**, Ege University; **Ülkü Öztürk**, Gediz University; **Cassondra Puls**, Anadolu University; **Yelda Sarikaya**, Cappadocia Vocational College; **Müge Şekercioğlu**, Ege University; **Melis Senol**, Canakkale Onsekiz Mart University, The School of Foreign Languages; **Patricia Sümer**, Kadir Has University; **Rex Surface**, Beykent University; **Mustafa Torun**, Kapadokya Vocational College; **Tansel Üstünloğlu**, Ege University; **Fatih Yücel**, Beykent University; **Şule Yüksel**, Ege University;

THE MIDDLE EAST **Amina Saif Mohammed Al Hashamia**, Nizwa College of Applied Sciences, Oman; **Jennifer Baran**, Kuwait University, Kuwait; **Phillip Chappells**, GEMS Modern Academy, U.A.E.; **Sharon Ruth Devaneson**, Ibri College of Technology, Oman; **Hanaa El-Deeb**, Canadian International College, Egypt; **Yvonne Eaton**, Community College of Qatar, Qatar; **Brian Gay**, Sultan Qaboos University, Oman; **Gail Al Hafidh**, Sharjah Women's College (HCT), U.A.E.; **Jonathan Hastings**, American Language Center, Jordan; **Laurie Susan Hilu**, English Language Centre, University of Bahrain, Bahrain; **Abraham Irannezhad**, Mehre Aval, Iran; **Kevin Kempe**, CNA-Q, Qatar; **Jill Newby James**, University of Nizwa; **Mary Kay Klein**, American University of Sharjah, U.A.E.; **Sian Khoury**, Fujairah Women's College (HCT), U.A.E.; **Hussein Dehghan Manshadi**, Farhang Pajooh & Jaam-e-Jam Language School, Iran; **Jessica March**, American University of Sharjah, U.A.E.; **Neil McBeath**, Sultan Qaboos University, Oman; **Sandy McDonagh**, Abu Dhabi Men's College (HCT), U.A.E.; **Rob Miles**, Sharjah Women's College (HCT), U.A.E.; **Michael Kevin Neumann**, Al Ain Men's College (HCT), U.A.E.;

LATIN AMERICA **Aldana Aguirre**, Argentina; **Claudia Almeida**, Coordenação de Idiomas, Brazil; **Cláudia Arias**, Brazil; **Maria de los Angeles Barba**, FES Acatlan UNAM, Mexico; **Lilia Barrios**, Universidad Autónoma de Tamaulipas, Mexico; **Adán Beristain**, UAEM, Mexico; **Ricardo Böck**, Manoel Ribas, Brazil; **Edson Braga**, CNA, Brazil; **Marli Buttelli**, Mater et Magistra, Brazil; **Alessandra Campos**, Inova Centro de Linguas, Brazil; **Priscila Catta Preta Ribeiro**, Brazil; **Gustavo Cestari**, Access International School, Brazil; **Walter D'Alessandro**, Virginia Language Center, Brazil; **Lilian De Gennaro**, Argentina; **Mônica De Stefani**, Quality Centro de Idiomas, Brazil; **Julio Alejandro Flores**, BUAP, Mexico; **Mirian Freire**, CNA Vila Guilherme, Brazil; **Francisco Garcia**, Colegio Lestonnac de San Angel, Mexico; **Miriam Giovanardi**, Brazil; **Darlene Gonzalez Miy**, ITESM CCV, Mexico; **Maria Laura Grimaldi**, Argentina; **Luz Dary Guzmán**, IMPAHU, Colombia; **Carmen Koppe**, Brazil; **Monica Krutzler**, Brazil; **Marcus Murilo Lacerda**, Seven Idiomas, Brazil; **Nancy Lake**, CEL-LEP, Brazil; **Cris Lazzerini**, Brazil; **Sandra Luna**, Argentina; **Ricardo Luvisan**, Brazil; **Jorge Murilo Menezes**, ACBEU, Brazil; **Monica Navarro**, Instituto Cultural A. C., Mexico; **Joacyr Oliveira**, Faculdades Metropolitanas Unidas and Summit School for Teachers, Brazil; **Ayrton Cesar Oliveira de Araujo**, E&A English Classes, Brazil; **Ana Laura Oriente**, Seven Idiomas, Brazil; **Adelia Peña Clavel**, CELE UNAM, Mexico; **Beatriz Pereira**, Summit School, Brazil; **Miguel Perez**, Instituto Cultural, Mexico; **Cristiane Perone**, Associação Cultura Inglesa, Brazil; **Pamela Claudia Pogré**, Colegio Integral Caballito / Universidad de Flores, Argentina; **Dalva Prates**, Brazil; **Marianne Rampaso**, Iowa Idiomas, Brazil; **Daniela Rutolo**, Instituto Superior Cultural Británico, Argentina; **Maione Sampaio**, Maione Carrijo Consultoria em Inglês Ltda, Brazil; **Elaine Santesso**, TS Escola de Idiomas, Brazil; **Camila Francisco Santos**, UNS Idiomas, Brazil; **Lucia Silva**, Cooplem Idiomas, Brazil; **Maria Adela Sorzio**, Instituto Superior Santa Cecilia, Argentina; **Elcio Souza**, Unibero, Brazil; **Willie Thomas**, Rainbow Idiomas, Brazil; **Sandra Villegas**, Instituto Humberto de Paolis, Argentina; **John Whelan**, La Universidad Nacional Autonoma de Mexico, Mexico

CONTENTS

READING ▶ previewing and predicting
VOCABULARY ▶ using the dictionary
WRITING ▶ organizing and developing an essay
GRAMMAR ▶ restrictive relative clauses

UNIT QUESTION

What makes someone admirable?

A Discuss these questions with your classmates.

1. Why do we like to read stories about admirable people?

2. Who do you admire? Why do you admire this person?

3. Look at the photo. What makes these people admirable?

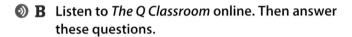

🔊 **B** Listen to *The Q Classroom* online. Then answer these questions.

1. Marcus says admirable people are brave and sacrifice themselves. What two examples does he give? Sophy says regular people can also be admirable. What examples does she give? What do you think makes someone admirable?

2. What qualities of an admirable person do Felix and Sophy discuss? Which qualities are most important in your opinion?

 C Go online to watch the video about the "big tipper." Then check your comprehension.

VIDEO VOCABULARY

tuition *(n.)* the money that you pay to be taught, especially in a college or university

knight in shining armor *(n.)* a person who rescues another

tip *(n.)* a piece of information to help someone do something

tip *(n.)* money given to someone who performs a service for another

 D Go to the Online Discussion Board to discuss the Unit Question with your classmates.

E Many different kinds of people have spoken about admirable qualities. Read the quotations below and discuss the following questions with a partner.

1. What does each quotation mean?

2. Do you agree with the quotation? Why or why not?

Words of Wisdom

1. Keep away from people who try to belittle your ambitions. Small people always do that, but the really great make you feel that you, too, can become great.
—*Mark Twain, American author*

2. No person was ever honored for what he received. Honor has been the reward for what he gave.
—*Calvin Coolidge, American President*

3. We must always remember with gratitude and admiration the first sailors who steered their vessels through storms and mists, and increased our knowledge of the lands of ice in the South.
—*Roald Amundsen, Norwegian explorer*

4. I've learned that people will forget what you said, people will forget what you did, but people will never forget how you made them feel.
—*Maya Angelou, American author*

F What qualities do you wish you had? In the chart, write down each quality and someone you know who has it. Share your ideas with your partner.

Quality	Name of person who has the quality

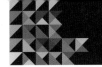

READING 1 | We All Need a Role Model

 You are going to read an essay about role models. Use the essay to gather information and ideas for your Unit Assignment.

PREVIEW THE READING

Reading Skill | Previewing and predicting

 for Success

When you write a research paper, you need to get information from a variety of sources. Previewing many books and articles will help you decide which ones are important for your research.

When you **preview** a text, you look through it quickly to learn general information. To preview:

- Read the title of the text.
- Look at any charts, graphs, pictures, or captions.
- Skim the text for subheadings. Subheadings indicate important ideas that will be developed in the text.

Previewing will help you **predict** what the text is about and prepare you to better understand it.

A. **PREVIEW** Read the title of the essay and look at the pictures. Write two things you think the text might be about.

1. _____

2. _____

B. Skim the essay and read the subheadings. Then look at the pairs of ideas below. Check (✓) one idea in each pair that you think might be developed in the text.

1. ☐ the qualities of role models
   ☐ a description of a specific role model

2. ☐ how people become role models
   ☐ what people may be role models

3. ☐ how role models can inspire us
   ☐ how we can inspire others

4. ☐ why role models do wrong things
   ☐ how role models learn from mistakes

C. Go online for more practice with previewing and predicting.

D. **QUICK WRITE** What qualities should a good role model possess? Write for 5–10 minutes in response. Be sure to use this section for your Unit Assignment.

E. **VOCABULARY** Check (✓) the words you know. Then work with a partner to locate each word in the reading. Use clues to help define the words you don't know. Check your definitions in the dictionary.

achievement (n.) 🔑	embody (v.)
acknowledged (for) (adj.) 🔑	inclined (adj.)
adversity (n.)	inherently (adv.)
aspire to (phr. v.)	pursue (v.) 🔑
confront (v.) 🔑	resolve (n.) 🔑
constrained (adj.)	version (n.) 🔑

🔑 Oxford 3000™ words

 F. Go online to listen and practice your pronunciation.

WORK WITH THE READING

A. Read the essay and gather information about what makes someone admirable.

We All Need a Role Model

1   Who do you turn to when you have a problem or don't know how to do something? If you have someone to help you, you are lucky. If you have someone who takes a personal interest in helping you, you are luckier still. You have a role model.

Definition of a Role Model

2   Just what is a role model? First, let's recognize what it is not. It is not necessarily the smartest, strongest, or most successful person you know—although it could be. A role model is a person who has the characteristics you want for yourself and who can help you develop those traits. In other words, a role model both **embodies** positive qualities and teaches others, directly or through example.

Who Can Be a Role Model?

3   For most of us, our parents are our first role models. From when we are young children, they help us learn how to interact with other people—how to share, how to ask for what we need, and how to disagree without hurting someone. They are **inherently** interested in us and want us to do well. Furthermore, our parents teach us how to be adults in our society. A mother demonstrates to her daughters how to be a daughter, a woman, a wife, and a mother. Lessons learned from our parents will stay with us throughout our lives.

4   Other family members also serve as role models. Grandparents, uncles and aunts, cousins, and even siblings can show us how to manage our daily lives. Other obvious candidates include teachers and community leaders.

5   Sometimes we find role models in unexpected places. A family story might inspire us to have the same generosity as our grandfather had. We might see a young child fall, pick herself up, fall again, and pick herself up again. Her **resolve** might inspire us to continue in our own struggles, just as she learns to stand, keep her balance, and take a step. We might even find a model within ourselves, remembering back to a time when we were brave, or imagining a different **version** of ourselves who has the quality we desire.

What Role Models Do

6   Besides showing us how to do different things, a good role model also inspires us to **pursue** our dreams and **achievements**. A wise lawyer may inspire one person to study law, while a competent, compassionate physician may lead another person to the medical profession. Role models should empower others to become good parents, leaders, and members of society, and to internalize the qualities that they value. Therefore, role models must do the right thing, even when no one is watching, even when they won't be **acknowledged for** what they have done.

When Things Go Wrong

7   It is easy to be a role model when everything is going well, but it is perhaps more important to be a role model when things go wrong. A role model can show us how to handle **adversity**. For instance, we all make mistakes, but what do we do when we realize that we have made one? Do we try to hide it or pretend that it never happened? Are we **inclined** to look for someone to blame? Do we get angry?

8   A role model can show us how to deal with mistakes. A parent or teacher can help us repair any damage that was done or soothe any feelings that were hurt. He or she can listen to us, advise us on alternative courses of action, and support us as we make amends. The example of a community leader might serve to guide us toward appropriate action, encouraging us to imagine what he would do in our circumstances.

A role model shows us how to do different things and how to handle adversity.

9   Other situations that we might find ourselves in include dealing with stress, illness, or other misfortunes. **Confronting** these predicaments and overcoming them is made easier by the knowledge that people we admire and respect have faced similar conditions. Asking ourselves what they would do might help us be brave for a little while longer or figure out how to deal with life when we feel **constrained** by difficulties.

10   We need role models throughout our lives, and we only need to look around us to find someone who has experienced what we are going through, who has faced difficult decisions, or who has accomplished something we **aspire to** do. Sometimes we only have to look as far as the mirror to see a role model for our children, our neighbors, or even ourselves. Who is your role model? Maybe it is time to say thank you.

B. VOCABULARY Here are some words and phrases from Reading 1. Read the sentences. Then write each bold word or phrase next to the correct definition. You may need to change verbs to their base form.

Vocabulary
Skill Review

Remember to read the whole sentence and consider the *context*. This can help you identify the correct meaning of a word.

1. My father **embodies** the quality of honesty; he never tells a lie.

2. The best athletes have the **resolve** to keep trying even when everything looks hopeless.

3. I will **pursue** my goal to be an engineer even though it will be difficult.

4. Winning the competition was an incredible **achievement** for such a young player.

5. When you set goals, don't be **constrained** by your present situation. If you can dream it, you can do it.

6. The athlete is suffering with a long-term injury, but he still **aspires to** race at the Olympics.

7. Skydiving is an **inherently** dangerous sport.

8. We all want to be **acknowledged for** our good deeds and the things we do to help others.

9. He had a hard life, but the **adversity** and challenges he faced made him a stronger person.

10. She had to **confront** the problem even though she was frightened.

11. I prefer my usual routine and am not **inclined** to try new things.

12. The first witness's **version** of the accident was quite different from the second witness's version.

a. _____ (*adj.*) recognized or shown appreciation for something

b. _____ (*n.*) a strong determination to do something

c. _____ (*adv.*) being a basic part of something that cannot be removed

d. _____ (*phr. v.*) to have a strong desire to do or become something

e. _____ (*adj.*) limited by something or someone

f. _____ (*n.*) a form of something that is different from another form of the same thing

g. _____ (*n.*) something that has been done successfully, especially through hard work or skill

h. _____ (*v.*) to deal with a problem or difficult situation

i. _____*embody*_____ (*v.*) to represent an idea or quality

j. _____ (*adj.*) wanting to do something

k. _____ (*n.*) a difficult or unpleasant situation

l. _____ (*v.*) to try to achieve something over a period of time

iQ ONLINE   **C.** Go online for more practice with the vocabulary.

D. Answer these questions.

1. What is the main idea of the essay? Write it in a complete sentence.

_____

2. The main idea is found in two places. Where did you find the main idea?

_____

E. Read the sentences. Number the main ideas in the order they are developed in the essay. (Use the subheadings in the essay to help you.)

____ a. Role models can show us how to deal with mistakes.

____ b. Role models can show us how to deal with problems.

_1_ c. A role model is a person with qualities that other people want to have.

____ d. Role models inspire us to develop our talents and abilities.

____ e. Many different kinds of people are role models.

F. Answer these questions.

1. Who are some of the people that can be role models?

_____

2. How can a lawyer or doctor serve as a role model?

_____

3. How can a role model help us deal with mistakes?

_____

_____

4. When is another time role models might help us?

_____

_____

G. Write *T* (true) or *F* (false) for each statement. Then correct each false statement to make it true. Write the paragraph number where you found information to support your answer.

____ 1. A role model is sometimes the most successful person you know.
(paragraph ____)

_____

____ 2. A teacher is usually our first role model.
(paragraph ____)

_____

____ 3. A young child can be a role model.
(paragraph ____)

_____

____ 4. A role model is supposed to do the right thing.
(paragraph ____)

_____

____ 5. A role model never makes mistakes.
(paragraph ____)

_____

____ 6. We need role models only when we confront adversity.
(paragraph ____)

_____

____ 7. It's hard to find a role model.
(paragraph ____)

_____

____ 8. You can be your own role model.
(paragraph ____)

_____

H. Complete the chart with two more people the essay identified as role models and what they can teach us.

Role models	What they can teach us
1. parents	1. how to interact with other people: -how to share -how to ask for what we need -how to disagree without hurting someone 2. how to be adults in our society
2.	
3.	

I. Go online to read *Taking Responsibility for Your Actions* and check your comprehension.

WRITE WHAT YOU THINK

A. Discuss these questions in a group.

1. Do athletes make good role models? Why or why not?

2. Who are you a role model for?

3. Imagine yourself 20 years from now. What would you like to hear people saying about you? What can you do between now and then so that people will say that?

B. Choose one question and write a paragraph in response. Look back at your Quick Write on page 6 as you think about what you learned.

READING 2 | Search for 100 Real-Life Heroes

You are going to read an article from the newspaper *The Guardian* about a journalist who spent two years searching for 100 real-life heroes. Use the article to gather information and ideas for your Unit Assignment.

PREVIEW THE READING

A. **PREVIEW** Read the title of the article and skim the first three paragraphs. Answer these questions.

1. What was Tithiya Sharma looking for?

   _____

2. Where was she looking?

   _____

3. How long did she look?

   _____

B. **QUICK WRITE** If you could do something to make your community better, what would you do? What would you need in order to accomplish this? Write for 5–10 minutes in response. Be sure to use this section for your Unit Assignment.

C. **VOCABULARY** Check (✓) the words you know. Use a dictionary to define any new or unknown words. Then discuss how the words will relate to the unit with a partner.

bear witness *(phr. v.)*	**inspirational** *(adj.)*
criteria *(n.)* 🔑	**navigate** *(v.)*
deconstruct *(v.)*	**notorious** *(adj.)*
disrupt *(v.)*	**pressing** *(adj.)*
drastic *(adj.)*	**reconciliation** *(n.)*
initiative *(n.)* 🔑	**underprivileged** *(adj.)*

🔑 Oxford 3000™ words

 D. Go online to listen and practice your pronunciation.

WORK WITH THE READING

A. Read the article and gather information about what makes someone admirable.

Search for 100 Real-Life Heroes

Indian Journalist Tithiya Sharma Visits 45 Countries over Two Years to Find Local Champions
by Kate Hodal and Tom Phillips

City of God favela in Rio de Janeiro, Brazil

1   Heroes are normally the stuff of mythology. But for Tithiya Sharma, whose journey to find them took two years and spanned 45 countries across six continents, heroes are part of everyday life.

2   Sharma spent the two years looking for 100 **inspirational** figureheads[1], community leaders, and social workers.

3   The only requirement? That these heroes were changing the future of their countries, from the clean boulevards of the west to the most **underprivileged** and conflict-ridden corners of the developing world.

4   Calling her quest the 100 Heroes Project, the New Delhi-born former journalist left the newsrooms of Mumbai, formerly Bombay, in May 2010 and in December 2011 touched down in South America, on one of the final stops on her global tour.

5   "I'd become so used to being a journalist in India, making really good money, renting a fancy apartment in the most expensive part of Bombay," says Sharma, 29, on her way to meet her latest hero in Rio de Janeiro's **notorious** City of God favela[2].

6   "It was such an easy trap to fall into and I knew that if I was going to make a change it had to be something really **drastic**. So I quit my job, sold all my stuff, moved back in with my parents, and decided I wanted to do this."

7   "This" means **navigating** her way alone through some of the world's trickiest corners, often with little more than a scrap of paper and some scribbled notes as her guide.

8   Sharma has no set **criteria** for her heroes, whom she finds by using Internet search engines and then relying on local contacts to determine the area's most **pressing** issues.

9   "What makes a hero, anyway? Is it that you're helping 1,000 people or two people?" she asks. "If you help the life of one single person but in a really meaningful way, I think you're a hero."

---

[1] **figureheads:** people in a high position in a country or organization but who have no real power or authority

[2] **favela:** a poor area in or near a Brazilian city, with many houses that are close together and in bad condition

10 Sharma's latest find—number "70-something," she says—is 50-year-old social worker Maria do Socorro Melo Brandão, a favela-born but university-educated psychiatrist who now runs City of God's Seed of Life Association.

11 The community group works with local job-seekers and offers extracurricular[3] activities to children and teens.

12 As Brandão describes her work providing counseling to slum[4] residents, Sharma underlines the effect just one individual can have on the rest of the world. "All it takes is that one person who takes it upon him or herself to put all of the pieces of the puzzle together, to inspire, to bring people together, that one person who doesn't give up," she says.

13 "Sometimes it's just about **deconstructing** the way people think. One amazing idea can **disrupt** the thinking of an entire community or country."

14 Determined to use "social media for social good," Sharma is raising money and awareness for the heroes she finds, using her journalistic background to blog, tweet, and publish articles about her experiences.

15 Donors have been impressed: while she has paid for her trip primarily through personal savings, Indian travel site MakeMyTrip has funded all her flights—its chief marketing officer, Mohit Gupta, says he was inspired by Sharma's drive to learn about and take in "the best the world has to offer."

16 Sharma admits that traveling alone has proven difficult at times. She has been in some dangerous situations, but these experiences have only strengthened her resolve.

17 Sharma notes that wherever she travels, she does so through the eyes of a woman, and in most situations, she feels wronged, unhappy, or unsettled by what she sees. "I now know I want to work in a women's rights organization," she says. She wants to work with and for the female heroes "in society who are clawing[5] every day to create a new normal."

18 By the end of her two-year journey, Sharma had seen the Northern Lights, churches of Lalibela, Ethiopia, and the pyramids of Egypt, crossed 45 countries over six continents, and found well over 100 heroes.

19 But only one thing stood out, she says. "After time, every church starts looking the same." What she remembers most about this trip is the people. Sharma talks about the love and hospitality she experienced everywhere she visited.

20 "It's a reminder of how lucky I am, how fortunate and privileged to be here and now and having this experience. To be able to **bear witness**. I could do this for the rest of my life."

Six of the 100 Heroes

Sonja Kruse (right) with a woman she met while writing her book, *The Ubuntu Girl*

---

[3] **extracurricular:** not part of the usual course of work or studies at a school or college

[4] **slum:** an area of a city that is very poor and where the houses are dirty and in bad condition

[5] **clawing:** slowly achieving something by using a lot of determination and effort

21 **Sonja Kruse** The 32-year-old "Ubuntu Girl" spent a year traveling through her native South Africa with nothing but a backpack, a camera, and 100 rand ($12.14) to prove that *ubuntu*—an African concept meaning "I am only because you are"—is alive and well. She is writing a book about her experiences.

22 **Yamam Nabeel** Iraqi-born, London-based Nabeel started FC Unity to bring together people from different social, religious, and ethnic backgrounds through soccer, and teach them to work as a team. Since its founding in 2006, the charity has created soccer-based education and development programs in Iraq, Sudan, England, and Ghana.

23 **Mahfuza Folad** From an office above a Kabul cookie shop, Folad serves as executive director of Justice for All Organisation, which offers free advice and support to Afghan women and works for women's and children's rights. Folad is also a judge in Kabul.

24 **Dr. Jo and Lyn Lusi** The husband and wife co-founded HEAL Africa, which provides medical and social care for women in Congo. Their charity heads one of Congo's three full-service hospitals and provides community-based **initiatives** such as safe houses and remote clinics, microlending schemes, and law-training programs.

25 **Felicite Rwemalika** The founder of the Association of Kigali Women in Sports, Rwemalika started Rwanda's first women's sports federation in 2001 to give young Hutu and Tutsi[6] girls a chance to find **reconciliation** in post-conflict Rwanda. Her organization also promotes women's rights and teaches healthy lifestyles and economic empowerment.

---

[6] **Hutu and Tutsi:** two ethnic groups inhabiting Rwanda and Burundi in Africa

B. **VOCABULARY** Work with a partner. Read the bold word or phrase and the three definitions in each row. Two of the definitions are similar and correct. A third is incorrect. Cross out the incorrect definition.

	a.	b.	c.
1. inspirational *(adj.)*	a. making someone want to be better or more successful	b. causing someone to have exciting new ideas	c. ~~making someone breathe~~
2. underprivileged *(adj.)*	a. having the position of power just below the manager	b. having less money and fewer opportunities than most people	c. not having rights or advantages that most people have
3. pressing *(adj.)*	a. needing to be dealt with immediately	b. required to complete a task	c. urgent

4. notorious *(adj.)*	a. well known for being bad	b. knowing a lot of bad words	c. famous for doing something wrong
5. drastic *(adj.)*	a. extreme in a sudden, serious way	b. hard to do	c. very different from normal
6. navigate *(v.)*	a. to sail on a ship	b. to find the direction you need to go in	c. to use a map to decide how to travel
7. criteria *(n.)*	a. principles used to help make a decision	b. rules for accepting or not accepting something	c. knowledge
8. deconstruct *(v.)*	a. to tear something down	b. to analyze something to understand it	c. to figure out how something works
9. disrupt *(v.)*	a. to make it difficult for something to continue in the normal way	b. to cause something to stop or change course	c. to hurt something without meaning to
10. bear witness *(phr. v.)*	a. to provide evidence of the truth of something	b. to experience something and tell others about it	c. to solve problems that other people can't
11. initiative *(n.)*	a. a plan for achieving a goal	b. a ceremony that makes a person a member of a group or organization	c. a plan for dealing with a problem
12. reconciliation *(n.)*	a. restarting a friendship that ended because of distance	b. an end to a disagreement and beginning of an agreement	c. the start of a good relationship after a fight

 C. Go online for more practice with the vocabulary.

D. Answer these questions.

1. How did Tithiya Sharma decide if someone was a hero?

   _____

2. What are two ways Sharma's decision to go on her journey changed her life?

   _____

3. Why did Sharma choose Maria do Socorro Melo Brandão as a hero?

   _____

4. Of the six heroes featured at the end of the article, which has the greatest influence on their community? Why?

   _____

   _____

5. What does Tithiya Sharma plan to do after her journey?

   _____

E. Write *T* (true) or *F* (false) for each statement. Then correct each false statement to make it true. Write the paragraph number where you found information to support your answer.

____ 1. Tithiya Sharma paid for her journey by herself.
   (paragraph ____)

   _____

____ 2. Sharma sometimes found herself in dangerous areas with just a few notes to guide her.
   (paragraph ____)

   _____

____ 3. Sharma provided counseling to slum residents in the City of God favela.
   (paragraph ____)

   _____

____ 4. Sharma tried to raise money for the 100 heroes by writing about them.
   (paragraph ____)

   _____

_____ 5. Mahfuza Folad runs a cookie shop in Kabul.
       (paragraph _____)

_____

_____ 6. Sharma's best memories of her journey are of the places she visited
       around the world.
       (paragraph _____)

_____

F. Complete the chart with information about the heroes from the article.

Name	Country	Why he/she is a hero
Maria do Socorro Melo Brandão		
	South Africa	
	England/Iraq	Created soccer-based education and development programs in Iraq, Sudan, England, and Ghana to teach people of different social, religious, and ethnic backgrounds to work as a team.
Mahfuza Folad		
Dr. Jo and Lyn Lusi		
	Rwanda	

G. Based on the chart above, what will be the lasting effects of each hero's actions for his or her community? Compare your ideas with a partner.

1. Maria do Socorro Melo Brandão

_____

_____

2. Sonja Kruse

_____

_____

3. Yamam Nabeel

_____

_____

4. Mahfuza Folad

_____

_____

5. Dr. Jo and Lyn Lusi

_____

_____

6. Felicite Rwemalika

_____

_____

WRITE WHAT YOU THINK

A. Discuss the questions in a group. Look back at your Quick Write on page 12 as you think about what you learned.

1. Have you ever volunteered to do something to help your community? If so, describe your experience.

2. Firefighters are often seen as admirable. What other people are seen as admirable because of their profession? Why?

3. How can you become a local champion? How could your actions help your community?

B. Think about the unit video, Reading 1, and Reading 2 as you discuss the questions. Then choose one question and write a paragraph in response.

1. Think of someone in the news who is a real-life role model. What makes this person a role model?

2. If you did something for your community, would you want to be publicly acknowledged for it? Why or why not?

Vocabulary Skill | Using the dictionary

When you look up a word in the dictionary, you will find the definition and other information about the word and how it is used. Different dictionaries may include slightly different information, but they are generally organized in a similar way. Notice the different parts of this dictionary entry from the *Oxford Advanced American Dictionary for learners of English*.

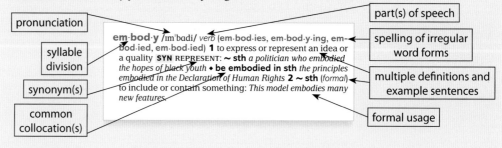

All dictionary entries are from the *Oxford Advanced American Dictionary for learners of English* © Oxford University 2011.

A. Look at the dictionary entry for *mentality*. Check (✓) the information that this entry has.

men·tal·i·ty **AWL** /mɛnˈtæləti/ *noun* [usually sing.] (*pl.* men·tal·i·ties) the particular attitude or way of thinking of a person or group **SYN** MINDSET: *I cannot understand the mentality of video gamers.* ♦ *a criminal/ghetto mentality* ➲ see also SIEGE MENTALITY

☐ syllable division
☐ pronunciation
☐ part(s) of speech
☐ spelling of irregular word forms

☐ multiple definitions
☐ example sentences
☐ formal usage
☐ synonym(s)
☐ common collocation(s)

Tip for Success

The abbreviations -*sth* and -*sb* mean "something" and "somebody." They show you whether a verb is followed by a noun for a thing (-*sth*), a person (-*sb*), or both.

con·front 🔑 /kənˈfrʌnt/ *verb*
1 ~ sb/sth (of problems or a difficult situation) to appear and need to be dealt with by someone: *the economic problems confronting the country* ♦ *The government found itself confronted by massive opposition.* **2 ~ sth** to deal with a problem or difficult situation **SYN** FACE UP TO: *She knew that she had to confront her fears.* **3 ~ sb** to face someone so that they cannot avoid seeing and hearing you, especially in an unfriendly or dangerous situation: *This was the first time he had confronted an armed robber.* **4 ~ sb with sb/sth** to make someone face or deal with an unpleasant or difficult person or situation. **5 be confronted with sth** to have something in front of you that you have to deal with or react to: *When confronted with a bear, stop and stay calm.*

1. How many definitions does *confront* have? ____

2. What synonym is given for *confront*? _____

3. What common expression is given that uses *confront*?

    _____

in·her·ent **AWL** /ɪnˈhɪrənt; -ˈhɛr-/ *adj.* **~ (in sb/sth)** that is a basic or permanent part of someone or something and that cannot be removed **SYN** INTRINSIC: *the difficulties inherent in a study of this type* ♦ *Violence is inherent in our society.* ♦ *an inherent weakness in the design of the machine* ▶ in·her·ent·ly **AWL** *adv.: an inherently unworkable system*

4. What part of speech is *inherent*? _____

    Inherently? _____

5. What synonym is given for *inherent*? _____

6. Where are the syllable divisions in *inherently*? Write the word and put a slash (/) after each syllable. _____

> **con·strain** **AWL** /kənˈstreɪn/ *verb (formal)* **1** [usually passive] **~ sb to do sth** to force someone to do something or behave in a particular way: *The evidence was so compelling that he felt constrained to accept it.* **2** [often passive] to restrict or limit someone or something: **~ sth** *Research has been constrained by a lack of funds.* ◆ **~ sb (from doing sth)** *She felt constrained from continuing by the threat of losing her job.*

7. In what form is *constrain* usually used? _____

8. How many example sentences are given for *constrain*? ____

9. What words often follow *constrain*? _____

> **a·chieve·ment** 🔑 **AWL** /əˈtʃiːvmənt/ *noun* **1** [C] a thing that someone has done successfully, especially using their own effort and skill: *the greatest scientific achievement of the decade* ◆ *It was a remarkable achievement for such a young player.* ◆ *They were proud of their children's achievements.* ↗ collocations at ACHIEVE **2** [U] the act or process of achieving something: *the need to raise standards of achievement in education* ◆ *Even a small success gives you a sense of achievement* (= a feeling of pride).

10. Where are the syllable divisions in *achievement*? Write the word and put a slash (/) after each syllable. _____

11. How many definitions does *achievement* have? ____

12. What common collocation is given that uses *achievement*?

_____

C. Work with a partner. Look up words from Reading 1 and Reading 2 in your dictionary. Take turns asking questions like the ones in Activity B.

iQ ONLINE **D.** Go online for more practice with using the dictionary.

WRITING

 **UNIT OBJECTIVE** At the end of this unit, you will write an analysis essay about the qualities that make someone admirable. This essay will include specific information from the readings, the unit video, and your own ideas.

 **Writing Skill** | **Organizing and developing an essay**

Tip for Success

The writer is responsible for producing text that others can understand. Write on one topic (unity) in a logical way (coherence).

An **analysis essay** examines a topic by breaking it down into smaller parts. Remember that an essay includes an **introduction**, one or more **body paragraphs**, and a **conclusion**.

Introduction

This paragraph should make the reader interested in your topic. It usually includes a "hook" to catch the reader's attention. It also provides background information or general statements about the topic. Within the introduction paragraph, include a **thesis statement**. The thesis statement contains the topic and the **controlling idea** (a specific idea or an opinion about the topic) of the essay. It tells the reader the purpose of the essay.

topic   controlling idea

Thesis statement: A role model inspires people to do their best.

Body paragraphs

For each body paragraph, include a **topic sentence** that states the topic of the paragraph and the controlling idea. Add supporting sentences that provide as much detail as possible to fully develop your thesis. Use supporting sentences that all relate to or develop the topic to create **unity**. Organize the supporting sentences in a logical way so there is a clear connection between the ideas to create **coherence**. Often **transition words** like *first*, *in addition*, and *for example* are used to show the relationship between supporting ideas.

Conclusion

The conclusion brings the essay to a close. This paragraph may restate the thesis statement in different words, summarize the main points, or do both. Write sentences that remind the reader of why he or she is reading the essay. You can also use the conclusion to help your reader look beyond the essay or think about further ideas that relate to your topic.

A. WRITING MODEL Read the model essay. Then follow the steps below.

Successful People

Are fame and fortune in your future? Do you dream of becoming a billionaire or a famous actor? For most of us, that is not too likely. Even though we may never see our picture on the cover of a glossy magazine, we all want to make something of ourselves and have a good life. We all want to succeed, and identifying what qualities make someone successful can help us to achieve that goal.

Successful people share three common qualities that allow them to stand out. First, people who are successful are organized. They don't waste time, and they work in ways that maximize their efficiency. They also work longer hours. Second, they are focused and single-minded. They can see where they want to go and only do the things that will get them there. For example, when they are working on something, they don't get lost in the details or overwhelmed by the tasks they need to do. Finally, people who are successful must be able to set and accomplish goals. Knowing what they want helps them stay both organized and focused.

If you want to be successful, you need to get organized, stay focused, and set and accomplish goals. Not many people succeed without these qualities, but don't despair. These behaviors can be learned and improved, and anyone can stand out if he or she develops organization, focus, and goals.

1. Read the introduction again. Circle the hook.

2. Find the thesis statement in the introductory paragraph. Underline the topic once. Underline the controlling idea twice.

3. Underline the topic sentence of the body paragraph.

4. One sentence in the body doesn't contribute to the unity of the essay because it doesn't develop the topic. Draw a line through it.

5. Circle the transition words that contribute to the coherence of the body paragraph.

6. Read the conclusion again. Circle the answer that best describes what the conclusion does.
   a. It restates the thesis statement and suggests further examination of the topic.
   b. It summarizes the main points and suggests ways to be successful.
   c. It restates the thesis statement and summarizes the main points.

B. In the chart on page 25, list two people you consider successful, the qualities you believe contributed to their success, and their accomplishments. List one family member or friend and a famous or well-known person.

Successful people	Qualities	Accomplishments
my mother	hardworking, organized, caring	worked as a nurse while raising my sisters and me

C. Work with a partner. Read the sentences and number them to make a meaningful body paragraph. First, identify the topic sentence. Then order the supporting sentences to create unity and coherence. Then write the whole paragraph in order and check for unity and coherence.

____ a. First, role models have a well-developed set of skills or qualities, but they may be unwilling or unable to help others develop them.

____ b. Mentors, on the other hand, may have the same skills or qualities, but they make it a point to train or teach others on a personal basis.

____ c. There are two important differences between role models and mentors.

_3_ d. For example, a research scientist may be great in the lab but not in the classroom.

____ e. Role models may or may not pay personal attention to those they inspire and may affect a large number of people at once, but mentors always have a few special people they work with individually.

____ f. A role model can inspire many people just by his or her actions, while a mentor is limited to inspiring a few people at a time.

____ g. This is because of the time it takes to work with someone individually.

____ h. A second factor is the number of people a role model or mentor can influence at one time.

D. The paragraph in Activity C is the body paragraph for an essay about role models and mentors. Answer the questions.

1. List some possible hooks for an introduction to this paragraph.

_____

_____

2. Choose the best thesis statement for the essay.
    a. We all need both role models and mentors.
    b. Role models and mentors are both admirable, but their effect on our lives will be very different.
    c. Both role models and mentors are admirable.

3. What is the best way to conclude this essay?

_____

 E. Go online for more practice with organizing and developing an essay.

Grammar   Restrictive relative clauses

1. **Restrictive relative clauses*** describe or identify nouns. Usually, they directly follow nouns, noun phrases, or indefinite pronouns (*something*, *everyone*, etc.).

> pronoun /
> noun   adjective clause
> A role model is <u>someone</u> **who makes a difference in people's lives.**
> Role models face <u>questions</u> **that we may also face.**

2. Most relative clauses begin with a relative pronoun.

   • Use *who* or *that* after nouns for people.

   > Role models are <u>people</u> **who may volunteer in their communities.**
   > <u>Ordinary people</u> **that we each know** can be role models.

   • Use *that* or *which* after nouns for things. (*Which* usually sounds more formal.)

   > <u>Biographies</u> **that tell stories of successful people** are very popular.
   > Role models do <u>things</u> **that we would like to do.**
   > Sarah works for a <u>company</u> **which helps the homeless.**

3. You can think of a sentence with a relative clause as a combination of two sentences about the same noun.

   • In a **subject relative clause**, the relative pronoun stands for the subject of the clause. It is followed by a verb.

   > A role model is someone. + ~~He or she~~ makes a difference in people's lives. =
   >   subject + verb
   > A role model is <u>someone</u> **who makes a difference in people's lives.**

   • In an **object relative clause**, the relative pronoun stands for the object of the clause. The relative pronoun is followed by a subject + verb.

   > Role models face questions. + We may also face ~~the questions~~. =
   >   object + subject + verb
   > Role models face <u>questions</u> **that we may also face.**

4. In object relative clauses, the relative pronoun can be omitted.

   > <u>Ordinary people</u> ~~that~~ **we each know** can be role models.
   > Role models do <u>things</u> ~~that~~ we **would like to do.**

*Also called *identifying adjective clauses*

A. Underline the relative clause in each sentence. Circle the noun, noun phrase, or indefinite pronoun it identifies.

1. Not every (person) <u>who makes his or her community a better place</u> is acknowledged for it.

2. They do <u>the things that they do</u> because they want to make their communities better.

3. At 19, Ahmed borrowed a novel that changed his life forever.

4. His father was an illiterate cattle merchant who insisted that his son have an education.

5. She reads storybooks to children who have no access to television.

6. Lisa started a youth environmental group which is trying to clean up the city.

7. The trash Lisa's group collects is carried away by bicycles.

B. Combine each pair of sentences using a restrictive relative clause with *who*, *that*, or *which*. Use the words in bold to help you.

1. We all aspire to do **something**. Other people will respect **it**.

   We all aspire to do something that other people will respect.

2. Role models may inspire us to help **people**. **They** cannot help themselves.

   _____

3. Role models have **qualities**. We would like to have **them**.

   _____

4. To me, **a person** is a role model. **He** inspires others to do good deeds.

   _____

5. Reading novels gives students **something**. They cannot get **it** in textbooks.

   _____

6. Caring for the environment is **something**. We can all do **it**.

   _____

7. **Someone** is a generous person. **He or she** donates money to charity.

   _____

C. Which sentences in Activity B can omit the relative pronoun? Cross out the relative pronoun if it can be omitted.

 D. Go online for more practice with restrictive relative clauses.

E. Go online for the grammar expansion.

 Write a three-paragraph analysis essay

---

 In this assignment, you are going to write a three-paragraph analysis essay. As you prepare your essay, think about the Unit Question, "What makes someone admirable?" Use information from Reading 1, Reading 2, the unit video, and your work in this unit to support your essay. Refer to the Self-Assessment checklist on page 30.

Go to the Online Writing Tutor for a writing model and alternate Unit Assignments.

PLAN AND WRITE

A. BRAINSTORM Follow these steps to help you organize your ideas.

1. In the chart below, list three people who you think are admirable. Describe the qualities that they possess and give an example of their accomplishments.

Person	Qualities	Accomplishments
1.		
2.		
3.		

2. Compare the people in your chart. What qualities do they share? How are their accomplishments similar or different?

Similarities	Differences

Writing **Tip**
Outlines help you put your ideas in order. Often when you write an outline for an essay, you include the thesis statement, notes about supporting ideas for your body paragraphs, and notes for the concluding paragraph.

B. PLAN **Follow these steps to plan your essay.**

1. Write a topic for your essay.

   _____

2. Write an opinion or a specific idea about the topic above. This will be your controlling idea for your thesis statement.

   _____

   _____

3. Now combine your topic from 1 and your controlling idea from 2 to form your thesis statement.

   _____

   _____

   _____

4. Go to the Online Resources to download and complete the outline for your analysis essay.

C. **WRITE** Use your **PLAN** notes to write your essay. Go to *iQ Online* to use the Online Writing Tutor.

1. Write your analysis essay about the qualities that make a person admirable. Be sure to have an introduction, a body paragraph, and a conclusion. Include restrictive relative clauses where appropriate. You may also use transition words from the box below to help connect your ideas.

In addition,	For example,	First,	Finally,
Also,	For instance,	Second,	Most importantly,

2. Look at the Self-Assessment checklist below to guide your writing.

REVISE AND EDIT

A. **PEER REVIEW** Read your partner's essay. Then go online and use the Peer Review worksheet. Discuss the review with your partner.

B. **REWRITE** Based on your partner's review, revise, and rewrite your essay.

C. **EDIT** Complete the Self-Assessment checklist as you prepare to write the final draft of your essay. Be prepared to hand in your work or discuss it in class.

SELF-ASSESSMENT		
Yes	**No**	
☐	☐	Does the essay have an introduction with a hook and thesis statement?
☐	☐	Are there enough details in the body paragraph to support the topic sentence?
☐	☐	If transition words are included, are they used appropriately?
☐	☐	Are relative clauses used correctly?
☐	☐	Does the essay include vocabulary from the unit?
☐	☐	Did you check the essay for punctuation, spelling, and grammar?

D. **REFLECT** Go to the Online Discussion Board to discuss these questions.

1. What is something new you learned in this unit?

2. Look back at the Unit Question—What makes someone admirable? Is your answer different now than when you started the unit? If yes, how is it different? Why?

Circle the words and phrases you have learned in this unit.

Nouns
achievement 🔑 AWL
adversity
criteria 🔑 AWL
initiative 🔑 AWL
reconciliation
resolve 🔑 AWL
version 🔑 AWL

Verbs
confront 🔑
deconstruct
disrupt
embody
navigate
pursue 🔑 AWL

Phrasal Verbs
aspire to
bear witness

Adjectives
acknowledged (for) 🔑 AWL
constrained AWL
drastic
inclined AWL
inspirational
notorious
pressing
underprivileged

Adverb
inherently AWL

🔑 Oxford 3000™ words

AWL Academic Word List

Check (✓) the skills you learned. If you need more work on a skill, refer to the page(s) in parentheses.

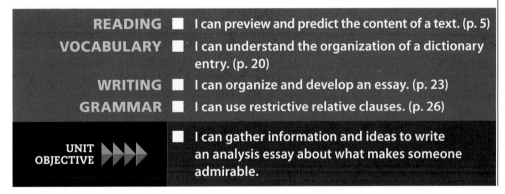

READING ☐	I can preview and predict the content of a text. (p. 5)
VOCABULARY ☐	I can understand the organization of a dictionary entry. (p. 20)
WRITING ☐	I can organize and develop an essay. (p. 23)
GRAMMAR ☐	I can use restrictive relative clauses. (p. 26)
UNIT OBJECTIVE ▶▶▶▶ ☐	I can gather information and ideas to write an analysis essay about what makes someone admirable.

UNIT **2**

Consumer Behavior

READING ▶ highlighting and annotating
VOCABULARY ▶ collocations with nouns
WRITING ▶ writing a descriptive essay
GRAMMAR ▶ definite and indefinite articles

UNIT QUESTION

What makes you want to buy something?

A Discuss these questions with your classmates.

1. What sorts of things do you like to shop for? What do you not enjoy shopping for?

2. How does the way something appears influence your decision to buy it?

3. Look at the photo. Would you buy something from this shop? Why or why not?

B Listen to *The Q Classroom* online. Then answer these questions.

1. Why are appearances important to Sophy when she makes a purchase? Do you share this value? Why or why not?

2. What does Marcus say about packaging and Felix about presentation? Give other examples of how packaging or presentation affects your decision to buy something.

 C Go to the Online Discussion Board to discuss the Unit Question with your classmates.

D Complete the questionnaire about your recent shopping purchases. Write down or check (✓) your answers. Then compare with a partner.

Why Do You Shop?

What was the last thing you bought because . . . ?	Item or service bought	Don't remember	Doesn't apply
1. you needed to satisfy a basic need (like food or medicine)		☐	☐
2. you had to replace something that was broken		☐	☐
3. you needed it for school		☐	☐
4. you were in a hurry (even though it wasn't exactly what you wanted)		☐	☐
5. the price was lower than it was before		☐	☐
6. you were bored and wanted something to do		☐	☐
7. you thought it was stylish or special		☐	☐
8. all your friends had one		☐	☐

E Read the descriptions of different kinds of shoppers below and discuss these questions with your partner.

1. Which descriptions sound like you and your partner?

2. Are you one specific type of shopper or a combination of types?

The practical shopper: You always go shopping with a list and only buy the things you need.

The convenient shopper: You only go shopping if something is easy to get or especially affordable.

The emotional shopper: You shop more often when you are happy or sad.

The trendy shopper: You typically buy stylish things or popular brand names.

The peer-pressure shopper: You often buy things because your friends are buying them.

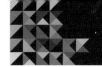

READING

READING 1 | So Much Dead Space

You are going to read an article from a business journal about how store windows are used to attract customers. Use the article to gather information and ideas for your Unit Assignment.

PREVIEW THE READING

Paco Underhill

A. **PREVIEW** Read the title and subtitle of the article by Paco Underhill, the CEO of a research firm that focuses on the relationships between people and stores and people and products. Answer these questions.

1. What does the title mean?

2. What do you think Paco Underhill thinks about most store windows?

3. Based on the subtitle, what is Underhill's purpose in writing the article?

B. **QUICK WRITE** Think about stores you typically pass by or shop in. What kinds of things do you usually see in the windows? Describe what is in a favorite store window. Write for 5–10 minutes in response. Be sure to use this section for your Unit Assignment.

C. **VOCABULARY** Check (✓) the words you know. Then work with a partner to locate each word in the reading. Use clues to help define the words you don't know. Check your definitions in the dictionary.

allude to *(phr. v.)*	**liberate** *(v.)*
concept *(n.)* 🔑	**pedestrian** *(n.)*
distinguish *(v.)* 🔑	**priority** *(n.)* 🔑
evolve *(v.)*	**promote** *(v.)* 🔑
focus on *(phr. v.)* 🔑	**sophisticated** *(adj.)*
individual *(n.)* 🔑	**urban** *(adj.)* 🔑

🔑 Oxford 3000™ words

 D. Go online to listen and practice your pronunciation.

WORK WITH THE READING

🔊 **A.** Read the article and gather information about what makes you want to buy something.

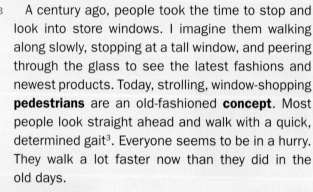

So Much Dead Space
Creating Store Windows Alive with Promise

1   I am a nerdy American researcher. No one has ever thought of me as fashionable. What I do know about is shops and shopping. I've always been good at watching people. Because I grew up with a terrible stutter[1] and was not comfortable talking, I learned to *observe* as a way of understanding social rules. I've turned this coping mechanism[2] into a profession. What I have done for the past twenty-five years is research shopping behavior: I simply walk around malls and shopping streets and figure out what motivates people to buy things. What makes someone stop and look at a store window? What makes someone go into a store? What makes someone buy something?

2   As I stroll around, I look closely at store windows, since they are an essential part of the shopping experience. In his delightful book *Made in America*, Bill Bryson writes about the history of stores and shopping in America. He describes the big store windows that were an important feature of most retail stores in the past century. When I look out my office window in New York City, I see many of those windows. They remain the same today as they were some 120 years ago.

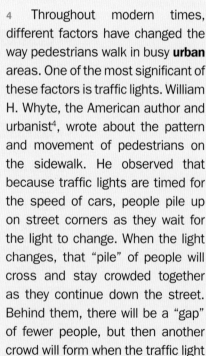

a store window display

3   A century ago, people took the time to stop and look into store windows. I imagine them walking along slowly, stopping at a tall window, and peering through the glass to see the latest fashions and newest products. Today, strolling, window-shopping **pedestrians** are an old-fashioned **concept**. Most people look straight ahead and walk with a quick, determined gait[3]. Everyone seems to be in a hurry. They walk a lot faster now than they did in the old days.

4   Throughout modern times, different factors have changed the way pedestrians walk in busy **urban** areas. One of the most significant of these factors is traffic lights. William H. Whyte, the American author and urbanist[4], wrote about the pattern and movement of pedestrians on the sidewalk. He observed that because traffic lights are timed for the speed of cars, people pile up on street corners as they wait for the light to change. When the light changes, that "pile" of people will cross and stay crowded together as they continue down the street. Behind them, there will be a "gap" of fewer people, but then another crowd will form when the traffic light changes again. This creates a pattern of crowds and gaps on urban shopping streets.

---

[1] **stutter:** difficulty speaking because you cannot stop yourself from repeating the first sound of some words

[2] **coping mechanism:** a technique to deal with a difficult matter or situation

[3] **gait:** a way of walking

[4] **urbanist:** a person who studies cities

5   Now, think about how **individuals** behave when walking in these crowds of people. Some people will speed up to get out of the crowd, and then the entire group will begin to walk more quickly. This behavior affects how people view the store windows that they pass by. Even if you wanted to slow down or stop to look in a window, you couldn't. You have to keep walking quickly so that you won't be in the way of other people. That's why window displays need to instantly grab attention. But many don't. Take the drugstores in my neighborhood, for example. The windows are filled with boxes of bleach and detergent, packages of razors and soap, and whatever else can be squeezed into the space. With the window so crowded, it is impossible to **focus on** any single product. Often, it's difficult to even see clearly what is really being **promoted**! Maybe in 1928, it was important for a store to advertise the large selection of products offered. Maybe then, shoppers had the time to really take a look at a window and examine the display. But these days, retailers are lucky if pedestrians just glance at their store windows.

> " *Especially since today's retail market is so competitive, if done right, windows can function as an important brand-identity tool.* "

6   The way our eyes and brain handle information has become more **sophisticated**. Thanks to television and computers, our ability to process images is faster. We no longer read letter by letter but rather in groups of words at a time. TV programs have **evolved** so that we see the stories of years— or even lifetimes—in just a few hours. A billboard can tell a more sophisticated joke today than it could 20 years ago. A 15-second commercial can **allude to** a full story. Likewise, when it comes to window displays, shoppers today can understand information more quickly.

7   Store windows today must be quick reads. They must be simple enough so that the products can be clearly identified, and they must be creative enough to catch the busy pedestrian's eye. Just a quick look at a store window should answer many questions for savvy[5] shoppers: Who is the core market[6] of the store? Does the store fit their personal style or not? How long will a typical trip into the store take? Especially since today's retail market is so competitive, if done right, windows can function as an important brand-identity[7] tool. As retailers, you must know who your customers are, and you must create windows that they will understand. For instance, Kiehl's, which sells all-natural bath and body products, uses its windows as a place for highlighting social issues, which fits with the **priorities** of its customers.

8   My favorite windows are in France. A man who runs his family's boutique off the main square in Strasbourg takes enormous pleasure in his windows. They tell jokes. Some are related to history. Sometimes his windows make me chuckle. The clothes are part of a larger story. His store always **distinguishes** itself from the other shops on the crowded square because his windows always make an impression. As busy as I might be as I walk down the street, his windows make me stop. Even more, they almost always tempt me to come inside the shop and take a good look around.

9   So what can stores do with their "dead space"? How can windows come alive? To modern retailers, I propose the following: Let's **liberate** our design teams. Stop filling windows with products. Tell a story. Make us laugh. Make us think. Learn from advertisers like Calvin Klein or Benetton who think outside the box with ads that catch our attention and motivate a response. Windows can be like literature. It's OK if not everybody understands the story you're telling. What is important is that the target customer gets it, and stops to look.

[5] **savvy:** having practical knowledge of something
[6] **core market:** the main group of people a store sells to

[7] **brand identity:** characteristics that quickly identify and distinguish a brand to shoppers

In Unit 1, you learned how to use the dictionary to find definitions and other information about a word. Look up the vocabulary words *liberate, promote,* and *urban* in the dictionary. How many definitions do they have? What other information about these words can you find?

B. **VOCABULARY** Here are some words and phrases from Reading 1. Read the sentences. Circle the answer that best matches the meaning of each bold word or phrase.

1. On a typical weekday, the sidewalks are filled with **pedestrians** who are window-shopping or looking for a place to stop and eat.
   a. people walking
   b. people bicycling

2. His **concept** for the advertisement was poorly thought out, so the design team chose another.
   a. product
   b. idea

3. Unlike quiet streets in rural areas, the crowded streets in **urban** areas are often filled with people.
   a. city
   b. country

4. Each **individual** in the survey was a professional designer.
   a. group of people
   b. single person

5. In a crowded store, it is easy to get overwhelmed and not be able to **focus on** what you like.
   a. concentrate
   b. remember

6. Because the business **promoted** its products successfully on the Internet, they sold well.
   a. developed
   b. advertised

7. After a year of study abroad, I had a more **sophisticated** view of the world.
   a. able to understand complicated ideas
   b. knowledgeable about a specific topic

8. Her poetry has **evolved** over the years because she has gained more confidence and developed her own style.
   a. kept the same form
   b. changed from an earlier form

9. She **alluded to** her work experience when she said, "I've been very busy the past few years."
   a. spoke indirectly about
   b. avoided speaking about

10. I had a lot to do and not much time, so I decided what my **priorities** were and I did those things first.
    a. the most important things
    b. the easiest things

11. The store **distinguishes** itself from its competitors by having lower prices.
    a. copies
    b. differs

12. Knowledge can **liberate** people and give them independence.
    a. control
    b. set free

C. Go online for more practice with the vocabulary.

D. Answer these questions.

1. What is the topic of the reading?

   _____

2. What is the controlling idea?

   _____

   _____

E. Circle the answer that best completes each statement.

1. The author is a researcher who ____.
   a. creates window displays
   b. observes how people shop
   c. compares shopping at different stores

2. The main reason that the article describes urban pedestrians is to ____.
   a. explain why store windows must be both simple and creative
   b. analyze their walking patterns
   c. contrast modern shoppers with shoppers in the past

3. The author thinks store windows should show ____.
   a. the products we can buy inside
   b. a piece of history
   c. something that catches our attention

4. The idea of "dead space" refers to ____.
   a. how the brain handles information from TV programs and billboards
   b. store windows that don't attract attention
   c. the empty space between pedestrians on the sidewalk

5. The author's intended audience is ____.
   a. shoppers
   b. pedestrians
   c. store owners

F. Answer these questions.

1. How is pedestrian behavior different now than in the last century?

   _____

2. What happens on sidewalks when people have to stop and wait for traffic lights to change?

   _____

3. What is the problem with the drugstore windows in the author's neighborhood?

   _____

4. What is one example the author uses to show how "our ability to process images is faster"?

   _____

5. What does the author mean when he says that store windows must be "quick reads"?

   _____

6. What does the author like about his favorite store windows? Give two examples.

   _____

G. The article refers to the work and research of others. Find the names of two authors and three stores in the reading. Complete the chart.

Name	Information about the author or store	Reason to include in the reading
Bill Bryson		
	author and urbanist	
	store selling all-natural bath and body products	
Calvin Klein Benetton		

H. Answer these questions.

1. According to Paco Underhill, what are seven things store windows should be and do?

   1. _____

   2. _____

   3. _____

   4. _____

   5. _____

   6. _____

   7. _____

2. What is one thing a store window should not be or do?

   _____

 I. Go online to read *Think Before You Buy* and check your comprehension.

WRITE WHAT YOU THINK

A. Discuss these questions in a group.

Critical Thinking **Tip**

The Write What You Think questions require you to discuss your ideas. Through **discussion**, you can clarify your understanding of new material, which will help you remember it better. Discussion also helps you clarify information for others who may not understand it.

1. Other than store windows, what are some ways store owners use appearance inside the store to attract customers?

2. Given that online shopping is more and more common, stores create online "windows" on their websites. How is shopping different when browsing or "window-shopping" online?

3. Think about a favorite store or website. Describe what is in the store window or on the website. Based on what you read, is the store window or website appealing? Explain.

B. Choose one question and write a paragraph in response. Look back at your Quick Write on page 35 as you think about what you learned.

The purpose of **highlighting** and **annotating** is to identify important ideas in a text. Both of these techniques will allow you to quickly find the information later, without having to reread the text.

Highlighting

Always decide the purpose of your highlighting before you begin. Then highlight, underline, or circle information in a text such as:

- the main idea or topic of a paragraph
- key words, details, or examples
- phrases that summarize the information

Use different-colored highlighter pens for different types of information. For example, use one color for main ideas and another for details. Or use a graphic system, such as solid lines, dotted lines, circling, etc.

Annotating

Annotating—writing directly on the page of a text—is a useful way to identify and mark important information. First, read a paragraph and decide what is important. Then write brief notes in the margin. You may use abbreviations such as:

T = thesis	S = summary	R = reason
MI = main idea	Ex = example	? = question

A. Read this paragraph from Reading 1 and look at the highlighting and annotations. Then answer the questions below.

S = people
understand
info faster now

R = TV,
computers

  The way our eyes and brain handle information has become more sophisticated. Thanks to television and computers, our ability to process images is faster. We no longer read letter by letter but rather in groups of words at a time. TV programs have evolved so that we see the stories of years—or even lifetimes—in just a few hours. A billboard can tell a more sophisticated joke today than it could 20 years ago. A 15-second commercial can allude to a full story. Likewise, when it comes to window displays, shoppers today can understand information more quickly.

1. What does the information highlighted in yellow show?

2. What does the information highlighted in pink show?

3. What purposes do the two annotations have?

Tip for Success

After annotating the text, you may want to write out your notes to use as a reference and study tool.

B. Highlight and annotate a paragraph from Reading 1 on page 43. Follow these steps. Then compare your notes with a partner.

1. Highlight in one color (or circle) the main idea of the paragraph.

2. Highlight in another color (or underline) the key details.

3. Write a brief note in the margin to summarize the paragraph.

4. Write a note in the margin that identifies a specific example.

> Store windows today must be quick reads. They must be simple enough so that the products can be clearly identified, and they must be creative enough to catch the busy pedestrian's eye. Just a quick look at a store window should answer many questions for savvy shoppers: Who is the core market of the store? Does the store fit their personal style or not? How long will a typical trip into the store take? Especially since today's retail market is so competitive, if done right, windows can function as an important brand-identity tool. As retailers, you must know who your customers are, and you must create windows that they will understand. For instance, Kiehl's, which sells all-natural bath and body products, uses its windows as a place for highlighting social issues, which fits with the priorities of its customers.

 C. Go online for more practice highlighting and annotating.

READING 2 | Now on Stage: Your Home!

 You are going to read an article from a design magazine about how to "stage" a home: how to make it more attractive to people who might buy it. Use the article to gather information and ideas for your Unit Assignment.

PREVIEW THE READING

A. PREVIEW Read the title of the article and look at the photos. Which room do you think is staged? Why?

before

after

B. **QUICK WRITE** Which version of the room do you like more? Write for 5–10 minutes in response. Include a description to help your reader form a mental picture. Be sure to use this section for your Unit Assignment.

C. **VOCABULARY** Check (✓) the words you know. Use a dictionary to define any new or unknown words. Then discuss how the words will relate to the unit with a partner.

feature *(v.)* 🔑	minimize *(v.)*	remove *(v.)* 🔑
in theory *(idm.)* 🔑	negative *(n.)* 🔑	residence *(n.)*
investment *(n.)* 🔑	neutral *(adj.)*	tend *(v.)* 🔑
mentally *(adv.)* 🔑	potential *(adj.)* 🔑	visualize *(v.)*

🔑 Oxford 3000™ words

 D. Go online to listen and practice your pronunciation.

WORK WITH THE READING

A. Read the article and gather information about what makes you want to buy something.

Now on Stage: Your Home!

by Douglas Nan

1 Tina Miller is busy at work in the kitchen of her New Jersey condominium[1], wrapping dishes in paper. Just outside, several large boxes stand near the front door, and in the living room, Miller's two sons are packing video games. "We've been here for almost ten years," she says, looking around. "I never realized how much stuff we had."

2 Two months ago, Tina's husband Evan accepted a job in another state, and now the family is getting ready to move. "There's a lot of work to do, but the hardest part seems to be selling this condo," she explains. "We've had it on the market[2]

for over a month and several people have come to see it. But so far, no luck."

3 **In theory**, the Millers' home should have sold quickly. It is in a modern building on a quiet street; shops and restaurants are within walking distance. The couple has even reduced the sale price by $10,000. Connie Tran, the real estate agent[3] working with the Millers, believes she knows what the problem is. "This is a nice condo. The rooms are large and there's lots of light, but the feel of the place is all wrong. The living room is full of boxes; the kitchen and bathroom are cluttered[4]; the paint on the walls is too dark. It doesn't make a great first impression on **potential** buyers."

4 To help sell their condo, Tran has suggested that the Millers hire someone to stage it. What exactly

---

[1] **condominium** (short form: **condo**): an apartment that is owned by the person who lives in it
[2] **on the market**: for sale

[3] **real estate agent**: a person who sells homes
[4] **cluttered**: messy and disorganized; filled with many things

does this mean? The main goal, professional stagers would say, is to prepare a house to sell by making it as attractive as possible. For most people, this simply involves fixing things that are broken or cleaning a place thoroughly. But even though these things are important, real estate agent Elizabeth Weintraub says that staging goes "beyond decorating and cleaning. It's about creating [a] mood[5]. Staging makes your house look bigger, brighter, cleaner, warmer, and best of all, it makes home buyers want to buy it."

5 The Millers have agreed to have their home staged. So what will a professional home stager suggest doing to help sell their condo?

6 **1.** *Minimize the clutter.* The Miller family has lived in their home for ten years, and though they are preparing to move, many of the rooms are still full of furniture, books, electronics, and other things that people collect over time. These things can make the place look crowded and smaller than it is. Packing and moving most of the unnecessary items out of the condo will make it look much larger—which will appeal to buyers.

7 **2.** *Store personal items.* The Millers also have to be aware of the small stuff: photos and magazines in the living room, a child's drawings on the refrigerator, and slippers in the bathroom. Not only do these things make the condo appear more cluttered, they also make it look like the *Millers'* home— and that's a problem. A buyer doesn't want to tour the place and see someone else's stuff. Professional home stager Barb Schwartz advises sellers to "clear all unnecessary objects throughout the house." Doing this will help a potential buyer to "**mentally** 'move in' with their own things"—and to **visualize** themselves in the home.

8 **3.** *Organize what's left.* Once each room is down to a few essential items, a professional stager will make sure these things are positioned in an attractive way that makes the rooms look good. Sandra Rinomato, the host of a popular TV show about selling houses, offers these suggestions:

- "**Feature** only a few pieces of furniture [in each room] and pull pieces away from walls to make rooms look bigger."

- "Bedrooms are difficult to stage because they are in daily use." To make these rooms appear spacious[6] and neat, Rinomato recommends using white sheets on the bed and "clearing everything off nightstands."

- "Open the drapes[7] or **remove** them completely. Light, bright rooms give the impression of a happy place—and everyone wants to move into a happy place."

9 **4.** *Repaint if necessary.* Four years ago, the Millers painted the walls in the living room a warm reddish color. They love it but a potential home buyer might not, for a couple of reasons. The color was a personal choice made by the Millers— which makes the condo still seem as if it is theirs. Dark colors can also make a room appear smaller. Repainting the walls a lighter, more **neutral** color will make the room look more spacious.

10 What if the Millers don't sell the condo before they move? Should they still have it staged if it is empty? Sveta Melchuk, of Home

---

[5] **mood:** a feeling

[6] **spacious:** open, with lots of room
[7] **drapes:** thick curtains used to cover windows

Staging Montreal, and many other real estate professionals say yes. Melchuk notes on her website that "most people have a hard time imagining [a] space as a potential home if it contains no furniture. The rooms will look too big or too small" and may invite buyers to "notice the **negatives**" (such as a scratch on the floor or old windows). For these reasons, many real estate agents will recommend furnishing some of the main rooms in a vacant home.

11   In some cases, staging a home can cost as much as $4,000, which has many sellers wondering if it's worth it. Barb Schwartz, who has staged thousands of **residences**, believes it is. According to her, the average home can take up to 212 days to sell, while a professionally staged one usually takes just 37. Schwartz and others in her field[8] also note that homes they prepare for viewing **tend** to sell for more money—often thousands of dollars more.

12   Ultimately, staging seems to be a good **investment**, especially if an owner is having difficulty selling a home. The Millers agree. "I hardly recognize this place anymore," laughs Tina. "It looks wonderful—like something you'd see in a magazine. And last week, we had two offers to buy. The trouble is, I like it here so much now that I don't want to move!"

[8] **field:** a profession or area of work (for example, the medical field)

B. VOCABULARY Complete the sentences with the vocabulary from Reading 2.

feature (v.)	mentally (adv.)	neutral (adj.)	residence (n.)
in theory (idm.)	minimize (v.)	potential (adj.)	tend (v.)
investment (n.)	negative (n.)	remove (v.)	visualize (v.)

1. Close your eyes and try to _____ this room full of furniture. Can you picture it?

2. The yellow paint on these walls is too bright. A(n) _____ color like tan or cream would be better.

3. Can you _____ the books and papers from the table and put them in your backpack?

4. We really like the apartment. The only _____ is that it doesn't come with parking.

5. They own a home in the country, but their primary _____ is in London.

6. Most people in this city _____ to live in apartments. Only a few live in large houses.

7. One way to _____ noise in the apartment is to put rugs on the floors. Then it will be quieter.

8. I can think of two _____ ways to use this room: as an office or as an extra bedroom.

9. This month's *House* magazine is going to _____ photos of famous people's homes.

10. Shopping for a new home can be _____ exhausting. Sometimes you get so tired, you can't think anymore.

11. Buying a house is a good _____. You can live in it now and sell it later.

12. _____, it should only take twenty minutes to rearrange my furniture, but I always take hours to think about where everything should go.

iQ ONLINE **C. Go online for more practice with the vocabulary.**

D. Circle the correct answer. Then explain more about your answer.

1. Who is the intended audience for this article?
   a. people selling a home
   b. new homeowners
   c. potential home buyers

   Why did you choose this answer?

   _____

2. People hire a professional home stager primarily to help them ___ a home.
   a. find and buy
   b. organize and decorate
   c. find a buyer for

   According to Elizabeth Weintraub, what is the most important thing a home stager can do?

   _____

3. Look at the numbered list in paragraphs 6–9. A good subheading for this section of the article would be ___.
   a. Four Reasons You Should Hire a Professional Home Stager
   b. Four Tips for Successfully Staging a Home
   c. Four Staging Mistakes Many Homeowners Make

   Why are there bullet points in paragraph 8?

   _____

4. Paragraph 10 describes why ____.
   a. it's helpful to stage a vacant home
   b. staged houses sometimes do not sell
   c. empty homes are easier to sell

   Where in paragraph 10 is this idea explicitly stated?

   _____

5. The purpose of paragraph 11 is to explain ____ a home.
   a. the cost of staging
   b. the time it takes to stage
   c. the benefits of staging

   Why does Barb Schwartz believe that paying for staging is worthwhile?

   _____

6. The author ends the article by saying he ____ home staging is a good idea.
   a. believes
   b. doesn't think
   c. isn't sure if

   The author uses an example to support this idea. What is surprising about the example?

   _____

E. Answer these questions about the Miller family.

1. Who are the Millers?

   _____

2. Why are they selling their home?

   _____

3. What are some good points about their home?

   _____

4. What are some things that are wrong with the Millers' home?

   _____

   _____

5. What did the Millers do to increase the chances of selling their home?

   _____

6. Were their efforts effective? How do you know?

_____

7. Why do you think the author included the Millers in this article?

_____

F. The article describes different home staging techniques. Complete the chart with the correct information.

Home staging technique	Reason for doing it
1. Pack and move unnecessary items out of the home.	makes a place look larger
2. Remove personal items from the rooms.	
3.	makes rooms look bigger
4. Use white sheets in the bedroom.	
5.	makes rooms seem bright and happy
6. Paint walls a neutral color.	
7. Furnish some of the main rooms in an empty home.	

WRITE WHAT YOU THINK

A. Discuss the questions in a group. Look back at your Quick Write on page 44 as you think about what you learned.

1. Draw a picture of one of the rooms in your home in as much detail as possible. Then look again at the tips in Reading 2. What changes would you need to make so that the room was more attractive to a potential buyer?

2. Do you think a stager's job is interesting? Could you do it? Why or why not?

B. Before you watch the video, discuss the question in a group.

1. In your opinion, what were the most important suggestions in the reading for staging a home?

2. What are some other suggestions for staging a home?

C. Go online to watch the video about staging homes. Then check your comprehension.

VIDEO VOCABULARY

accentuate *(v.)* to emphasize something to make it noticeable

commodity *(n.)* a product that can be bought or sold

enlist *(v.)* to persuade someone to help

languish *(v.)* to suffer something unpleasant for a long time

D. Think about the unit video, Reading 1, and Reading 2 as you discuss the questions. Then choose one question and write a paragraph in response.

1. Reading 1 ends with "It's OK if not everybody understands the story you're telling. What is important is that the target customer gets it, and stops to look." What story do home sellers want to tell?

2. What lesson from staging a home could window designers use? How would that idea need to be modified to fit a store window instead of a home?

Vocabulary Skill   Collocations with nouns

Collocations are words that often occur together. While there are no rules to help you learn collocations, it is important to pay attention to the patterns of words in a text. These patterns are clues that show you which words collocate. There are several common collocation patterns with nouns.

Adjective + noun

> Does the store fit the shopper's **personal style** or not?
> Most people have a **hard time** imagining a space as a potential home if it contains no furniture.

Verb + noun/noun phrase

> Maybe in the past, shoppers had the time to really **take a look** at a window.
> The condo doesn't **make a great first impression** on potential buyers.

Preposition + noun/noun phrase

> Everyone seems to be **in a hurry**.
> **In theory**, the Millers' home should have sold quickly.

A. Circle the word that usually goes together with the noun in each sentence. Look back at Reading 1 (R1) and Reading 2 (R2) to check your answers.

a shopping mall

1. (**Social** / **Society**) **rules** tell people what behavior is acceptable. (R1, para. 1)

2. In **the** (**old** / **past**) **days**, no one researched how people shop. (R1, para. 3)

3. There have been many changes to advertising in (**current** / **modern**) **times**. (R1, para. 4)

4. A good advertisement should (**grab** / **grasp**) **the shopper's attention**. (R1, para. 5)

5. The mover can only carry two boxes (**at** / **by**) **a time**. (R1, para. 6)

6. We had a feeling that we weren't hearing the (**full** / **total**) **story**. (R1, para. 6)

7. A book in the window (**caught** / **held**) **his eye**, so he went into the store. (R1, para. 7)

8. The house was not attractive, so the buyers only took a (**sudden** / **quick**) **look** at it. (R1, para. 7)

9. While some people (**have** / **take**) **pleasure** in shopping, many others hate it. (R1, para. 8)

10. The latest computer technology has just come (**at** / **on**) **the market**. (R2, para. 2)

11. Stores try to (**create** / **make**) **a mood** using displays and lighting. (R2, para. 4)

12. (**During** / **Over**) **time**, the value of most homes will increase. (R2, para. 6)

13. You can only take two (**personal** / **private**) **items** on a plane. (R2, para. 7)

14. The salesperson gave advice (**in** / **on**) **a way** that was helpful and practical. (R2, para. 8)

15. Light-colored walls (**make** / **give**) **the impression** of a large living space. (R2, para. 8)

16. She is one of the best researchers (**in** / **of**) **her field**. (R2, para. 11)

Tip for Success

Some collocations are **idioms**. This means that when the words are combined, they take on a unique meaning. Some examples of idioms are *window-shopping* and *in theory*.

B. Choose five collocations from Activity A. Write a sentence for each.

I like to have the newest computer technology on the market.

 C. Go online for more practice with collocations with nouns.

WRITING

At the end of this unit, you will write a descriptive essay about a product, business, or service. This essay will include specific information from the readings, the unit video, and your own ideas.

Writing Skill — Writing a descriptive essay

A **descriptive essay** describes a person, place, or thing in a way that gives the reader a clear mental picture of the subject of the essay.

Organization

- The **introduction** should make the reader interested in what you are describing. It should include a **thesis statement** that tells why the person, place, or thing is your focus.
- Write one or more **body paragraphs** that contain the details of your description.
- Finish with a **conclusion** that gives your final thoughts or opinion about what you are describing.

Descriptive language

A good descriptive essay gives a clear mental picture of the subject of the essay. The reader should be able to imagine that he or she is with the person described, at the place described, etc. Include strong **imagery** (language that helps create these mental pictures) in your body paragraphs.

Not descriptive

She walked into the room.

He was dressed formally.

The street was filled with people selling food.

Descriptive

She walked **slowly** and **nervously** into the **dark** room.
  (with adjectives and adverbs)

He wore **a light suit, a tie, and shiny shoes**.
  (with details and specific language)

The street was filled with **loud men shouting out orders above the smoky smell of grilling meat**.
  (with sensory language related to sounds, smells, etc.)

A. **WRITING MODEL** Read the model descriptive essay. Then follow the steps below.

My Favorite Restaurant

One of my favorite restaurants is Ben's Diner on Fourth Street because it's perfect for a casual, delicious meal. Ben's is a family business that has been serving the local community for over sixty years. Look for their red neon sign with its flashing knife and fork. When you see it, you know you can expect good food that was cooked with fresh, local ingredients.

As soon as you step through the door at Ben's, you'll be glad you came. The restaurant is brightly lit and spotlessly clean, with gleaming tables and sparkling floors. You'll get a warm welcome from one of the staff, who will take you to a comfortable seat. I like the soft red leather seats in the booths, or sometimes I sit at the smooth marble counter. The pleasant noise of conversation and the soothing clatter of dishes will surround you. If you're not already hungry, the rich smell of homemade chicken soup coming from the kitchen will get you ready to eat.

Ben's menu has some old favorites and some unexpected surprises.

Their perfectly grilled burger is made of 100% prime beef. Served on a soft toasted bun, it's crunchy on the outside and moist and peppery inside. Add some sharp cheddar cheese for a satisfying treat. Their Greek salad is famous for its fresh ingredients: bright green lettuce leaves, deep red tomatoes, and tangy purple olives. Or how about chicken fajitas, served beside your table in a sizzling skillet, with a spicy aroma I can't resist?

So, whether you're looking for somewhere new to get some great food or just passing through, I suggest you head over to Ben's. You'll feel right at home and enjoy some good cooking, too.

1. Underline the thesis statement and the concluding sentence.

2. Find at least two sensory details for each sense.

   a. sight: _red neon sign,_____

   b. sound: _____

   c. taste: _____

   d. smell: _____

   e. touch: _____

B. Read the sentences. Rewrite them to make them more descriptive. Add adjectives and adverbs, details and specific language, and sensory language. Be creative.

1. The man lived in a house far from the city.

   <u>The old man lived quietly in a small farmhouse far from the busy city.</u>

2. The room was filled with roses, daisies, and lilacs.

   _____

3. The chicken and potatoes were good.

   _____

4. We went on a hike though the forest.

   _____

5. His aunt entered the room.

   _____

6. I didn't get to watch the soccer game on TV.

   _____

C. **WRITING MODEL** Read the model descriptive essay. Then answer the questions on page 55.

Adventure Seekers Wanted

Do you live for your next escape from your everyday routine? Are you a strong and healthy outdoor person seeking your next great adventure? The Adventurer sport utility vehicle (SUV) is the right vehicle to buy for adventure and outdoor fun if you are a thrill-seeking, athletic person who spends time outdoors. The Adventurer is the best, most reliable SUV to take you, your thrill-seeking friends, and all your gear where you're going, and it will get you there in great comfort and style.

Do you spend time climbing snow-capped mountains, rafting through red rock canyons on a raging river, or cruising the rocky shoreline of a vast ocean seeking the perfect wave? If you answered yes to any of these questions, then you know that you need to be driving a powerful, all-wheel-drive vehicle to arrive at your destination. The new Adventurer delivers that power and maneuverability. Don't be fooled by the quiet, comfortable ride. The new Adventurer is the perfect off-road vehicle. It is a powerful, all-wheel-drive vehicle that is as at home on steep,

---

rough dirt roads as it is on a flat, smooth highway. And, as a hybrid, it is the environmentally friendly vehicle you want to drive.

Do you plan to take friends and need to carry a lot of gear to your next adventure? There is plenty of room for all the equipment you'll need. The interior of the Adventurer is roomy and comfortable, so you can bring along as many as five fun-loving friends. The seats, of the softest, finest-quality leather, will keep you cool in the heat of the summer and warm in the winter. The climate control air system keeps the interior at a steady, regulated temperature.

Each adventure seeker creates his or her own story. Whatever your story, the Adventurer is the means to get you there. You will want the Adventurer because it is the right choice for your healthy, active lifestyle. Test-drive yours today!

1. What is the product?

   _____

2. What is the controlling idea about the product?

   _____

3. Who is the target customer for the product?

   _____

4. What makes the product appealing?

   _____

   _____

   _____

5. What does the conclusion do?

   _____

6. Can you form a mental picture of the Adventurer SUV? Explain your answer.

   _____

   _____

   _____

D. Below is a cluster diagram the author used to organize the description of the Adventurer. Complete the cluster diagram with ideas from the essay and your own ideas.

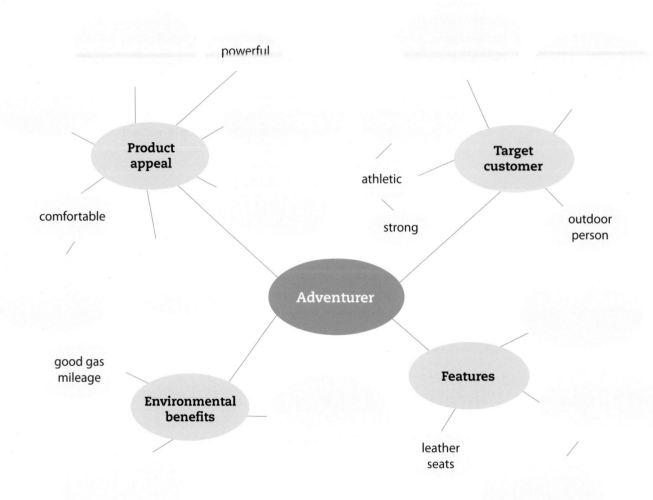

E. Go online for more practice with descriptive essays.

A noun (a person, place, thing, or idea) is often introduced by an article. Different types of nouns can use different articles. Understanding the context in which a noun occurs will help you use articles correctly.

	Singular count noun	Plural count noun	Noncount noun
Indefinite article	*a* + consonant sound *an* + vowel sound	no article	no article
Definite article	*the*	*the*	*the*

Indefinite articles with nonspecific nouns

Use *a/an* or no article when a noun is not specifically identified or is unknown to the reader; for example, the first time you mention a noun.

> We were excited to have **a new car**. (This is the first reference to *a new car*.
>   The reader does not know about it yet.)
> We bought **fish** for dinner. (No article is used with noncount nouns.)

You also use no article with plural count nouns or noncount nouns to refer to something in general.

> **Shoppers** can get a great deal of information from window displays.
>   (*Shoppers* refers to any shopper, not a specific shopper.)

Definite articles with specific nouns

Use *the* when a noun is specifically identified. Both the reader and the writer know the noun because they share information about it. For example:

- The noun was already introduced.

> We were excited to have <u>a new car</u>, but **the car** we chose was terrible!
> (*A new car* was introduced earlier in the sentence.)

- The noun relates directly to something else that you introduced.

> Let's go to Ben's Diner. **The owners** are really friendly, and **the soup** is delicious.
> (The reader and writer both know that *the owners* refers to the owners of Ben's
>   Diner, and *the soup* is served at Ben's Diner.)

- The noun is unique so the reader will know what you are referring to.

> **The Internet** has changed the way people look for homes.
> (There is only one Internet. It is unique.)
> **The government** should do more about false advertising.
> (You can assume the reader will know which government you are referring to.)

Tip for Success

Using *the* is not the only way to refer to a specific noun. You may also identify specific nouns with possessive adjectives (*my, your, their,* etc.), demonstrative adjectives (*this, that, these,* or *those*), or quantifiers (*two, many,* or *some*).

A. Complete the email. Write the correct articles: *a/an*, *the*, or Ø for no article.

To: Louis Rogers

From: Felix Thompson

Subject: Big news!

Hi Louis,

Sorry I haven't been in touch for a while, but I have __Ø__
                                                        1

big news. I got ____ job that I told you about, so I'm selling
                   2

my house! You know that ____ housing market is very tough
                         3

right now, but I'm happy because there is already ____
                                                   4

couple who are interested in my place. ____ potential
                                        5

buyers are coming over in two weeks. I want to stage ____
                                                     6

house so that everything looks perfect. I'm wondering if

you might be able to help me, so I thought I'd tell you what I'm planning.

This weekend, I'm going to clean ____ house all over and repaint all ____
                                 7   8

doors. I also bought ____ awesome dining table to put in ____ kitchen.
                     9   10

(I need some help picking it up!) Then I want to paint ____ main bedroom—
                                                       11

probably in ____ soft blue color. And when ____ weather is nice, I want to
            12   13

clean up ____ yard and plant ____ flowers.
         14   15

Real estate agents always say that when ____ buyers are looking at ____
                                         16   17

houses, they want to feel like they already live there, so I know this will be

worth all ____ effort.
          18

Let me know if you can help me. Oh, and one other question. Do you

know where I can find ____ good hardware store?
                      19

Felix

B. Go online for more practice with definite and indefinite articles.

C. Go online for the grammar expansion.

UNIT OBJECTIVE ▶▶▶▶▶▶ In this assignment, you are going to write an essay describing and selling features of a product, business, or service. As you prepare your essay, think about the Unit Question, "What makes you want to buy something?" Use information from Reading 1, Reading 2, the unit video, and your work in this unit to support your essay. Refer to the Self-Assessment checklist on page 60.

 Go to the Online Writing Tutor for a writing model and alternate Unit Assignments.

PLAN AND WRITE

A. **BRAINSTORM** Follow these steps to help you organize your ideas.

1. Think of some products, businesses, and services that you have strong opinions about. These could be things like restaurants, stores, or products like new technology.

2. Answer these questions for each product, business, or service.
   a. How would you describe it? Think about descriptive language you can use.
   b. What are the main features or qualities of the product, business, or service?
   c. What do you like or dislike about the qualities or features?

3. Choose one product, business, or service that you would like to sell.

 Writing **Tip**

You can use a **cluster diagram** to help you organize and develop your ideas. See page 56 for an example.

B. **PLAN** Follow these steps to plan your essay.

1. Choose two or three main features or qualities of the product, business, or service from question 2 in Activity A.

2. Brainstorm some descriptive language to give a clear mental picture of each feature or quality you selected.

 3. Go to the Online Resources to download and complete the outline for your descriptive essay.

C. **WRITE** Use your **PLAN** notes to write your essay. Go to *iQ Online* to use the Online Writing Tutor.

1. Write your essay describing a product, business, or service. Be sure to include a thesis statement telling why it is your focus and body paragraphs with the specific features or qualities of your product, business, or service.

2. Look at the Self-Assessment checklist below to guide your writing.

REVISE AND EDIT

A. **PEER REVIEW** Read your partner's essay. Then go online and use the Peer Review worksheet. Discuss the review with your partner.

B. **REWRITE** Based on your partner's review, revise, and rewrite your essay.

C. **EDIT** Complete the Self-Assessment checklist as you prepare to write the final draft of your essay. Be prepared to hand in your work or discuss it in class.

SELF-ASSESSMENT		
Yes	**No**	
☐	☐	Does the thesis statement have a topic and controlling idea?
☐	☐	Does the essay use descriptive language to create a clear mental picture of the subject?
☐	☐	Are correct articles used?
☐	☐	Did you use collocations from the unit correctly?
☐	☐	Does the essay include vocabulary from the unit?
☐	☐	Did you check the essay for punctuation, spelling, and grammar?

D. **REFLECT** Go to the Online Discussion Board to discuss these questions.

1. What is something new you learned in this unit?

2. Look back at the Unit Question—What makes you want to buy something? Is your answer different now than when you started the unit? If yes, how is it different? Why?

TRACK YOUR SUCCESS

Circle the words and phrases you have learned in this unit.

Nouns
concept 🔑 AWL
individual 🔑 AWL
investment 🔑 AWL
negative 🔑 AWL
pedestrian
priority 🔑 AWL
residence AWL

Verbs
distinguish 🔑
evolve AWL
feature 🔑 AWL
liberate AWL
minimize AWL
promote 🔑 AWL
remove 🔑 AWL
tend 🔑
visualize AWL

Phrasal Verbs
allude to
focus on 🔑 AWL

Adjectives
neutral AWL
potential 🔑 AWL
sophisticated
urban 🔑

Adverb
mentally 🔑 AWL

Collocations

Adjective + Noun
full story
hard time
modern times
personal item
personal style
quick look
social rules
the old days

Verb + Noun
catch the eye
create a mood
give an impression
grab attention
make an impression
take a look
take pleasure

Preposition + Noun
at a time
in a hurry 🔑
in a way
in the field
in theory 🔑 AWL
on the market
over time

🔑 Oxford 3000™ words
AWL Academic Word List

Check (✓) the skills you learned. If you need more work on a skill, refer to the page(s) in parentheses.

READING ☐	I can highlight and annotate a text. (p. 42)
VOCABULARY ☐	I can recognize and use collocations with nouns. (p. 50)
WRITING ☐	I can write a descriptive essay. (p. 52)
GRAMMAR ☐	I can use definite and indefinite articles. (p. 57)
UNIT OBJECTIVE ▶▶▶▶ ☐	I can gather information and ideas to write a descriptive essay about a product, business, or service.

READING ▶ making inferences
VOCABULARY ▶ prefixes and suffixes
WRITING ▶ writing a narrative and varying sentence patterns
GRAMMAR ▶ past perfect and past perfect continuous

Developmental Psychology

UNIT QUESTION

What important lessons do we learn as children?

A Discuss these questions with your classmates.

1. What are some significant memories from your childhood?

2. What are some things that parents and their children disagree about?

3. Look at the photo. How do you think the children feel? What important lesson will they learn?

B Listen to *The Q Classroom* online. Then answer these questions.

1. What important lessons did Felix, Sophy, and Yuna learn as children? What is one lesson you learned?

2. What does Marcus say about what he learned from his parents? Sophy disagrees with Marcus. Who do you agree with? Why?

 C Go to the Online Discussion Board to discuss the Unit Question with your classmates.

D Use the survey to interview a partner. Take notes on the answers.

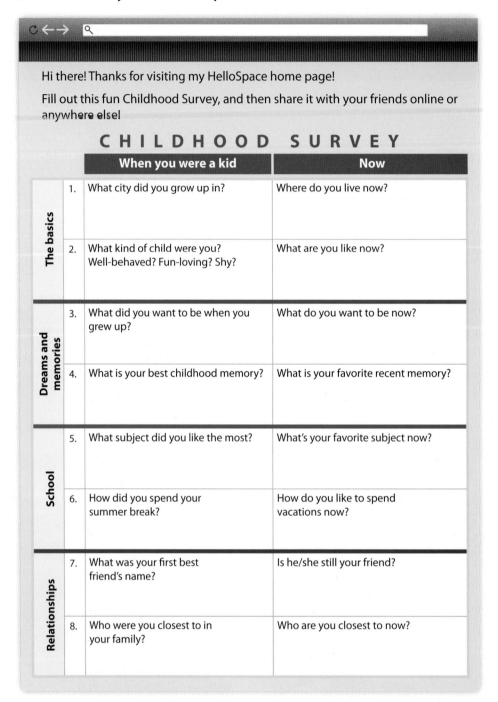

Hi there! Thanks for visiting my HelloSpace home page!

Fill out this fun Childhood Survey, and then share it with your friends online or anywhere else!

CHILDHOOD SURVEY

		When you were a kid	Now
The basics	1.	What city did you grow up in?	Where do you live now?
	2.	What kind of child were you? Well-behaved? Fun-loving? Shy?	What are you like now?
Dreams and memories	3.	What did you want to be when you grew up?	What do you want to be now?
	4.	What is your best childhood memory?	What is your favorite recent memory?
School	5.	What subject did you like the most?	What's your favorite subject now?
	6.	How did you spend your summer break?	How do you like to spend vacations now?
Relationships	7.	What was your first best friend's name?	Is he/she still your friend?
	8.	Who were you closest to in your family?	Who are you closest to now?

E Look at the responses to the survey. Find three to five ways your partner has changed and discuss these questions.

1. In what way has your partner changed the most?

2. What else can your partner tell you about the changes?

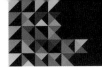

READING

READING 1 | The Good Teen

 You are going to read a magazine article that examines commonly held beliefs about the behavior of teenagers. Use the article to gather information and ideas for your Unit Assignment.

PREVIEW THE READING

A. **PREVIEW** The word *adolescence* describes the period of growth and change from childhood to adulthood—often called *the teenage years*. Besides physical changes, what kinds of changes do people go through from childhood to adulthood? Discuss your ideas with a partner.

B. **QUICK WRITE** What are some things people believe about the behavior of teenagers? Think about their moods and emotions, their relationships with their families, and their relationships with their friends. Write for 5–10 minutes in response. Be sure to use this section for your Unit Assignment.

C. **VOCABULARY** Check (✓) the words you know. Then work with a partner to locate each word in the reading. Use clues to help define the words you don't know. Check your definitions in the dictionary.

accurately *(adv.)* 🔑	**extracurricular** *(adj.)*
assumption *(n.)*	**innate** *(adj.)*
colleague *(n.)* 🔑	**nurture** *(v.)*
competence *(n.)*	**period** *(n.)* 🔑
consistent with *(phr.)* 🔑	**select** *(v.)* 🔑
equipped with *(phr.)*	**theoretically** *(adv.)*

🔑 Oxford 3000™ words

 D. Go online to listen and practice your pronunciation.

A. **Read the article and gather information about the important lessons we learn as children.**

The Good Teen

1   Eliza Parks is a high school senior. She gets good grades, is president of the senior class, and writes for the school newspaper. As a junior, she received her school's top prizes in English and history, and was **selected** to represent the school at a statewide speech contest. Not surprisingly, Eliza has been accepted at Yale University next year, where she has been awarded a scholarship. Even with all her **extracurricular** activities and academic commitments, Eliza makes time to be with her brother and her parents. Whenever possible, they eat dinner as a family, and often take trips together on weekends. Eliza also has a strong network of friends who her parents know well. "I talk with my parents very freely about my friends, my life, whatever," she says.

2   What is the secret to Eliza's happy adolescence? We often think of adolescence as a difficult **period**: the stereotypical[1] teenager makes poor decisions, hangs out with the wrong friends, or takes dangerous risks. Many parents often dread these years because they think their children will stop talking to them and refuse to follow their rules. However, recent research suggests that this common **assumption** about adolescence is often not true. Many teens not only survive these years, they thrive[2]. Instead of rebelling[3], many adopt the values of their parents. Instead of getting into trouble, they learn to work hard. Instead of forming negative relationships, they look for good role models and find supportive friends. In particular, teens **equipped with** specific skills and qualities may be better at avoiding the dangers others experience.

3   Dr. Richard Lerner, Director of the Institute for Applied Research in Youth Development at Tufts University, agrees that "most teens do not have a stormy adolescence." In order to discover how teens navigate these years happily and successfully, Lerner and his **colleagues** have conducted a long-range study of teens and their parents. This research, the 4-H Study of Positive Youth Development, examines how young people interact with others. It pays close attention to the activities they are involved in. It also looks at the adults who guide and support these children. The study identifies five interconnected characteristics for positive development in

[1] **stereotypical:** an image that people have of a type of person or thing which is often not true

[2] **thrive:** to become successful, strong, and healthy
[3] **rebelling:** fighting against or refusing to obey rules

adolescents, called the *Five Cs*: **competence**, confidence, connection, character, and caring. Researchers suggest that young people who have the Five Cs will also demonstrate a sixth C—contribution to self, family, community, and society. Teens with the Five Cs are more likely to become capable adults. And, **theoretically**, young people without the Five Cs would be at higher risk for a variety of social and personal problems.

4   How does Eliza fare[4] in terms of these characteristics? She has social and academic skills which allow her to excel in school (competence). Perhaps because of her talents, she has a good feeling about herself and her abilities (confidence). She has positive bonds with family, friends, and people at school (connection), and a good sense of right and wrong (character). And finally, Eliza cares about other people (caring). Her qualities and experience reflect all Five Cs. At least in Eliza's case, having the Five Cs **accurately** predicts her success.

5   But could it be that kids like Eliza are happier because they have fewer problems than others? That doesn't seem to be true. The 4-H Study has found that teens from any background can thrive. It doesn't matter if they are rich or poor, from the city or the country, living in a high-crime area or a low-crime area—anyone can do well with a little help. Researchers say that even adolescents with very serious problems can be successful if they are resilient. This means that even when they get knocked down by life, they can bounce back and recover quickly from the negative experience.

6   So, how do teens develop the Five Cs and become more resilient? Lerner's study found that families, schools, and communities are key[5]. "Quality time spent with teachers, parents, mentors, or in effective out-of-school programs put [young people] on a positive path to community contributions," he says.

According to Lerner, teens need opportunities that **nurture** positive interactions with adults, develop life skills (skills that will help them deal with the challenges of everyday life), and give them the chance to show leadership.

7   For parents, contact is critical. Although teens are starting to pull away, parents need to stay connected. One way is to participate in out-of-school activities. For example, kids and parents could volunteer to take care of a park or build a playground. But parents don't have to work on long-term projects to have an effect. Just spending time with teens can help. For example, one of the strongest predictors[6] of positive youth development was that a family ate dinner together on a regular basis. It is also important for parents to give teens time and space to explore their own interests and passions.

8   All these recommendations are **consistent with** the advice of psychologist Laurence Steinberg of Temple University. According to Steinberg, author of *The 10 Basic Principles of Good Parenting*, parents should be involved in their children's lives and give them plenty of love. In his book, Steinberg says that good parenting encourages "elements like honesty, empathy[7], self-reliance, kindness, cooperation, self-control, and cheerfulness." Sounds a lot like the Five Cs. Steinberg recognizes that for some people, good parenting is **innate**, but all parents can improve their skills through practice.

9   The message for parents is a good one. Your teenagers will not necessarily suffer and neither will you. Their connections to *both* friends and family will help them succeed during this period. But letting them have the one thing they really want—some independence—may actually help by giving them a sense of competence and control. During these years, parents need to find a balance between staying connected and letting go. This may be the best rule a parent can make.

---

[4] **fare:** to be successful or unsuccessful in a particular situation
[5] **key:** most important

[6] **predictors:** information that can show what will happen in the future
[7] **empathy:** the ability to understand another person's feelings

In Unit 2, you learned
that there are
common collocations
with nouns. Look
at the words in
the sentences in
Activity B. What
four adjective +
noun collocations
can you find?

B. **VOCABULARY** Complete the sentences with the vocabulary from Reading 1.

accurately *(adv.)*	**competence** *(n.)*	**extracurricular** *(adj.)*	**period** *(n.)*
assumption *(n.)*	**consistent with** *(phr.)*	**innate** *(adj.)*	**select** *(v.)*
colleague *(n.)*	**equipped with** *(phr.)*	**nurture** *(v.)*	**theoretically** *(adv.)*

1. For our research project, my _____ and I looked at the reasons that some teenagers do well in school.

2. We decided to conduct a second experiment, and we were pleased to see that the new results were _____ the previous ones.

3. _____, getting a college degree should help you get a good job.

4. I'll need more information in order to _____ answer the question.

5. His _____ activities include the school soccer team and the debate club.

6. You should carefully review the information in the guide before you _____ your classes for the term.

7. University classrooms are _____ a lot of technology to enhance students' learning opportunities.

8. The director said she was impressed with the _____ Victor showed in his role as student council president.

9. Good parents will _____ their children's dreams and help them realize their goals.

10. It's easy to make a judgment about someone based on a false _____.

11. Even writers with _____ talent need formal training, too.

12. We often think of the years between childhood and adulthood as a difficult _____.

 C. Go online for more practice with the vocabulary.

D. Answer these questions.

1. What assumption about adolescence does the research examine?

2. What are the Five Cs?

3. In what way is Eliza like other successful teens?

4. According to Dr. Lerner, what do teens need to develop the Five Cs?

5. According to Dr. Steinberg, what does good parenting encourage?

E. Circle the correct answer. Then discuss your answers with a partner.

1. What is the purpose of the first paragraph?
   a. It gives an example of the topic of the article.
   b. It gives a definition of the topic of the article.
   c. It gives a suggestion for a solution to a problem.

2. What is the main idea of paragraph 2?
   a. Eliza has a secret to being happy.
   b. People think that adolescents have lots of problems because they do.
   c. People think that adolescents have lots of problems, but they don't.

3. The 4-H Study of Positive Youth Development looked at ____.
   a. troubled adolescents and institutions that deal with them
   b. activities that successful teens are involved in
   c. how schools change their programs to deal with troubled teens

4. The purpose of paragraph 4 is to show ____.
   a. how Eliza's experiences and skills compare with the Five Cs
   b. that the Five Cs do not apply to Eliza
   c. how Eliza could do better if she knew about the Five Cs

5. How does being resilient help teens?
   a. It teaches leadership skills that they can use in later life.
   b. It helps them succeed in spite of problems.
   c. It allows them to get better more quickly when they are sick.

6. According to the article, ____.
   a. teens need to do things with supportive adults
   b. teens need their parents to work on long-term projects with them
   c. parents don't need to interact with their teenagers

7. The author probably included paragraph 8 ____.
   a. to show the opposite view by giving another expert's ideas
   b. to support his view by using another expert's ideas
   c. to question whether the 4-H Study was right

8. The audience for this reading is probably ____.
   a. teenagers   b. researchers   c. parents

F. Write *T* (true) or *F* (false) for each statement. Then correct each false statement to make it true. Write the paragraph number where you found information to support your answer.

_____ 1. Eliza Parks has a good relationship with her parents. (paragraph _____)

_____ 2. Many people assume that teens will make poor decisions. (paragraph _____)

_____ 3. Lawrence Steinberg conducted the 4-H Study. (paragraph _____)

_____ 4. The 4-H Study says that teens with the Five Cs are more likely to help in their communities. (paragraph _____)

_____ 5. Eating dinner as a family is important to positive youth development. (paragraph _____)

_____ 6. Steinberg thinks that parents can become better through practice. (paragraph _____)

_____ 7. Parents should try to control their children during adolescence. (paragraph _____)

 G. Go online to read *Siblings and Social Skills* and check your comprehension.

WRITE WHAT YOU THINK

A. Discuss these questions in a group.

1. Choose three of the activities in the box and discuss which of the Five Cs each one involves. (There will be more than one C for each activity.) Explain your answers.

coaching younger athletes	playing on a sports team	speaking in public
finding a career	reading to young children	

Critical Thinking Tip

Question 3 asks you to **relate** the Five Cs to your own childhood. When you connect new information to your own experience, you deepen your understanding of it.

2. What other kinds of activities do you think help adolescents develop the traits that help them become responsible adults?

3. How can you relate the Five Cs to your childhood? Give an example from your experience in which your development was affected by one of these characteristics.

B. Choose one question and write a paragraph in response. Look back at your Quick Write on page 65 as you think about what you learned.

Writers don't usually state all their ideas directly. Usually, they expect the reader to **infer** some ideas that the information suggests. Making inferences about a text means that you use your knowledge to make a logical conclusion about the information that is given. Look at this excerpt from Reading 1.

> The 4-H Study has found that teens from any background can thrive. It doesn't matter if they are rich or poor, from the city or the country, living in a high-crime area or a low-crime area—anyone can do well with a little help.

In order to make these claims, the researchers had to do the right kind of research. So you can infer:

- They chose to research teens from many backgrounds.
- They also looked at the kind of help those teens received in order to be successful.

Making inferences helps you improve your comprehension and understand a text more deeply.

A. Read the paragraph from Reading 1. Check (✓) the statements that can be inferred from the text. Then compare your answers with a partner. Explain what information in the paragraph led to the inference.

Tip for Success

Your inferences should always depend on the author's words first and your experience second. Make sure your inferences are not contradicted by statements that are made later in the text.

Eliza Parks is a high school senior. She gets good grades, is president of the senior class, and writes for the school newspaper. As a junior, she received her school's top prizes in English and history, and was selected to represent the school at a statewide speech contest. Not surprisingly, Eliza has been accepted at Yale University next year, where she has been awarded a scholarship. Even with all her extracurricular activities and academic commitments, Eliza makes time to be with her brother and her parents. Whenever possible, they eat dinner as a family, and often take trips together on weekends. Eliza also has a strong network of friends who her parents know well. "I talk with my parents very freely about my friends, my life, whatever," she says.

☐ 1. Eliza likes schoolwork.

☐ 2. Eliza is also very good at math.

☐ 3. Eliza speaks well in public.

☐ 4. Eliza succeeds at everything she tries.

☐ 5. Eliza's family does not have a lot of money.

☐ 6. Eliza is a very busy person.

☐ 7. Eliza enjoys spending time with her parents.

☐ 8. Eliza's mother is a good cook.

☐ 9. Eliza's parents help her choose her friends.

☐ 10. Eliza is a confident person.

B. Read the paragraph. Circle the answer(s) to each question. You may circle *a*, *b*, or both. Then compare your answers with a partner. Explain your answers.

> I have always had to struggle to get out of bed in the morning. When I was a young child, the problem wasn't so bad. Because I didn't want to miss anything that my older siblings were doing, I made myself get up. But as each one of them went away to college, I had less and less enthusiasm to get up in the mornings. After they were all gone, my father used to come to my bedroom door, knock, and say, "It's 6:00. Wake up and get out of bed." I would respond, "One or the other, Dad. One or the other."

1. What can you infer about the writer?
   a. The writer is an adult.
   b. The writer is male.

2. What can you infer about the writer's family?
   a. The writer had four older siblings.
   b. The writer was the youngest child.

3. What can you infer about the writer's problem?
   a. The writer still struggles to get out of bed.
   b. It was easier to get out of bed as a child than as a teenager.

4. What can you infer about the writer's father?
   a. He used to get up early.
   b. He was annoyed because the writer wouldn't get up.

5. What can you infer from the writer's response to the father?
   a. The writer has a good sense of humor.
   b. The writer would get up right away.

 C. Go online for more practice making inferences.

READING 2 | Bird by Bird

 You are going to read an excerpt from author Anne Lamott's memoir, *Bird by Bird: Some Instructions on Writing and Life*. In it, she looks back at her childhood and the influence that her father had on her. Use the excerpt to gather information and ideas for your Unit Assignment.

PREVIEW THE READING

A. **PREVIEW** Skim the excerpt. Check (✓) the correct statement.

☐ Anne Lamott decided to become a writer because of her father.

☐ Despite her family's wishes, Anne Lamott decided to become a writer.

B. **QUICK WRITE** Who influenced you most as a child? Write for 5–10 minutes in response. Be sure to use this section for your Unit Assignment.

C. **VOCABULARY** Check (✓) the words you know. Use a dictionary to define any new or unknown words. Then discuss how the words will relate to the unit with a partner.

capture *(v.)* 🔑	impassioned *(adj.)*	refuge *(n.)*
creative *(adj.)* 🔑	motivate *(v.)*	resentful *(adj.)*
episode *(n.)*	profound *(adj.)*	significance *(n.)*
exaggerate *(v.)* 🔑	rely on *(phr. v.)* 🔑	suspect *(v.)* 🔑

🔑 Oxford 3000™ words

 D. Go online to listen and practice your pronunciation.

WORK WITH THE READING

A. Read the excerpt and gather information about the important lessons we learn as children.

BIRD BY BIRD

1   Every morning, no matter how late he had been up, my father rose at 5:30, went to his study, wrote for a couple of hours, made us all breakfast, read the paper with my mother, and then went back to work for the rest of the morning. Many years passed before I realized that he did this by choice, for a living, and that he was not unemployed or mentally ill. I wanted him to have a regular job where he put on a necktie and went off somewhere with the other fathers and sat in a little office. . . . But the idea of spending entire days in someone else's office doing someone else's work did not suit my father's soul. I think it would have killed him. He did end up dying rather early, in his mid-fifties, but at least he had lived on his own terms.

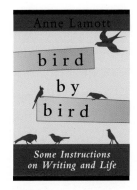

2   So I grew up around this man who sat at his desk in the study all day and wrote books and articles about the places and people he had seen and known. He read a lot of poetry. Sometimes he traveled. He could go anyplace he wanted with a sense of purpose. One of the gifts of being a writer is that it gives you an excuse to do things, to go places and explore. Another is that writing **motivates** you to look closely at life, at life as it lurches by[1] and tramps around[2].

3   Writing taught my father to pay attention; my father in turn taught other people to pay attention and then to write down their thoughts and observations. His students were the prisoners at San Quentin[3] who took part in the creative-writing program. But he taught me, too, mostly by example. He taught the prisoners and me to put a little bit down on paper every day, and to read all the great books we could get our hands on. He taught us to read poetry. He taught us to be bold and original and to let ourselves make mistakes. . . . But while he helped the prisoners and me to discover that we had a lot of feelings and observations and memories and dreams and opinions we wanted to share, we all ended up just the tiniest bit **resentful** when we found the one fly in the ointment[4]: that at some point we had to actually sit down and write.

4   I believe writing was easier for me than for the prisoners because I was still a child. But I always found it hard. I started writing when I was seven or eight. I was very shy and strange-looking, loved reading above everything else, weighed about forty pounds at the time, and was so tense that I walked around with my shoulders up to my ears. I saw a video once of a celebration I went to in the first grade, with all these cute little boys and girls playing together like puppies, and all of a sudden I scuttled across the screen like Prufrock's crab[5]. I was very clearly the one who was going to grow up to . . . keep dozens and dozens of cats. Instead, I got funny. I walked in a strange way: I think I was trying to plug my ears with my shoulders, but they wouldn't quite reach. So first I got funny and then I started to write, although I did not always write funny things.

5   I started writing a lot in high school: journals, **impassioned** antiwar pieces, parodies of the writers I loved. And I began to notice something important. The other kids always wanted me to tell them stories of what had happened, even—or especially—when they had been there. Blowups[6]

---

[1] **lurches by:** makes a sudden, unsteady movement forward or sideways
[2] **tramps around:** travels or wanders on foot
[3] **San Quentin:** a state prison in California
[4] **fly in the ointment:** something that spoils the enjoyment
[5] **Prufrock's crab:** a shy, timid character that appears in a well-known poem by T. S. Eliot
[6] **blowup:** a fight or conflict

in the classroom or on the school yard, scenes involving their parents that we had witnessed—I could make the story happen. I could make it vivid and funny, and even **exaggerate** some of it so that the event became almost mythical, and the people involved seemed larger, and there was a sense of larger **significance**, of meaning.

6   I'm sure my father was the person **on** whom his friends **relied** to tell their stories, in school and college. I know for sure that he was later, in the town where he was raising his children. He could take major events or small **episodes** from daily life and shade or exaggerate things in such a way as to **capture** their shape and substance, capture what life felt like in the society in which he and his friends lived and worked. . . . People looked to him to put into words what was going on.

7   I **suspect** that he was a child who thought differently than his peers, who may have had serious conversations with grown-ups, who as a young person, like me, accepted being alone quite a lot. I think that this sort of person often becomes either a writer or a career criminal. Throughout my childhood I believed that what I thought about was different from what other kids thought about. It was not necessarily more **profound**, but there was a struggle going on inside me to find some sort of **creative** or spiritual or aesthetic way of seeing the world and organizing it in my head. I read more than other kids; I luxuriated in books. Books were my **refuge**. I sat in corners with my little finger hooked over my bottom lip, reading, in a trance[7], lost in the places and time to which books took me. And there was a moment during my junior year in high school when I began to believe that I could do what other writers were doing. I came to believe that I might be able to put a pencil in my hand and make something special happen.

8   Then I wrote some terrible, terrible stories.

---

[7] **trance:** a condition in which you don't notice what is going on around you

B. **VOCABULARY** Complete the sentences with the vocabulary from Reading 2.

capture (v.)	exaggerate (v.)	profound (adj.)	resentful (adj.)
creative (adj.)	impassioned (adj.)	rely on (phr. v.)	significance (n.)
episode (n.)	motivate (v.)	refuge (n.)	suspect (v.)

1. Studying a new language can _____ a person to travel.

2. My friends _____ their stories so much it's hard to know

    which parts are true.

3. My brother speaks Italian very well, so whenever we go to Italy,

   I _____ him to translate.

4. The writer used descriptive words to _____ the mood of the place.

5. Many of the things my parents told me as a child seemed unimportant at

   the time, but I now realize the _____ of their words.

6. My aunt is a great storyteller. She can describe a simple

   _____ from the past in a really exciting way.

7. As the storm got worse, they had to find _____.

8. I _____ that my friends are planning to surprise me,

   but I'm not really sure.

9. Marcos was furious about the article in the newspaper, and he

   wrote a(n) _____ letter in response.

10. Ben should study geography. He's always interested in having

    _____ discussions about the environment.

11. I have a hard time coming up with ideas. I wish I were more _____.

12. Ivan was _____ because he wasn't allowed to play in

    the soccer game.

iQ ONLINE **C. Go online for more practice with the vocabulary.**

D. Each of these sentences gives the main idea of a paragraph in the reading. Write the correct paragraph number (1–7) next to each sentence.

____ a. Her father taught his students how to write: for instance, to write a little every day, to read great books, and not to be afraid of making mistakes.

____ b. Writing gave her father a reason to explore things and motivated him to look at life closely.

____ c. In high school, she discovered that her classmates really liked stories about things that had happened when they were there.

____ d. Because she had a different way of thinking about things, she started to believe that she could be a writer.

_____ e. Her father had made the choice to work at home and be a writer.

_____ f. Because she was nervous and shy, she learned to be funny and started writing.

_____ g. Her father wrote about major events and small episodes from daily life in a way that expressed the atmosphere or feeling of the place and time.

E. **Answer the questions about Anne Lamott. Write the paragraph number where you found the information for your answer.**

1. What do you think Lamott means by "life as it lurches by and tramps around"?

2. How does she describe herself as a child?

3. What is her purpose in describing herself as a child?

4. Why did the other kids in high school want her to tell them stories of what happened even when they were there?

5. Why does she call books her refuge?

F. **Anne Lamott writes about both her father and herself as storytellers. Find a sentence in the reading that describes how each of them told stories. Write the paragraph number and highlight the sentence.**

Anne Lamott: Paragraph _____   Her father: Paragraph _____

G. **Find these sentences in the excerpt. What can you infer from each sentence? Circle the best answer. Then explain your answer to a partner.**

1. **Paragraph 1:** "I wanted him to have a regular job where he put on a necktie and went off somewhere with the other fathers and sat in a little office."
   a. The author wanted her father to spend more time out of the house.
   b. The author wanted her father to have a more "normal" job.

2. **Paragraph 2:** "Sometimes he traveled. He could go anyplace he wanted with a sense of purpose."
   a. When he traveled, he was thinking about how he could write about it.
   b. Because he worked at home, his schedule allowed him time to travel a lot.

3. **Paragraph 3:** ". . . we all ended up just the tiniest bit resentful when we found the one fly in the ointment: that at some point we had to actually sit down and write."
   a. The author thinks her father gave them too many writing assignments.
   b. The author thinks writing down your ideas is difficult.

4. **Paragraph 7:** "I suspect that he was a child who thought differently than his peers, who may have had serious conversations with grown-ups, who as a young person, like me, accepted being alone quite a lot."

    a. The author thinks that she and her father were very similar as children.

    b. The author thinks her father should have been more outgoing as a child.

WRITE WHAT YOU THINK

A. Discuss the questions in a group. Look back at your Quick Write on page 73 as you think about what you learned.

1. Think about a profession you are familiar with or interested in. What qualities does a person in that profession have or need to have?

2. Think about a person who influenced you as a child or teenager. How did that person affect who you are today?

B. Before you watch the video, discuss the questions in a group.

1. Have you ever wanted to quit doing an activity you originally liked? What did you do?

2. Should children be allowed to quit doing after-school activities, like playing on a soccer team or ice skating? Why or why not?

C. Go online to watch the video about children who want to quit doing an activity. Then check your comprehension.

> **VIDEO VOCABULARY**
>
> **couch potato** *(n.)* a person who spends a lot of time sitting and watching television
>
> **instill** *(v.)* to make someone feel a particular way over time
>
> **rule of thumb** *(n.)* a practical method of measuring something, usually based on past experience
>
> **stamina** *(n.)* physical or mental strength that enables you to do something for long periods

D. Think about the unit video, Reading 1, and Reading 2 as you discuss the questions. Then choose one question and write a paragraph in response.

1. Reading 1 describes the five Cs that help adolescents move successfully into adulthood. Which of the five Cs does the author of Reading 2 display?

2. Did you ever want to quit an activity like a sports team when you were a child? How did quitting or not quitting affect who you are now?

A **prefix** is a group of letters that comes at the beginning of a word. When you add a prefix to a word, it usually changes the word's meaning. Study the chart of prefixes from Readings 1 and 2 and other common examples.

Prefix	Meaning	Example
anti-	against	antiwar
co-	together	cooperation
extra-	more	extracurricular
in-	not	independence
inter-	go between	interact
mid-	middle	mid-fifties
mis-	incorrect, badly	misunderstanding
re-	again	reread

A **suffix** is a group of letters that comes at the end of a word. When you add a suffix to a word, it usually changes the part of speech of that word. For example, adding the suffix *-tion* to the verb *inform* makes it the noun *information*. Study the chart of suffixes from Readings 1 and 2.

Suffixes that form nouns	-ence / -ance	competence, significance
	-tion	assumption, connection
Suffixes that form adjectives	-ent / -ant	consistent, important
	-ful	resentful, successful
Suffixes that form verbs	-ate	exaggerate, motivate
	-ize	organize, realize

A. Complete the word in each sentence with the correct prefix from the Vocabulary Skill box above. Then check your answers in the dictionary.

1. He _____ pronounced the word, so she didn't understand what he had said.

2. They were both _____ ordinary students. They excelled at school and were talented in sports and poetry as well.

3. Many parts of the brain are _____ connected. They work together to enable the brain's many functions.

4. His job required that he _____ locate often, so he had lived in many places.

5. Terry knew she wasn't ready for _____ term exams, but she hoped she'd do better on the final.

6. People assumed Jin was _____ social because he rarely spoke with other children.

7. Some siblings have to learn to _____ exist peacefully together.

8. We're going to have a(n) _____ formal gathering tonight. Come by if you want.

B. Read each word. Check (✓) the correct part of speech. Use information from the Vocabulary Skill box on page 79 to help you. Then check your answers in the dictionary.

	Noun	Adjective	Verb
1. recognize	☐	☐	☐
2. reliance	☐	☐	☐
3. peaceful	☐	☐	☐
4. demonstrate	☐	☐	☐
5. resilient	☐	☐	☐
6. contribution	☐	☐	☐
7. confidence	☐	☐	☐
8. significant	☐	☐	☐
9. substance	☐	☐	☐
10. navigate	☐	☐	☐
11. imagination	☐	☐	☐
12. cheerful	☐	☐	☐

C. Choose five words from Activity B. Write a sentence for each.

 D. Go online for more practice with prefixes and suffixes.

WRITING

 **UNIT OBJECTIVE** At the end of this unit, you will write a narrative essay about someone or something that influenced you. This essay will include specific information from the readings, the unit video, and your own ideas.

Writing Skill | **Writing a narrative essay and varying sentence patterns**

A **narrative essay** tells a story about a personal experience, event, or memory.

Organization

- The **introduction** sets the scene for the reader. It should give information about the people, place, and time, and should create interest in the story. The introduction may include a **thesis statement** that tells why the story is important or memorable.

- There can be one or more **body paragraphs**. These tell the main events or actions of the story. They are usually in the order in which the events happened. They may also include important or interesting details to support the ideas in the main event.

- The **conclusion** gives the outcome or result of the actions in the story. It often tells what the writer learned from the experience.

Expressing the order of events

In a narrative essay, you use **time words** and **time clauses** to explain when the events happened in the story and the order of events.

> **Prepositions: in** 1978, **on** June 5, **before/after** class, **for** five years
> **Time expressions:** a week **ago, last** month, **earlier** this year, the week **before**, an hour **later**, the **next** day
> **Time clauses: after** we spoke, **before** I ate, **as** they were leaving, **when** we met

Varying sentence patterns

Varying sentence patterns in your writing will help the reader maintain interest and focus on important information. Here are some ways to add variety to your writing.

- Shorter sentences emphasize or stress one important point.
- Longer sentences combine closely related ideas. Longer sentences can be made by using conjunctions, subordinators, or relative clauses to combine shorter sentences.

> **Shorter:** There was a sudden noise.
> **Longer** (with conjunction): Then a cat jumped out of the bushes **and** ran up the path.
> **Longer** (with subordinator): **Even though** it was only a cat, my heart started beating faster.
> **Longer** (with relative clause): The next noise **that I heard** was definitely not a cat.

A. Brainstorm ideas for a narrative essay.

Writing Tip

Using a **timeline** is a good way to plan a narrative essay. A timeline can help you map out important events in the order in which they occurred.

1. Draw a timeline of four or five events that you remember from your childhood. Put on your timeline how old you were and a short phrase indicating what happened.

Example:

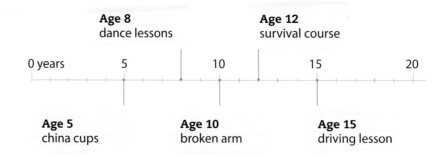

2. Choose one of the events on your timeline and answer these questions.

   a. What happened?

   _____

   b. Who was with you?

   _____

   c. Where were you?

   _____

   d. When did it happen?

   _____

   e. What did you learn?

   _____

My Mother's China Cups

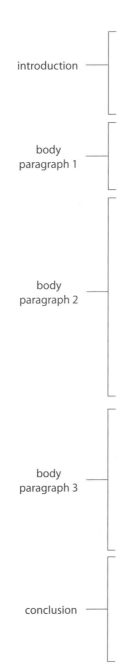

introduction

When I think about my mother, one thing I remember is her collection of china cups and saucers. She had collected them throughout her life, and they were very important to her. They were displayed on shelves in our kitchen. Some of them were quite old; some she had gotten from faraway places. And each one had a special memory for her.

body paragraph 1

From a very young age, I always wanted to take down those beautiful cups and wash them. It was my chance to see them up close. My mother never really wanted to let me do it. She knew the cups were fragile and I could easily break them. But sometimes I begged until she let me take them down and clean them.

body paragraph 2

My earliest memory of this was when I was five. I pulled a chair near the kitchen table and took down the small cups. I started with my favorites: the very old blue and white one that had belonged to my great-grandmother and the one from Japan with exotic buildings on it. I moved them all, one by one, to the kitchen counter. After I had put them on the counter, I moved my chair to the sink, filled the sink with soapy water, and began to wash the tiny cups.

body paragraph 3

I had only washed a few when the beautiful blue and white cup slipped from my small hands and fell back into the sink. The handle broke off. My mother's special cup was ruined, and I was sure she would be angry. I cried and waited for quite a while before I could find the courage to tell her. My mother, who was probably upset, only smiled and said we would glue it back together. I happily finished washing the precious cups. When I had cleaned and dried them all, we carefully placed them back on the shelves. Then my mother glued the handle back on the broken cup before we set it back in its place, too.

conclusion

I washed those cups many times as a child, and almost every time, I broke one. By the time I was grown, several showed the signs of my efforts. I am an adult now and my mother is gone, but I will always remember that she cared more about encouraging me than about her valuable cups. Now, as a mother myself, I understand the patience it took to allow me to handle her precious things. I try to demonstrate that same level of caring to my own children.

1. Who are the people in the narrative?

_____

2. Where does the action take place?

_____

3. When does the action take place?

_____

Writing Tip

When writing a
narrative, use details
and descriptive
language to make
the story come alive
for the reader. See
the Writing Skill on
page 52 for more
information.

C. Complete the outline of the essay. You do not have to use the writer's exact words.

I. Introductory ideas: _____

_____

II. Body paragraph 1: Main event in story

  When I was a child, I always wanted to wash my mother's china cups.

   A. Important or interesting detail: _____

   _____

   B. Important or interesting detail: _____

   _____

III. Body paragraph 2: Main event in story

   _____

   A. Important or interesting detail: I started with my favorites—

      the old blue and white one and the one from Japan.

   B. Important or interesting detail: _____

   _____

IV. Body paragraph 3: Main event in story

   _____

   A. Important or interesting detail: _____

   _____

   B. Important or interesting detail: My mother glued the handle on

      the cup before we put it back on the shelf.

   V. Conclusion (what I learned): _____

   _____

D. Look at body paragraph 3 of "My Mother's China Cups" on page 83. Circle the conjunctions. Underline the subordinators. Put a star (*) next to the relative clause. Then answer these questions.

1. Write the shortest sentence here. _____

2. How many conjunctions did you find? ____

3. How many subordinators? ____

4. The relative clause has commas around it. Who does the relative clause

   describe? _____

Tip for Success

You do not have to use all the techniques in everything you write. Just be sure to vary the patterns that you use.

E. Work with a partner to rewrite the paragraph below. Vary the sentence patterns by keeping some shorter sentences and by using conjunctions, subordinators, and relative clauses to make longer sentences.

The toughest weekend of my life was also one of the best. I was 12. My father and I attended a short survival course. I will never forget it. I woke up early on a Saturday morning. It was still dark. I wanted to go back to sleep. My father was wide awake. My father was excited about the day ahead. We ate a quick breakfast. We drove to the school at the edge of the desert. We arrived at 7 a.m. The desert was already hot. I felt nervous. I didn't want to show it. The other students arrived. One was a boy. He was about my age. He was with his father, too. The instructor came out to greet us.

Example: The toughest weekend of my life was also one of the best. When I was 12, my father and I attended a short survival course that I will never forget.

F. Go back to your paragraph from Activity E. Circle the conjunctions. Underline the subordinators. Put a star (*) next to the relative clauses. Then answer these questions.

1. How many short sentences do you have? ____

2. How many sentences have conjunctions? ____

3. How many sentences have subordinators? ____

4. How many sentences have relative clauses? ____

G. Read the rest of the essay from Activity E.

The instructor—a tall, athletic man—looked at us seriously. "You are going to learn about survival," he said. "This may be the most challenging and rewarding weekend of your life." I looked at my father. I wasn't sure that I wanted to continue, but he was still very excited. "You will learn how to do such things as find food, find shelter, and keep warm. I won't tell you that it is going to be easy. In fact, it won't be. However, at the end of the weekend, I hope you'll think that it was worth the effort."

We set out with only our water bottles and knives. We hiked through the desert for miles in the hot sun. I was afraid that we would run out of water, but our guide said that we would be fine as long as we didn't waste any. Along the way, we looked for food. We found an edible plant that people call a barrel cactus. We also caught a lizard that people can boil and eat, but no one wanted to. We were hungry and tired when the instructor had us stop near some flowering cactus. We ate the flowers, which tasted OK, and we rested in the shade of some large rocks.

I don't remember much about the rest of the first day, but I do remember that the air got cold quickly when the sun set, and I was happy to sit close to my father, near the fire that we had helped build. I looked up at the stars and smiled. They were so beautiful, out away from the city. I looked up at my father and saw his face more peaceful than I could remember ever seeing it before.

It was a tough weekend, but I am glad we went. I learned about the desert and how to survive in it, but more importantly, I learned about myself and my father. We had shared a difficult time in the desert, and we grew closer because of it. Long afterward, whenever we saw the stars, one or the other would say, "Remember that night in the desert?" and we would both smile.

Choose one of the paragraphs in the essay. Circle the conjunctions. Underline the subordinators. Put a star (*) next to the relative clauses.

H. Go online for more practice with narrative essays and varying sentence patterns.

Grammar | Past perfect and past perfect continuous

Order of events in the past

The **past perfect** shows that one event happened before another event in the past. The past perfect expresses the earlier event. The simple past is often used to express the later event. The past perfect often gives background information about events or situations. It has the same form for all subjects: subject + *had* (+ *not*) + past participle.

Past perfect with past time clauses

The past perfect is often used in sentences with **past time clauses**. A past time clause usually begins with a subordinator such as *when*, *until*, or *by the time*. Notice the use of a comma when the past time clause comes first.

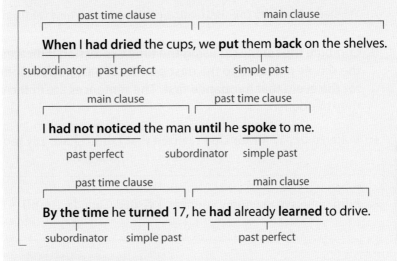

Past perfect continuous

The **past perfect continuous** is used for actions that began in the past and continued up to another past event or state in the past. It is often used with *for* to indicate how long a situation lasted. Like the past perfect, it often gives background information. The past perfect continuous is *had + been + verb + -ing*.

I **had been living** there for six months when the Smiths moved next door.

She **had been writing** stories for many years when her first story was published.

When she finally arrived, **he'd been waiting** for her for two hours.

A. Read the sentences. Underline the past perfect and past perfect continuous verbs and circle the simple past verbs in each example. Label the verbs *1* for the earlier event and *2* for the later event.

1. My mother (had) a collection of very small china cups and saucers.
   She had collected them throughout her life.

2. I had only washed a few when the beautiful blue and white cup slipped from my small hands.

3. I had forgotten to call my brother, so he was angry with me.

4. She had thought seriously about studying medicine, but in the end she decided to study business.

5. Until he got an internship at a big ad agency, he hadn't been interested in working in advertising.

6. I didn't answer the man because I hadn't heard him clearly.

7. We had been working on the project for hours when we finally finished it.

B. Combine the sentences using the time expression indicated. Change the simple past verb to the past perfect or past perfect continuous for the event that happened first. The sentences are in the order that they happened.

I didn't have any money.

1. I offered to pay for lunch. I realized that I didn't have any money. (when)

   _____

2. I did not leave my home country. I visited Canada. (until)

   _____

3. He already finished reading the book. He watched the DVD. (when)

   _____

4. They recalled important events from their past. The students wrote stories about their memories of childhood. (after)

   _____

   _____

5. I had lunch. She arrived at the restaurant. (by the time)

   _____

6. She was studying English. She moved to the United States. (when)

   _____

C. Go online for more practice with the past perfect and past perfect continuous.

D. Go online for the grammar expansion.

In this assignment, you are going to write a narrative essay about someone or something that influenced you when you were younger. As you prepare your essay, think about the Unit Question, "What important lessons do we learn as children?" Use information from Reading 1, Reading 2, the unit video, and your work in this unit to support your essay. Refer to the Self-Assessment checklist on page 90.

iQ ONLINE Go to the Online Writing Tutor for a writing model and alternate Unit Assignments.

PLAN AND WRITE

A. BRAINSTORM Follow these steps to help you organize your ideas.

1. Write down the names of some people or things that influenced you when you were younger.

2. Think about memories associated with those people or things. Write notes about the memories and specific details such as people, times, and places.

 Tip for Success

To help you remember all the details of your memory, ask and answer the six *wh*-questions: *who, what, where, when, why,* and *how.*

People	Memories	Details
My older brother	The time I fell off my bike when we were kids	I was 6. We were in Greenway Park. I cut my head. We went to see Dr. Garcia.

Things	Memories	Details
Greenwich Elementary School	My first day of school	I was lost on my first day. Mrs. Lu found me in the school playground. She took me back to class.

B. PLAN Follow these steps to plan your essay.

1. Choose one of the people or things from Activity A to write about.

2. Circle the most interesting memories and the most important details.

iQ ONLINE 3. Go to the Online Resources to download and complete the outline for your narrative essay.

C. **WRITE** Use your **PLAN** notes to write your essay. Go to *iQ Online* to use the Online Writing Tutor.

1. To clearly express the order of the events, use time words and time clauses, the past perfect and past perfect continuous, and other past verb forms.

2. Look at the Self-Assessment checklist below to guide your writing.

REVISE AND EDIT

A. **PEER REVIEW** Read your partner's essay. Then go online and use the Peer Review worksheet. Discuss the review with your partner.

B. **REVISE** Based on your partner's review, revise, and rewrite your essay.

C. **EDIT** Complete the Self-Assessment checklist as you prepare to write the final draft of your essay. Be prepared to hand in your work or discuss it in class.

SELF-ASSESSMENT		
Yes	**No**	
☐	☐	Does the introduction tell why the story is important?
☐	☐	Are the events in the order in which they happened?
☐	☐	Does the conclusion tell why the memory is important today?
☐	☐	Are time words and time clauses used to clearly express the order of the events?
☐	☐	Are the past perfect and past perfect continuous used appropriately to give background for other past events or situations?
☐	☐	Does the essay include vocabulary from the unit?
☐	☐	Did you check the essay for punctuation, spelling, and grammar?

D. **REFLECT** Go to the Online Discussion Board to discuss these questions.

1. What is something new you learned in this unit?

2. Look back at the Unit Question—What important lessons do we learn as children? Is your answer different now than when you started the unit? If yes, how is it different? Why?

TRACK YOUR SUCCESS

Circle the words and phrases you have learned in this unit.

Nouns
assumption AWL
colleague 🔑 AWL
competence
episode
refuge
period 🔑 AWL
significance AWL

Verbs
capture 🔑
exaggerate 🔑
motivate AWL
nurture
select 🔑 AWL
suspect 🔑

Phrasal Verb
rely on 🔑 AWL

Adjectives
creative 🔑 AWL
extracurricular
impassioned
innate
profound
resentful

Adverbs
accurately 🔑 AWL
theoretically AWL

Phrases
consistent with 🔑 AWL
equipped with AWL

Prefixes
anti- 🔑
co-
extra-
in-
inter-
mid-
mis-
re- 🔑

Suffixes
-ate
-ence / -ance
-ent / -ant
-ful
-ize
-tion

🔑 Oxford 3000™ words
AWL Academic Word List

Check (✓) the skills you learned. If you need more work on a skill, refer to the page(s) in parentheses.

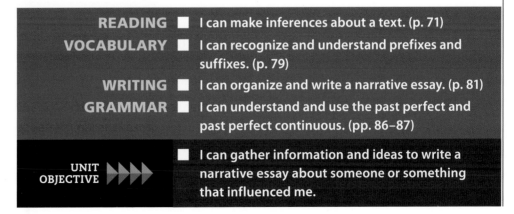

READING ■	I can make inferences about a text. (p. 71)
VOCABULARY ■	I can recognize and understand prefixes and suffixes. (p. 79)
WRITING ■	I can organize and write a narrative essay. (p. 81)
GRAMMAR ■	I can understand and use the past perfect and past perfect continuous. (pp. 86–87)
UNIT OBJECTIVE ▶▶▶▶ ■	I can gather information and ideas to write a narrative essay about someone or something that influenced me.

UNIT QUESTION

How important is it to write by hand?

A Discuss these questions with your classmates.

1. Do you like to write by hand? Why?

2. Why is it important to preserve the skill of writing?

3. Look at the photo. Why are these people writing by hand? Why might this be important to them?

B Listen to *The Q Classroom* online. Then answer these questions.

1. What are Marcus's reasons for not writing by hand?

2. What are reasons the other students give for writing by hand? Who do you agree with? Why?

 C Go to the Online Discussion Board to discuss the Unit Question with your classmates.

UNIT
OBJECTIVE ▶▶▶▶ Read an article from an education journal and a biography and gather information and ideas to write an essay comparing and contrasting two forms of writing.

93

D Work with a partner. Read these quotations about writing and the creative process and discuss the questions.

1. What does each quotation mean?

2. Do you agree with the quotations? Check (✓) *Agree* or *Disagree*.

The Writer's Way

AGREE DISAGREE

1. That which we persist in doing becomes easier, not that the task itself has become easier but that our ability to perform it has improved.
   —Ralph Waldo Emerson (1803–1882)

☐ ☐

2. Here is a golden rule… Write legibly. The average temper of the human race would be perceptibly sweetened, if everybody obeyed this rule.
   —Lewis Carroll (1832–1898)

☐ ☐

3. Energy and persistence alter all things.
   —Benjamin Franklin (1705–1790)

☐ ☐

4. It's not the hours you put in your work that count, it's the work you put in the hours.
   —Sam Ewing (1949–)

☐ ☐

E Work in a group and discuss your answers. Explain why you checked *Agree* or *Disagree*.

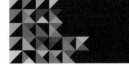
READING 1 | Two Styles of Writing

You are going to read an article from an education journal on two different styles of writing English text. Use the article to gather information and ideas for your Unit Assignment.

PREVIEW THE READING

A. **PREVIEW** Think about how you write. What is important to you when you start to write something? Check (✓) all the characteristics that you pay attention to.

☐ My handwriting is legible.

☐ I write quickly.

☐ My handwriting is neat.

☐ My handwriting looks nice.

☐ My handwriting is different from everyone else's.

☐ I write using a certain type of pen or color of ink.

B. **QUICK WRITE** Think about learning to write the characters in your language and/or the letters in English. Were the characters difficult to learn? Did you ever tear the paper or have trouble making the writing look nice? How is your handwriting now? Write for 5–10 minutes in response. Be sure to use this section for your Unit Assignment.

C. **VOCABULARY** Check (✓) the words you know. Use a dictionary to define any new or unknown words. Then discuss how the words will relate to the unit with a partner.

advocate *(v.)*	**legible** *(adj.)*
alternative *(n.)* 🔑	**maintain** *(v.)* 🔑
attain *(v.)*	**nerve** *(n.)* 🔑
by hand *(phr.)*	**proficient** *(adj.)*
distinctive *(adj.)*	**stimulate** *(v.)*
ensure *(v.)* 🔑	**worthwhile** *(adj.)*

🔑 Oxford 3000™ words

D. Go online to listen and practice your pronunciation.

WORK WITH THE READING

A. Read the article and gather information about how important it is to write by hand.

Two Styles of Writing

a child learning to write

1   What does it mean to learn a language? Of course, we need to produce the sounds that make up words, put words together into meaningful units, and understand others who speak to us. To be literate, we also need to read and write. We should be able to write the letters of the alphabet, but with all the other parts of the language that need to be practiced, is it important to learn two ways to write them?

2   Educators have long seen the connection between learning to read and learning to write the letters that make up words. In one study, adults who learned to write a new alphabet with paper and pencil were better able to recognize and remember letters than their counterparts, who only studied the printed letters but did not try to form them. In addition, children develop fine motor skills and control when learning to write **by hand**. They must pay attention to the shape of the letters, for example, in order to produce a "d" that is distinct from a "b." Likewise, they must judge how much pressure to apply so as to avoid poking holes in the paper or accidentally tearing it. They must learn to move their hands and not smudge their work while writing. Also, they need to keep the words in a straight line and pay attention to how the letters are placed with respect to one another. For example, the stem of a "b" rises, while the stem of a "p" falls.

3   Educators also employ tactile[1] and kinesthetic[2] methods to help young children learn to form their letters. Children may trace letters on sandpaper to **stimulate** nerve endings in their fingers. Similarly, they may use their whole arm and shoulder to write giant letters in the sand or on big pieces of paper. Using these large muscle groups helps to establish important **nerve** connections between the muscles and the brain.

4   With so many subjects competing for attention, some parents and teachers have raised questions about how **worthwhile** it is to teach children both to print, to form letters in much the same way as they are seen in books, and to write in cursive, a kind of writing that connects the letters of a word together. Is it worth the time spent on learning both forms, or is it enough to learn just to print, leaving more time for other subjects, such as reading or computer skills?

[1] **tactile:** related to touch
[2] **kinesthetic:** related to motion

5   Supporters of learning both forms **maintain** that cursive writing is faster than printing—an advantage when composing papers or taking notes. Brian Palmer, writing in the online magazine *Slate*, states that cultures have favored connected script throughout time, and writers will often develop their own **distinctive** methods of linking letters so as to take advantage of the faster means of forming words. These individual scripts can be problematic for readers, however, so teachers **advocate** the use of a standard script so as to better **ensure** legibility.

6   Furthermore, because cursive writing is highly individualistic, it is used as a means to establish identity. Analysts can use handwritten documents to determine whether two samples of writing most likely came from the same person or not. This is useful to historians who find unsigned papers or to police looking at evidence.

7   Yet another reason for continuing to teach cursive writing is that it is part of our culture and, therefore, valuable to link us to our past. Indeed, cursive writing is often seen as a more mature type of writing, and if we want to continue to read historic documents that predate the printing press, we will almost certainly need to continue to teach children this form of writing.

8   Those who disagree with continuing to teach this form are not opposed to cursive writing in itself. They contend that not everyone needs to be **proficient** in this skill and that there are other solutions to the problems cursive writing addresses.

9   First of all, the neurological benefits of learning to write are developed both with printing and with cursive writing. As long as we continue to have children write with their hands, or do other skills with their hands that involve fine motor control, we will continue to build nerve connections. These benefits do not change.

Many people find typing a useful alternative.

10   In addition, even with instruction, children and adults do not always develop **legible** handwriting. Some people prefer to print and can actually **attain** writing speeds comparable to those of people writing in cursive. Many people find typing a useful **alternative** and have increased their speed so that they can take notes comfortably on a computer. Writers themselves have a responsibility to their readers to produce clear texts by printing or typing their words if their writing is illegible.

11   Options also exist for using handwriting as a means of identification. Instead of asking for a signature, a legal paper could carry a thumbprint or a fingerprint. Some people might choose to learn to read and write in cursive much like some people learn to make clothes, speak Latin, or build houses. These people could be called on to use their skills when an old document needs to be read or when a special document is created.

12   No one seems to be suggesting that we stop teaching children to write by hand. After all, even if we had the technology to replace writing, technology sometimes fails or is unavailable. As with any skill, handwriting needs to be practiced, and schools are under pressure to have time to practice many different skills. The question lies in whether we want to take the time and make the effort to teach children a second, related, form of writing. What do you think?

In Unit 3, you learned
about prefixes that
change a word's
meaning and suffixes
that change the part
of speech. As you
learn new words,
find out whether
you can apply these
prefixes or suffixes to
make related words.

B. **VOCABULARY** Here are some words and phrases from Reading 1. Read the sentences. Circle the answer that best matches the meaning of each bold word or phrase.

1. My computer stopped working, so I wrote my essay **by hand.**
   a. using a machine
   b. easily
   c. with the hand(s)

2. When his heart stopped, the doctors **stimulated** it to keep him alive.
   a. made up
   b. made active
   c. made quiet

3. Your hands are sensitive because you have a lot of **nerves** in them.
   a. things that let you move or feel pain
   b. lines
   c. shaking

4. All our practice was **worthwhile** because we won the game.
   a. useless
   b. hard work over a long time
   c. good to spend time on or put effort into

5. Some people **maintain** that writing in cursive is still necessary.
   a. keep at the same level
   b. keep stating that something is true
   c. keep repaired

6. My teacher identified my **distinctive** handwriting when she looked at my note.
   a. different from others
   b. unpleasant in sound
   c. not loud enough to hear

7. He is going to **advocate** for a typing class next semester.
   a. publically support
   b. work hard at
   c. give legal advice to

8. Her mother **ensured** that she studied for the test.
   a. gave money when something happened
   b. made sure that something happened
   c. found out why something happened

9. It took hard work to become **proficient** in writing Chinese script.
    a. able to identify something
    b. able to support something
    c. able to do something well

10. A teacher's writing needs to be **legible** to students.
    a. legal; able to stand in court
    b. able to be selected
    c. clear enough to read

11. After four years, we will **attain** a university degree.
    a. put into
    b. succeed in getting
    c. understand

12. We didn't like our decision, but we didn't like the **alternative,** either.
    a. something that you change
    b. something that you charge
    c. something that you choose

iQ ONLINE   **C.** Go online for more practice with the vocabulary.

D. Circle the answer that best completes each statement.

1. Some benefits of writing by hand include ___.
    a. understanding differences in letters and gaining muscle control
    b. learning how to tear and poke holes in paper
    c. knowing different ways of writing

2. People disagree about whether ___.
    a. children should learn to write in school
    b. adults should learn to identify letters in another language
    c. children should learn to write in two different ways

3. Some benefits of writing in cursive are ___.
    a. it is faster and more legible than printing
    b. it is more attractive and stimulates more nerves
    c. it is faster and individualistic

4. People agree that ___.
    a. cursive writing is unnecessary
    b. children should learn to write by hand
    c. documents should be written by hand

E. Each subheading below refers to a main section of the text.
Match the subheadings with the paragraph numbers in the box.

paragraphs 2–3	paragraphs 5–7
paragraph 4	paragraphs 8–11

1. Benefits of Writing by Hand: _____

2. Reasons for Teaching Cursive Writing: _____

3. Explanation of the Problem with Teaching Cursive Writing:

   _____

4. Reasons against Teaching Cursive Writing: _____

F. Write *T* (true) or *F* (false) for each statement. Then correct each false statement to make it true.

_____ 1. People who study letters in print and how to form them by hand learn the alphabet more quickly.

_____ 2. Tactile and kinesthetic methods of teaching can develop brain and nerve connections.

_____ 3. Brian Palmer states that most cultures through history have preferred printing over cursive writing.

_____ 4. Researchers can match a person's identity to a piece of handwriting.

_____ 5. Children must learn cursive in order to refine nerve connections and develop good motor skills.

 G. Go online to read *Handmade Paper* and check your comprehension.

 # WRITE WHAT YOU THINK

A. Discuss these questions in a group.

1. Have you learned to write in two different ways? Why or why not?

2. Is it more important to learn to write by hand or to learn to use a computer keyboard? Why?

3. Do you think people will always write with pen and paper? Why or why not?

B. Choose one question and write a paragraph in response. Look back at your Quick Write on page 95 as you think about what you learned.

Writers **compare and contrast** information in order to examine the similarities and differences between two subjects. Comparisons show the subjects' similarities, while contrasts examine their differences. There are many different ways that texts can be organized when writers compare and contrast information. You can use a simple **T-chart** to quickly identify and separate the information about the two subjects. For example, look at the paragraph and the chart below.

> There are a number of differences between printing and writing in cursive. The most obvious is that the <u>letters in print are separate</u> while the <u>letters in cursive writing are connected</u>. <u>Printed letters</u> also tend to be <u>more legible</u>, whereas <u>letters written in cursive</u> tend to be <u>less clear and harder to read</u>. Most children used to learn to write in both styles by the time they were ten years old.

Printing	Cursive
separate letters	connected letters
more legible	less clear; harder to read

You can also divide the information further by adding categories or topic areas down the side of the chart. (Look at the chart below.) After you chart the information, you can easily examine the ideas for similarities and differences.

A. Reread paragraphs 5–11 of Reading 1 on page 97. Underline the good and bad points about print and cursive. Then write the information in the chart below.

Critical Thinking Tip

In Activity A, you have to **categorize** information from Reading 1. When you categorize information, you can see more clearly how ideas are similar and different.

	Print	Cursive
Speed		
Legibility		
Choice		
Part of culture		

B. Discuss your chart with a partner and add any points that you missed. Do you see similarities and differences in the points?

C. Go online for more practice understanding compare and contrast organization.

READING 2 | Haji Noor Deen—A Chinese Muslim Calligrapher

You are going to read a brief biography of Haji Noor Deen, a famous artist who does calligraphy. Calligraphy is beautiful handwriting that people do with a special pen or brush. Use the biography to gather information and ideas for your Unit Assignment.

PREVIEW THE READING

A. **PREVIEW** You will learn about Haji Noor Deen's work as a calligrapher and how he feels about it. What do you expect to learn about his work as a calligrapher? Add three things to the list.

   why he likes calligraphy _____

   _____

   _____

   _____

B. **QUICK WRITE** Would you want to learn calligraphy? Write for 5–10 minutes in response. Be sure to use this section for your Unit Assignment.

C. **VOCABULARY** Check (✓) the words you know. Then work with a partner to locate each word in the reading. Use clues to help define the words you don't know. Check your definitions in the dictionary.

complement (n.)	inspire (v.)
craft (n.) 🔑	recognize (v.) 🔑
determination (n.) 🔑	talent (n.) 🔑
essentially (adv.) 🔑	undertake (v.)
exhibit (v.) 🔑	unique (adj.) 🔑
imagery (n.)	

🔑 Oxford 3000™ words

D. Go online to listen and practice your pronunciation.

WORK WITH THE READING

A. Read the biography and gather information about how important it is to write by hand.

HAJI NOOR DEEN—A CHINESE MUSLIM CALLIGRAPHER

1   Today, there are approximately twenty million Muslims in China, and Haji Noor Deen is one of them. Born in 1963 in Shangdong province, China, Haji Noor Deen Mi Guang Jiang is a well-known and respected calligrapher. What makes him **unique** is that he is a master of Arabic calligraphy. **Essentially**, his work is a calligraphic technique which combines both Chinese and Arabic scripts.

Haji Noor Deen

2   Of his work Deen has said, "As a Chinese Muslim calligrapher, I have a deep sense of responsibility in promoting, propagating, and carrying forward this intricate skill and precious cultural heritage." He has **undertaken** the task of not only producing his own style of calligraphy, but also of **inspiring** others through lectures and workshops. He has taught his **craft** in lectures and workshops at many prestigious institutions in the U.S. and the U.K., such as Harvard University, the University of Cambridge, the University of California, and Boston University.

3   In 1997, Haji Noor Deen was awarded the Certificate of Arabic Calligrapher in Egypt. He was the first Chinese person to be given this prestigious award. In 2000, Deen taught the first Arabic Calligraphy course at the Zhengzhou Islamic College in China. In 2008, he became the first Chinese student to study traditional Arabic calligraphy when he traveled to Istanbul and studied under two distinguished calligraphers, Shiek Hassan Jalabi and Dawoud Baktash. In an article in ArabNews.com, Afra Naushad names Deen as one of the "top influential Muslims of 2009."

4   Deen's work has been collected and displayed in museums around the world, where he is **recognized** for being the first Chinese/Arabic calligrapher. He has **exhibited** his work in many countries, including the U.S. (in a San Francisco museum and the Harvard University Museum), the U.K. (in the British Museum and the National Museum of Scotland), Ireland, Australia, Canada, and Singapore. In the Middle East, his work has been shown in the United Arab Emirates, Qatar, and Kuwait.

5   Naushad says, "Most of the pieces of his calligraphic work are a creative exaltation[1] celebrating the glory of God with the verses of the Holy Qur'an." Naushad describes Deen's calligraphy as a revival of Islamic creativity and the role it has played in the preservation of the Qur'an's message.

Haji Noor Deen's calligraphy

6   Deen's website states that some of the most beautiful names of Allah and the **imagery** of prostration[2] are presented using a combination of the Chinese and Arabic alphabets. In 2005, a piece of his calligraphy entitled *The 99 names of God* was acquired by the British Museum and is now permanently displayed there.

7   Deen's work reflects a dedication to the presentation of the unity of Arabic and Chinese cultures. Chinese and Arabic calligraphy are two of the world's most beautiful styles of writing. They are both opposites and **complements**. Deen's calligraphy demonstrates that when combined, the result is a writing style of unique beauty.

8   "With **determination** and perseverance, with my hands and with the knowledge and **talent** bestowed on me by Allah the Almighty, I will seek to continue to craft the majestic and aesthetically[3] pleasing cultural tradition," Deen said.

---

[1] **exaltation:** a feeling of very great joy or happiness
[2] **prostration:** the act of stretching out with one's face on the ground, often in prayer
[3] **aesthetically:** beautifully; in a pleasing manner

B. **VOCABULARY** Here are some words from Reading 2. Read the sentences. Then write each bold word next to the correct definition. You may need to change verbs to their base form and nouns to the singular form.

1. It takes many years of practice to perfect the **craft** of calligraphy.

2. The children's stories were **exhibited** in the classroom.

3. They work well together because their methods of working are **essentially** the same.

4. A good teacher should be capable of **inspiring** his or her students to do well.

5. I believe he has the **determination** to achieve his goals.

6. These two foods are often eaten together because they are **complements**.

7. They were **recognized** for their acts of kindness to others.

8. The **imagery** in the story helped the young readers understand and feel sympathy for the characters.

9. Joshua has always had a **talent** for math. At a young age, he could see patterns and relationships between numbers and was able to understand complex equations.

10. I have never seen another book like that one. It is **unique**.

11. William is going to **undertake** the task of organizing the stories the students wrote into a book.

a. _____ (*n.*) an activity involving a special skill at making things with your hands

b. _____ (*adv.*) basically; when you consider the most important part of something

c. _____ (*v.*) to give someone the desire or enthusiasm to do well

d. _____ (*n.*) a natural skill or ability

e. _____ (*v.*) to agree that you will do something; to carry out

f. _____ (*v.*) to show something to the public

g. _____ (*n.*) the use of descriptions and comparisons in language in order to have a strong effect on people's imagination and emotions

h. _____ (*n.*) a thing that goes together well with something else

i. _____ (*adj.*) unlike anything else; being the only one of its type

j. _____ (*n.*) the continuation of something even though it is difficult or people say you cannot do it

k. _____ (*v.*) to show that you think something that someone has done is good

iQ ONLINE **C.** Go online for more practice with the vocabulary.

D. Write *T* (true) or *F* (false) for each statement. Then correct each false statement to make it true. Write the paragraph number where you found information to support your answer.

Haji Noor Deen . . .

____ 1. learned calligraphy at Harvard University. (paragraph ___)

_____

____ 2. has exhibited his calligraphy in museums. (paragraph ___)

_____

____ 3. teaches and gives workshops. (paragraph ___)

_____

____ 4. is well known in the world. (paragraph ___)

_____

____ 5. considers calligraphy an important cultural heritage. (paragraph ___)

_____

____ 6. has just retired from calligraphy. (paragraph ___)

_____

____ 7. was born in China. (paragraph ___)

_____

E. Number the events in the order in which they occurred.

___ 1.   Haji Noor Deen was awarded the Certificate of Arabic Calligrapher in Egypt.

___ 2.   The British Museum acquired a piece of Deen's calligraphy.

___ 3.   Deen became the first Chinese student to study traditional Arabic calligraphy.

___ 4.   Deen taught the first Arabic Calligraphy course at the Zhengzhou Islamic College.

___ 5.   Deen was listed in the "top influential Muslims."

F. Answer these questions to add information to each event in Haji Noor Deen's life from Activity E.

1.   What is noteworthy about his being awarded the Certificate of Arabic Calligrapher in Egypt?

   _____

2.   What is the name of the piece of calligraphy in the British Museum?

   _____

3.   Where did he study traditional Arabic calligraphy?

   _____

4.   Outside of China, where has Haji Noor Deen taught calligraphy?

   _____

5.   Where and by whom was he listed in the "top influential Muslims"?

   _____

G. List the reasons why Haji Noor Deen combines the styles of Arabic and Chinese calligraphy in his work.

   _____

   _____

   _____

WRITE WHAT YOU THINK

A. Discuss the questions in a group. Look back at your Quick Write on page 102 as you think about what you learned.

1. Why does Haji Noor Deen feel he has a responsibility to promote calligraphy?

2. Is it possible for anyone to learn calligraphy?

B. Before you watch the video, discuss the questions in a group.

1. What are three reasons for continuing to teach cursive writing in school?

2. Is cursive writing as important a skill as calligraphy?

3. Is learning cursive a good use of time in school? Are there other subjects that are more important?

C. Go online to watch the video about the importance of handwriting. Then check your comprehension.

> **bill** *(n.)* a plan for a possible new law
>
> **cognition** *(n.)* conscious mental activity
>
> **heritage** *(n.)* the history, traditions, and qualities that a country or society has had for many years and that are considered an important part of its character
>
> **infusion** *(n.)* the addition of something that is needed or helpful
>
> **nostalgia** *(n.)* a feeling of affection, mixed with sadness, for things that are in the past

VIDEO VOCABULARY

D. Think about the unit video, Reading 1, and Reading 2 as you discuss the questions. Then choose one question and write a paragraph in response.

1. What are some similarities between English writing and Arabic calligraphy?

2. What are some differences between English writing and Arabic calligraphy?

Finding the correct meaning

There are many words that have the same spelling and pronunciation but different meanings. These words are called **homonyms**.

> **bank (n.)** *an organization that provides various financial services*
> My salary is paid directly into my **bank**.
> **bank (n.)** *the side of a river and the land near it*
> She jumped into the river and swam to the opposite **bank**.

Some homonyms may be different parts of speech, for example, a noun with one or more meanings and a verb with other meanings.

> **place (n.)** *a particular position, point, or area*
> This would be a good **place** for a picnic.
> **place (v.)** *to put something in a particular place, especially when you do it carefully*
> He carefully **placed** his hand on his son's shoulder.

Advanced dictionaries will list all the word forms and definitions for them. When using a dictionary to find the correct meaning of a word, it is important to read the entire sentence and consider the use and context.

All dictionary entries are from the *Oxford Advanced American Dictionary for learners of English* © Oxford University Press 2011.

A. Look at the dictionary entry for *craft*. Check (✓) the correct information.

1. *Craft* can be used as:
   - ☐ an adjective
   - ☐ an adverb
   - ☐ a noun
   - ☐ a verb

2. *Craft* can mean:
   - ☐ a boat
   - ☐ a skill
   - ☐ frightening
   - ☐ strange
   - ☐ to make
   - ☐ to give

> **craft** 🔑 /kræft/ *noun, verb*
> • *noun* **1** [C, U] an activity involving a special skill at making things with your hands: *traditional crafts like basket-weaving* ♦ *a craft fair/workshop* ⮑ see also ARTS AND CRAFTS **2** [sing.] all the skills needed for a particular activity: *chefs who learned their craft in five-star hotels* ♦ *the writer's craft* **3** [U] (*formal, disapproving*) skill in making people believe what you want them to believe: *He knew how to win by craft and diplomacy what he could not gain by force.* **4** [C] (*pl.* **craft**) a boat or ship: *Hundreds of small craft bobbed around the liner as it steamed into the harbor.* ♦ *a landing/pleasure craft* **5** [C] (*pl.* **craft**) an aircraft or SPACECRAFT
> • *verb* [usually passive] ~ **sth** to make something using special skills, especially with your hands **SYN** FASHION: *All the furniture is crafted from natural materials.* ♦ *a carefully crafted speech* ⮑ see also HANDCRAFTED

B. Read the sentences and phrases from Readings 1 and 2. Look up each bold word in your dictionary. Write the part of speech and the correct definition based on the context.

Reading 1 (pages 96–97)

1. Children may trace letters on sandpaper to **stimulate** nerve endings in their fingers. (paragraph 3)

   _____

2. Using these large muscle groups helps to establish important **nerve** connections between the muscles and the brain. (paragraph 3)

   _____

3. Supporters of learning both forms **maintain** that cursive writing is faster than printing. (paragraph 5)

   _____

4. Some people prefer to print and can actually **attain** writing speeds comparable to those of people writing in cursive. (paragraph 10)

   _____

Reading 2 (pages 103–104)

5. What makes him **unique** is that he is a master of Arabic calligraphy. (paragraph 1)

   _____

6. He has **undertaken** the task of not only producing his own style of calligraphy . . . (paragraph 2)

   _____

7. . . . but also of **inspiring** others through lectures and workshops. (paragraph 2)

   _____

8. . . . some of the most beautiful names of Allah and the **imagery** of prostration . . . (paragraph 6)

   _____

 C. Go online for more practice with using the dictionary to distinguish between homonyms.

WRITING

UNIT OBJECTIVE

At the end of this unit, you will write an essay comparing and contrasting two forms of writing. This essay will include specific information from the readings, the unit video, and your own ideas.

Writing Skill   Writing a compare and contrast essay

A **compare and contrast essay** describes the similarities and differences between two subjects. Comparisons show their similarities, while contrasts examine their differences.

Introduction

The introduction describes the two subjects being compared and contrasted. It has a thesis statement that explains the relationship between the two subjects or gives reasons why the relationship is important.

Body paragraphs

There are many different ways to organize the body paragraphs of a compare and contrast essay. Before you write a compare and contrast essay, it is important to decide which organization is best for your essay. Here are two ways to organize your ideas:

- In a **point by point essay,** you choose three or more key points to compare and contrast. Each body paragraph compares and contrasts one key point. This organization can be best when you want to balance your essay evenly between your two subjects.

- In a **similarities and differences essay,** the first body paragraph explains what is similar about the two subjects. The second body paragraph explains what is different about the two subjects. The third body paragraph discusses the most important similarities and differences. This organization can be best when you want to explain why one subject is better than the other subject.

Conclusion

The conclusion summarizes the similarities and differences and gives the writer's opinion about the topic. It can explain why one of the subjects is better than the other or why they are of equal value.

A. **WRITING MODEL** Read the model compare and contrast essay. Then answer the questions on page 113.

Writing in the Digital Age

As we move more firmly into the digital age, we are writing as much or more with keyboards as with pen and paper. Computers and smartphones are basic equipment in the business community, and students are more likely to have to type their papers than to write by hand. While both methods serve the purpose of putting words into visible text, there are also some important differences.

Both handwriting and typing are used to convey information. They both use the same groups of letters to form words and the same groups of words to form sentences. However, in handwritten text, all of the beauty and the flaws are attributed to the writer, and more information about the author, especially emotion, can come out. The appearance of handwritten text can change easily with fatigue or excitement, while typewritten words look the same regardless of whether they were produced by a tired author or by a delighted one. Because type is standardized, there are no flourishes or misshapen letters to worry about.

Speed is a second factor in writing. Writers like to be able to get their ideas down, in ink or electrons, as they come, moving them from the brain, through the hand, to the paper or screen. Taking notes in a meeting or a class, which requires the writer to process someone else's ideas, is facilitated by having fluency in writing or typing. Using a pen and paper requires an author to keep an eye on the words so that they are legible—in a line, not overlapping, not too big or too small. Learning to "touch-type," on the other hand, frees the writer from looking at the words, so more attention can be paid to the actual ideas.

Both types of writing convey information to a reader, whether the reader is a stranger, a close friend, or the writer himself. Misspellings, awkward sentences, and incorrect grammar can be found in both handwritten and typed text. It is much easier to get away with an error in handwriting than in print. In handwritten text, a character can be ambiguous—is that an *a* or an *o*?—whereas a choice must be made when a keyboard is used. Although a person writing by hand must usually rely on himself for spacing within and between words, for respecting margins, and for correcting errors, most word processing programs take care of such spacing and layout concerns automatically, and some will correct common misspellings and other errors.

In short, words convey ideas, whether they are handwritten or typed. They use the same symbols, with some minor variations, and can be produced at varying speeds. The more personalized handwriting lends itself to showing individualization, paying attention to the skill, and error, while the mechanized writing demonstrates regularity, automatic responses, and a nudge toward corrections. Which is better? That might be in the hands of the writer—or in the eyes of the reader. Either way, we will no doubt have both forms with us for years to come.

1. What is the thesis statement? Underline it.

2. How is the essay organized? _____

3. Why do you think the author organized it this way?

   _____

B. Reread the essay on page 112. Complete the chart with both the similarities and the differences for each key point. Then compare with a partner.

Compare and Contrast Essay: Point by Point		
Key points	Handwriting	Typing
1. individualization	beauty and flaws are writers'	same characters; no variety in shape
2. attention to forms		
3. corrections		

C. Work with a partner. Complete the chart below. Reorganize the information in the essay into a plan for a similarities and differences essay. Use the chart in Activity B to help you.

Compare and Contrast Essay: Similarities and Differences		
Similarities	Differences	
	Handwriting	Typing
convey information	beauty and flaws are writers'	same characters; no variety in shape

D. You can use the same type of chart to help you brainstorm your ideas. Use the chart below to help you think of examples of what you could write about cooking 100 years ago and cooking now.

Compare and Contrast Essay: Similarities and Differences in Cooking 100 Years Ago and Now		
Similarities	Differences	
	100 years ago	Now

E. Choose another craft or activity you are familiar with. Create a chart for that activity like the one in Activity D.

Compare and Contrast Essay: Similarities and Differences in _____		
Similarities	Differences	
	100 years ago	Now

F. **WRITING MODEL** Read the model compare and contrast essay. Then answer the questions on page 116.

Do-It-Yourself, Then and Now

Tap, tap, tap. "Ouch!" I had hit my thumb one more time with the hammer, so I decided to take a break from building a new bookcase. I realized that I was actually enjoying working on this project, despite the pain in my thumb, because I liked doing something practical and having something new at the end of the day. I had become part of a trend of crafters making things by hand, not because they have to but because they want to. In the past few years, do-it-yourself (DIY) projects have become increasingly popular, but they are different from how they used to be.

In the past, getting food, clothing, and shelter often required having the skills to raise animals and plants for food, to make clothes, and to build and repair houses and other structures. There were no prepackaged foods, so girls, mostly, learned to cook. Because ready-made clothes were expensive, girls were taught how to make their own. Both girls and boys tended gardens and animals to supplement their families' diets. Boys often learned to construct and repair simple furniture and buildings by learning elementary carpentry, masonry, and plumbing. These skills were necessary to remain fed, clothed, and protected from the elements.

Nowadays, on the other hand, people can choose which, if any, of these skills they want to learn. With more available off-the-shelf products and more disposable income, more people buy food and clothing rather than making them themselves. They can move into existing housing and hire someone to do the necessary repairs. Despite all this, there has been a rise in the number of people learning these skills. Some cite the enjoyment of doing something practical with their hands, while others mention the satisfaction of creating, or helping to create, food, clothing, structures, or other materials by themselves. Furthermore, these skills are not typically divided by gender: Men may cook new types of food, and women may find themselves with a hammer and a blueprint.

Learning practical skills, like sewing and woodworking, may not be for everyone, but many people are finding that they enjoy the process of creating their own items, whether a new sweater, an additional closet, or a meal from their own garden. Without the necessity of making many things ourselves, we can enjoy the art and satisfaction of doing things ourselves. Why don't you give it a try?

1. What is the thesis statement? Underline it.

2. How is the essay organized? _____

   Why do you think the author organized it this way? _____

   _____

 G. Go online for more practice with writing a compare and contrast essay.

Grammar   Subordinators and transitions to compare and contrast

You can use a number of different words and phrases to compare and contrast ideas.

Subordinators showing contrast

You can use some adverb clauses to show an idea that contrasts with the main clause. The subordinators *although* and *though* show contrasting ideas. *Whereas* and *while* often show more direct opposition. Notice the comma when the adverb clause comes first.

main clause	adverb clause
In handwritten text, a character can be ambiguous	**whereas a choice must be made when** (subordinator) **a keyboard is used.**

adverb clause	main clause
Although a person writing by hand must (subordinator) **usually rely on himself,**	most word processing programs take care of layout concerns automatically.

Transitions showing comparison

You can use some transition words to show comparison. Some common transition words to show comparison are *similarly*, *likewise*, and *in addition*. These are used to discuss similarities.

> Children may trace letters on sandpaper. **Similarly**, they may use their whole arm and shoulder to write giant letters.
> They must pay attention to the shape of the letters. **Likewise**, they must judge how much pressure to apply.

Transitions showing contrast

You can use some transition words to show contrast, or differences.

Contrast	More direct opposition	Concession	
however	on the other hand	nevertheless	in spite of this
though	in contrast	nonetheless	despite this

> Both handwriting and typing use the same groups of letters to form words.
> **However**, in handwritten text, all of the beauty and the flaws are attributed to the writer.
>
> Using a pen and paper requires an author to keep an eye on the words. Learning to "touch-type," **on the other hand**, frees the writer from looking at the words.

A. Read each sentence. Underline the word or phrase that indicates a comparison or a contrast. Then write CP (comparison) or CT (contrast).

____ 1. Although some calligraphers use this craft as their job, others use it just for enjoyment.

____ 2. Writing well takes practice. Similarly, doing well at any activity takes commitment and training.

____ 3. There are professionals in many activities. Nonetheless, amateurs can also benefit from trying their hands at different hobbies.

____ 4. Whereas some hobbies require a lot of time to learn, others can be learned easily.

____ 5. Hobbies can help us relax. Likewise, they can help us enjoy time with others.

B. Circle the best phrase to complete each sentence.

1. John likes to use his hands to make things while Robert (prefers to play sports / makes things by hand, too).

2. John put together his own computer. Similarly, his brother (would rather go fishing / built a computer, too).

3. Robert likes to go fishing and camping. Though he enjoys both, he (likes camping better / likes them both equally).

4. Robert hopes to spend his weekend on the beach. John, too, plans to (study in the library / go to the beach).

5. Robert and John spend a lot of time studying. Nonetheless, they find they (need to study / appreciate having time to relax).

6. Although Robert wants to sleep in a tent, John will (sleep outside / sleep in a tent, too).

C. Complete these sentences using your own ideas. Make sure you use correct punctuation.

1. I don't enjoy fishing very much. Nevertheless ,_I enjoy cooking and eating_ _the fish._

2. Although many people enjoy fishing _____ _____

3. Not many people become professional athletes. Likewise _____ _____

4. Professional soccer players often have rigorous training. On the other hand _____ _____

5. I like both soccer and handball. However _____ _____

6. Whereas some athletes end their careers early _____ _____

7. Athletes need ambition to succeed. Similarly _____ _____

D. Go online for more practice with subordinators and transitions to compare and contrast.

E. Go online for the grammar expansion.

In this assignment, you are going to write a five-paragraph essay to compare and contrast two methods of writing. As you prepare your essay, think about the Unit Question, "How important is it to write by hand?" Use information from Reading 1, Reading 2, the unit video, and your work in this unit to support your essay. Refer to the Self-Assessment checklist on page 120.

iQ **ONLINE** Go to the Online Writing Tutor for a writing model and alternate Unit Assignments.

PLAN AND WRITE

Writing **Tip**

When you brainstorm ideas using both a point by point chart and a similarities and differences chart, it will help you discover which organization works best for your subject, and you may get more ideas.

A. **BRAINSTORM** Follow these steps to help you organize your ideas.

1. Work with a partner. Discuss pairs of methods of writing, such as writing in Chinese and writing in English or printed Arabic and handwritten Arabic, that you think have an interesting or important relationship to each other.

2. Choose the two methods of writing you would like to use as your subject to compare and contrast.

3. Write points to compare and contrast and similarities and differences for your subject. (Refer to the charts on page 113 to help you organize your ideas.)

B. **PLAN** Follow these steps to plan your essay.

1. Look at your ideas from question 3 in Activity A. Decide whether your essay would be best organized as a point by point essay or a similarities and differences essay.

iQ **ONLINE** 2. Go to the Online Resources to download and complete the graphic organizer for your compare and contrast essay (point by point or similarities and differences).

3. Go to the Online Resources to download and complete the outline for your compare and contrast essay.

iQ **ONLINE** **C.** **WRITE** Use your **PLAN** notes to write your essay. Go to *iQ Online* to use the Online Writing Tutor.

1. Write your essay comparing and contrasting two methods of writing. Be sure to include an introduction with a thesis statement, three body paragraphs, and a conclusion.

2. Look at the Self-Assessment checklist on page 120 to guide your writing.

REVISE AND EDIT

A. **PEER REVIEW** Read your partner's essay. Then go online and use the Peer Review worksheet. Discuss the review with your partner.

B. **REWRITE** Based on your partner's review, revise, and rewrite your essay.

C. **WRITE** Complete the Self-Assessment checklist as you prepare to write the final draft of your essay. Be prepared to hand in your work or discuss it in class.

Yes	No	SELF-ASSESSMENT
☐	☐	Does the thesis statement explain the relationship between the two subjects or give reasons why the relationship is important?
☐	☐	Is the essay organized using one of the compare and contrast essay types?
☐	☐	Does the essay contain an introduction, three body paragraphs, and a conclusion?
☐	☐	Does the essay use subordinators and transitions to compare and contrast?
☐	☐	Does the essay include vocabulary from the unit?
☐	☐	Did you check the essay for punctuation, spelling, and grammar?

D. **REFLECT** Go to the Online Discussion Board to discuss these questions.

1. What is something new you learned in this unit?

2. Look back at the Unit Question—How important is it to write by hand? Is your answer different now than when you started the unit? If yes, how is it different? Why?

TRACK YOUR SUCCESS

Circle the words and phrases you have learned in this unit.

Nouns
alternative 🔑 AWL
complement AWL
craft 🔑
determination 🔑
imagery AWL
nerve 🔑
talent 🔑

Verbs
advocate AWL
attain AWL
ensure 🔑 AWL
exhibit 🔑 AWL
inspire
maintain 🔑 AWL
recognize 🔑
stimulate
undertake AWL

Adjectives
distinctive AWL
legible
proficient
unique 🔑 AWL
worthwhile

Adverb
essentially 🔑

Phrase
by hand

🔑 Oxford 3000™ words
AWL Academic Word List

Check (✓) the skills you learned. If you need more work on a skill, refer to the page(s) in parentheses.

READING	☐	I can understand compare and contrast organization. (p. 101)
VOCABULARY	☐	I can use the dictionary to distinguish between homonyms. (p. 109)
WRITING	☐	I can write a compare and contrast essay. (p. 111)
GRAMMAR	☐	I can use subordinators and transitions to compare and contrast. (pp. 116–117)
UNIT OBJECTIVE ▶▶▶▶	☐	I can gather information and ideas to write an essay comparing and contrasting two forms of writing.

READING ▶ recognizing bias
VOCABULARY ▶ cause and effect collocations
WRITING ▶ writing a cause and effect essay
GRAMMAR ▶ agents with the passive voice

UNIT QUESTION

Should science influence what we eat?

A Discuss these questions with your classmates.

1. Do you think you have a generally healthy diet? What have you eaten so far today?

2. Which is more important to you: eating for pleasure or eating for health? Why?

3. Look at the photos. Would you eat food that was grown in a lab? Why or why not?

🔊 **B** Listen to *The Q Classroom* online. Then answer these questions.

1. Who agrees that science should influence what we eat? What reasons do they give?

2. Who thinks science shouldn't influence what we eat? What reasons do they give? Do you think science should influence what we eat? Why or why not?

iQ ONLINE **C** Go online to watch the video about genetically modified food. Then check your comprehension.

VIDEO VOCABULARY

certified *(adj.)* officially approved as having met a standard

contaminate *(v.)* to add a substance that will make something dirty, harmful, or impure

dispute *(n.)* a disagreement or argument between people

organic *(adj.)* produced by or using natural materials, not chemicals

iQ ONLINE **D** Go to the Online Discussion Board to discuss the Unit Question with your classmates.

E Cover the answers at the bottom of the page. Complete the questionnaire and compare with a partner. Then check the answers. How many did you get right? Did any information surprise you?

Food Facts and Fiction

You often hear these eight ideas about food, but not all of them are true. How much do you really know about what you're eating? Take this quiz. Can you tell the myths from the facts?

	Myth	Fact
1 You'll gain weight if you regularly have dinner after 9 p.m.	☐	☐
2 Adding salt to water makes it boil faster.	☐	☐
3 The tomato is a fruit, not a vegetable.	☐	☐
4 Eating carrots will help you see in the dark.	☐	☐
5 Frozen fruit and vegetables can be more nutritious than fresh.	☐	☐
6 Boiling vegetables removes all their nutrients.	☐	☐
7 Chocolate is bad for your teeth.	☐	☐
8 Eating fat-free food products will help you to lose weight.	☐	☐

Answers

1. Myth. What you eat has a direct effect on your weight, but when you eat doesn't.

2. Myth. A small amount of salt adds flavor, but it won't affect how quickly the water boils. (A large amount of salt will actually make the water take longer to boil.)

3. Fact. Scientifically speaking, the tomato is a fruit similar to a blueberry or raspberry.

4. Myth. Carrots do contain beta carotene, which the body uses to produce vitamin A. And vitamin A does help you see in poor light. But if you need to see in the dark, buy a flashlight!

5. Fact. Fruits and vegetables are often picked when they are freshest and then immediately frozen, so the nutrients are kept in the foods. Fresh (unfrozen) produce ripens quickly and loses its nutrients faster.

6. Myth. A certain quantity of vitamins may boil out of the food but most will remain. It is always good advice not to overcook any food, however.

7. Myth. Although eating chocolate should not replace good dental hygiene, there are parts of the chocolate plant that are actually good for your teeth.

8. Myth. Fat-free does not equal calorie-free. Many fat-free products contain a lot of sugar.

READING

READING 1 | Eating Well: Less Science, More Common Sense

You are going to read an article from a health magazine about ways that we can eat well. Use the article to gather information and ideas for your Unit Assignment.

PREVIEW THE READING

A. **PREVIEW** Read the title and look at the pictures. Answer these questions.

1. Does the author think science should help us choose the foods we eat?

_____

_____

2. What suggestions for eating well do you think the author will talk about?

_____

_____

B. **QUICK WRITE** How do you know what to eat? Do you pay attention to scientific studies about food? Write for 5–10 minutes in response. Be sure to use this section for your Unit Assignment.

C. **VOCABULARY** Check (✓) the words you know. Use a dictionary to define any new or unknown words. Then discuss how the words will relate to the unit with a partner.

access (n.) 🔑	**expert** (n.) 🔑
approach (n.) 🔑	**finding** (n.)
benefit (n.) 🔑	**link** (n.) 🔑
challenge (v.) 🔑	**participate** (v.) 🔑
eliminate (v.) 🔑	**physical** (adj.) 🔑
encourage (v.) 🔑	**practical** (adj.) 🔑

🔑 Oxford 3000™ words

 D. Go online to listen and practice your pronunciation.

A. Read the article and gather information about how science influences what we eat.

Eating Well: Less Science, More Common Sense

1   Food is life. We eat it to grow, stay healthy, and have the energy to do everyday activities. The food we consume makes all of these things possible, but not all food is created equal. Studies have shown, for example, that children who eat a nutritious breakfast do better in school than those with a poor diet. The well-fed child is able to pay attention longer, remember more, and **participate** more actively in class. Research has also shown that adults who have a healthy diet perform better on the job and miss fewer days of work. The **findings**, then, are clear. Because our food choices affect our health and behavior, we must do more than just eat; we must eat *well*. For many people today, though, making healthy food choices is not easy.

2   We are surrounded by information telling us what's good for us and what isn't, but usually this information is more confusing than helpful. In fact, different research about the same food often produces contradictory[1] results. Take one example: food studies done on eggs. For years, research showed a **link** between eating eggs and high cholesterol[2]. To prevent dangerous diseases like cancer or heart disease, people were **encouraged** to limit or completely **eliminate** eggs from their diets. However, recent studies now say that eggs are actually good for you and that most people can—and even *should*—eat one a day. It's hard to know who to believe.

3   Shopping for food can also be challenging. During a visit to a supermarket, we often need to make many different choices. Should you buy this cereal or that one? Regular or fat-free milk? Tofu or chicken? It's hard to know which to choose, especially when two items are very similar. Many shoppers read product labels to help them decide. Not surprisingly, people are more likely to buy items with the words "doctor-recommended," "low-fat," or "all-natural" on them. But are these foods *really* better for you? Probably not. Indeed, many food labels are often misleading. For instance, because doctors sometimes recommend that people eat yogurt for their digestion, a yogurt maker might then use the label "doctor-recommended" so that you buy their product. In reality, though, their specific yogurt isn't preferred by doctors, but shoppers may think it is because of the food label.

Product labels can be misleading.

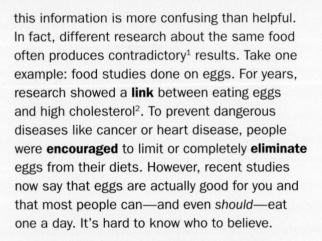

---

[1] **contradictory:** differing; opposite
[2] **cholesterol:** a substance found in foods like meat, milk, and cheese that can cause health problems

4   So how *do* we make healthy choices? Michael Pollan is a professor at the University of California, Berkeley who has written many books about eating well (including the bestseller *In Defense of Food*). In his opinion, our food needs to be defended against "needless complications" from "nutrition science and from the food industry." According to Pollan, we need to stop reading labels and listening to the so-called[3] scientific "**experts**." Instead, he offers some simple, yet **practical** tips for eating well and staying healthy.

5   Tip 1: "**Eat food. Not too much. Mostly plants.**" In other words, says Pollan, only eat "real food" or things your great-grandparents would recognize as food. Make fruit and vegetables your main source of food and limit your meat intake. And when you eat, says Pollan, do so in moderation. He quotes the Okinawan people of Japan who have an expression: "*Hara Hachi Bu*: eat until you are 80% full."

6   Tip 2: "**Get out of the supermarket whenever possible.**" Shopping for meat or dairy products at the market is probably OK, but a supermarket is also full of items like instant noodles, diet sodas, and similar products—the ones that aren't good for us. Instead, try to shop at a farmers' market or a local store when you can. The food there is fresher and healthier.

7   Tip 3: Pollan says that eating is not only about **physical** health and nutrition. "**Food is also about pleasure, about community and family.**" In other words, choosing the right food to eat is only the first step. Learning how to cook and sharing a meal with others are also important parts of eating well and being healthy.

8   Thinking like Michael Pollan's is **challenging** the "scientific **approach** to eating." It is also helping people to reconnect[4] with food traditions. In cities around the world, for example, urban gardens—common since ancient times—are becoming popular again. On small pieces of land, neighbors are working together to grow fruit and vegetables. What are the **benefits** of these gardens? Better nutrition for one thing; people have **access** to more fresh fruit and vegetables, especially poorer people who are less likely to spend money on these items. The food also costs less than it would in a supermarket (where it was probably driven in from farms or shipped in from another country). There are other benefits, too. Working together in the garden helps people to exercise; it also promotes community and sharing.

the Edible Schoolyard program

9   Urban gardens have also been used to teach children about food production and healthy eating. At the Edible Schoolyard—a program at a public school in the U.S.—children learn how to plant and harvest[5] fruit and vegetables. They also learn how to clean and prepare them for meals—a skill that they will be able to use all their lives. And best of all, because the children want to eat the things they have grown, they learn to develop healthy eating habits.

10   Ultimately, making healthy food choices and eating well do not have to be difficult. Doing simple things—changing your shopping habits, learning to cook, planting a garden, and limiting your intake of certain foods—can result in a better diet and a healthier you. *Bon appétit*[6]!

---

[3] **so-called:** used to show that the word being introduced is not accurate or true
[4] **reconnect:** to discover a relationship with something again

[5] **harvest:** to pick and collect fruit, vegetables, and other plants
[6] **bon appétit:** a French expression used in English, said at the start of a meal to mean "Enjoy the food."

In Unit 4, you used
the dictionary to
find homonyms that
are different parts
of speech. Five of
the 12 vocabulary
words in Activity B
are homonyms—
words that have the
same spelling and
pronunciation but
different meanings.
Use your dictionary
to identify the
five homonyms.

B. **VOCABULARY** Complete the sentences with the vocabulary from Reading 1.

access *(n.)*	**challenge** *(v.)*	**expert** *(n.)*	**participate** *(v.)*
approach *(n.)*	**eliminate** *(v.)*	**finding** *(n.)*	**physical** *(adj.)*
benefit *(n.)*	**encourage** *(v.)*	**link** *(n.)*	**practical** *(adj.)*

1. If you want to lose weight, you should _____ junk food from your diet.

2. Dr. Carlson is a medical _____ who specializes in women's health and nutrition.

3. One _____ of a vegetarian diet is that you'll probably live longer.

4. Is there a _____ between taking vitamins and better health?

5. Millions of people don't have _____ to clean drinking water. What can we do about this problem?

6. Do you want to _____ in our school's health study? You only have to answer a few questions.

7. One _____ from the study is that organic food is not always better for you.

8. You can _____ children to eat vegetables by eating more of them yourself.

9. Eating a large meal before bed isn't very _____. You won't be able to sleep.

10. To quit smoking, Leo tried chewing gum and exercising but neither _____ has worked.

11. My dad had a _____ exam today, and the doctor says he's in great health.

12. For years, people thought eating chocolate was bad for your skin, but recent studies _____ that belief. Research now says chocolate is good for you!

 C. **Go online for more practice with the vocabulary.**

D. Read the statements. Would the author of the magazine article agree with them? Write *Y* (yes) or *N* (no). Discuss your answers with a partner. Find the part of the article that supports your answer.

_____ 1. Scientific research about diet and health usually gives us helpful information.

_____ 2. Reading food labels has made us better-informed, healthier consumers.

_____ 3. We don't need experts to tell us what to eat.

_____ 4. A lot of food found in a supermarket is not "real food."

_____ 5. The purpose of eating is mainly for health and nutrition.

_____ 6. An urban garden is an old tradition that works well in modern cities.

_____ 7. Making healthy food choices is hard.

E. Circle the correct answer.

1. According to the reading, which question is difficult for many people to answer today?
   a. Why do some people have a healthier diet than others?
   b. How does our diet affect our health and behavior?
   c. Which are the healthiest foods to eat?

2. In paragraph 2, the studies on eggs are an example of _____ from the scientific community.
   a. confusing results
   b. helpful advice
   c. similar findings

3. Food labels that read "low-fat" or "all-natural" _____.
   a. are usually on products recommended by doctors
   b. are mainly used to sell a product
   c. often help shoppers make healthy food choices

4. Which piece of advice would Michael Pollan probably agree with?
   a. Try to eat only one meal per day; you'll feel better and be healthier.
   b. Selecting healthy food and learning how to cook it are both important.
   c. Never shop at a supermarket; the food there is unhealthy.

5. At the Edible Schoolyard in the U.S., what are children *not* learning to do?
   a. plant fruit and vegetables
   b. cook and eat healthy meals
   c. read and understand nutrition labels

F. Paragraph 8 of the article lists four benefits of having an urban garden. Write them below.

1. _____

2. _____

3. _____

4. _____

G. Complete the cause and effect chart on the benefits of an urban garden.

Causes	Effects (Benefits)
1. access to more fresh fruits and vegetables	
2. food doesn't have to be brought to supermarkets	
3. working in a garden	
4. working together	
5. participating in the Edible Schoolyard program	

  H. Go online to read *Turning Food into Science* and check your comprehension.

WRITE WHAT YOU THINK

A. Discuss these questions in a group.

1. Do you pay attention to the results of scientific food studies? What advice have you taken seriously?

2. Look again at Michael Pollan's tips for eating well in paragraphs 5–7 of Reading 1. Then describe the last three meals you have eaten and explain: Do you think you eat well? If yes, which of Pollan's tips are you following? If no, what do you need to do differently?

3. Look again at the benefits of an urban garden you listed in Activity F. Think of at least one more advantage and explain how it helps people.

B. Choose one question and write a paragraph in response. Look back at your Quick Write on page 125 as you think about what you learned.

Bias means a strong feeling for or against something. Writers may present information in ways that support their biases in order to influence a reader's opinion. It is important to recognize a writer's bias in order to better evaluate his or her arguments and ideas. Look at these examples from Reading 1. They show some techniques that writers use to influence readers.

1. Choosing descriptive language and vocabulary that states or implies the author's bias (It is not necessarily supported with facts, examples, etc.)

> The food we consume makes all of these things possible, but **not all food is created equal**. (paragraph 1)
>
> [Pollan] offers some **simple, yet practical** tips for eating well and staying healthy. (paragraph 4)

2. Expressing direct criticism of the opposing point of view

> Our food needs to be **defended against "needless complications"** from "nutrition science and from the food industry." (paragraph 4)

3. Using adverbs like *in fact*, *in reality*, and *indeed* to emphasize particular points

> **In fact**, different research about the same food often produces contradictory results. (paragraph 2)

4. Claiming that the reader shares the author's bias by using pronouns like *we* and *our*

> Because **our** food choices affect **our** health and behavior, **we** must do more than just eat; **we** must eat *well*. (paragraph 1)

A. Read these sentences from Reading 1. Look at the words in bold. Write the number of the technique used from the Reading Skill box for each sentence. Some items have two answers.

__2, 4__ a. **We are surrounded** by information **telling us what's good for us** and what isn't, but usually **this information is more confusing than helpful**. (paragraph 2)

_____ b. Shopping for food can also be **challenging**. (paragraph 3)

_____ c. **Indeed**, many **food labels are often misleading**. (paragraph 3)

_____ d. **In reality**, though, their specific yogurt isn't preferred by doctors, but shoppers may think it is because of the food label. (paragraph 3)

_____ e.   So how *do* **we make** healthy choices? (paragraph 4)

_____ f.   According to Pollan, **we** need to **stop reading labels and listening to the so-called scientific "experts."** (paragraph 4)

_____ g.   A supermarket is also full of items like instant noodles, diet sodas, and similar products—**the ones that aren't good for us**. (paragraph 6)

_____ h.   The food [at a farmers' market or a local store] is **fresher and healthier**. (paragraph 6)

Tip for Success

Pay attention to a writer's tone and choice of words to decide if he or she is biased. Writers may express strong opinions. However, those opinions need to be supported with facts, reasons, and examples.

B. These statements each contain an example of bias. Underline language that shows bias. For each sentence, write the number of the technique used from the Reading Skill box on page 131.

__2__ a.   You may have read that my colleagues do not agree with me on this topic. But let me make this clear: <u>my colleagues have ignored</u> the latest research data.

_____ b.   Not all fats are bad for you. In reality, some are very good for you.

_____ c.   Nutrition advice can sometimes be difficult to understand.

_____ d.   We are all concerned about our weight getting out of control, so let's do something about it.

_____ e.   Research into nutrition has been going on for decades, but in fact, much is still unknown about foods as simple as the carrot.

_____ f.   You and I both know that candy isn't good for our teeth, so why do we continue to eat it?

_____ g.   Everyone wants to eat healthily. Many food manufacturers, however, are more interested in keeping costs down than in using healthy ingredients.

_____ h.   You won't believe how delicious the cheesecake is: It's an absolute dream.

cheesecake

iQ ONLINE   **C.** Go online for more practice recognizing bias.

READING 2 | Anatomy of a Nutrition Trend

 UNIT OBJECTIVE You are going to read an article from the online newsletter *Food Insight* about trends in nutrition. The author discusses how trends develop and where people get their information about health and nutrition. Use the article to gather information and ideas for your Unit Assignment.

PREVIEW THE READING

A. **PREVIEW** Check (✓) the source of information about nutrition you think is the most common.

- ☐ nutritionists
- ☐ magazines
- ☐ television
- ☐ friends and family

B. **QUICK WRITE** Where do you get your information about nutrition: from nutritionists, magazines, television, or friends and family? Why? What have you learned from them? Write for 5–10 minutes in response. Be sure to use this section for your Unit Assignment.

C. **VOCABULARY** Check (✓) the words you know. Then work with a partner to locate each word in the reading. Use clues to help define the words you don't know. Check your definitions in the dictionary.

contribute *(v.)* 🔑	primarily *(adv.)* 🔑
currently *(adv.)* 🔑	shift *(v.)* 🔑
major *(adj.)* 🔑	sink in *(phr. v.)*
milestone *(n.)*	source *(n.)* 🔑
modify *(v.)*	stable *(adj.)* 🔑

🔑 Oxford 3000™ words

 D. Go online to listen and practice your pronunciation.

WORK WITH THE READING

🔊 **A.** Read the article and gather information about how science influences what we eat.

Anatomy[1] of a Nutrition Trend

1　Have you ever wondered how nutrition trends get started? Why did "fat-free" become all the rage[2] in the 1990s? Why is "low-carb" **currently** the "in"[3] thing? Consumers complain that health advisors "keep changing their minds." On the other hand, consumers also change their priorities when it comes to the nutrition topics they are interested in. Are trends really that hard to understand?

Trend Starters

2　Felicia Busch, a nutrition consultant, believes that "there are really two different kinds of trends. The first kind develops from a groundswell[4] of interest. It can come from a new book or a study that presents a new theory. Scientific research often **contributes** to new nutrition trends. These kinds of trends are usually promoted by the media and continue until the public [loses interest]. The second kind of trend occurs when a major **milestone** happens. When there's a food recall[5] or people die from a food-related disease, people stop and think. A milestone can either start a trend or support other trends that are already out there." Trends that arise from groundswells are more common than those that arise from major milestones.

Trend Influencers

3　Consumers' desires and needs depend on their beliefs and attitudes. Here are just a few of the many factors that affect public opinion:

- beliefs about what keeps us healthy and how we get sick

- attitudes about our ability to control our health and eating habits
- reactions to hearing or reading news stories, and reading books
- talking with friends and family members about the latest nutrition trend

4　Consumer surveys have shown that the public depends on the media for most of their information about health and nutrition. Of course, people ask their health-care providers for information as well. According to the *Shopping for Health* survey from the Food Marketing Institute (FMI), most people rely **primarily** on magazines (75%) and books (72%). After that they turn to health-care professionals (63%), friends or family (58%), newspapers (51%), and television (49%). Twenty-five percent turn to nutritionists.

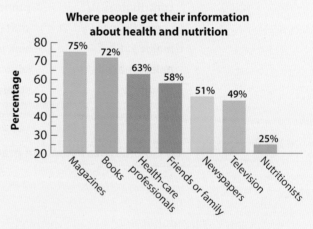

Where people get their information about health and nutrition

Source: *Shopping for Health* survey from the Food Marketing Institute (FMI)

---

[1] **anatomy:** the examination of what something is like or why it happens
[2] **all the rage:** very popular and fashionable
[3] **in:** popular and fashionable

[4] **groundswell:** a sudden increase
[5] **recall:** an official order to return something, often because of a problem

5   Linda Gilbert, president of HealthFocus International in Atlanta, Georgia, is a market researcher who specializes in health and nutrition trends. Gilbert believes that the media have a powerful influence on trends but that there is another crucial factor: repetition. "Hearing the same things from a number of **sources** is key. It's not just the media that affect trends. Sources like friends and families, nurses, and even coffee shop conversation remind consumers that 'I've heard that before.' When it comes to beliefs about nutrition and health, repetition is so important. You have to be exposed to ideas for a while before the message **sinks in**."

> " There was so much information coming out at once. No wonder the public was confused. "

6   Felicia Busch agrees that the media influence what people hear and read about nutrition and health. "People get their information from the media. And the media often depend on a few top sources. Reporters tend to 'feed' off each other. A newspaper article can lead to a TV story or magazine article and vice versa."

7   The Food Marketing Institute (FMI) in Washington, DC, has studied consumer attitudes about nutrition and health for the last 20 years. FMI's survey data shows that the percentage of consumers reporting that they are "very concerned about the nutritional content of what they eat" was relatively **stable** from the mid-1980s through the mid-1990s. Since then, this percentage has fallen a bit.

8   Some trend watchers think the drop in concern about nutrition is partly due to public opinion about health advisors. Felicia Busch explains, "During the period from 1980 until 1995, we had to keep **modifying** our positions about fats as we learned more about the relationship between dietary fat and health. First we had people follow no-cholesterol diets, then it was low-fat diets. After that, it became low-saturated fats, now we're talking about low-trans-fat diets. I think this changing advice has had an impact on people just giving up." In defense of nutritionists, Busch adds, "There was so much information coming out at once. No wonder the public was confused. It's hard to have people understand that science is an ongoing process."

Where Do We Go from Here?

9   Trends in nutrition come and go. Some trends become cultural norms because everyone is doing it. Others die because different needs and interests eclipse[6] them. According to data from a HealthFocus International survey, consumers are now very interested in the health benefits that certain foods may provide.

10   The media's interest in nutrition has also **shifted** more toward the subject of functional foods, meaning foods that claim to have specific health benefits. The International Food Information Council (IFIC) recently conducted a media analysis that offered some interesting results. News stories about vitamin and mineral intake, antioxidants[7], and specific functional foods accounted for 12% of all media discussions about diet, nutrition, and food safety. The other topics reported on most often were biotechnology[8] (12%), disease prevention (9%), and food-borne

[6] **eclipse:** to make something seem unimportant by comparison
[7] **antioxidants:** substances that remove dangerous molecules from the body
[8] **biotechnology:** the use of living cells in industrial processes

illness (8%). Also, news stories about fat have shifted from a focus on low-fat foods to how certain types of fat such as omega-3 and omega-6 fatty acids can have health benefits.

11 Certainly, nutrition is still a hot topic among consumers, even though they may be less concerned now than they were in the 1990s.

Nutrition trends, like all trends, change with time. They depend on consumer needs and interests, scientific reports, media coverage of issues, and sometimes, **major** events. For most of us, watching trends is easier than predicting them. Studying them can be a fascinating way to look at our society and culture.

B. VOCABULARY Complete the sentences with the vocabulary from Reading 2.

contribute (v.)	**modify** (v.)	**source** (n.)
currently (adv.)	**primarily** (adv.)	**stable** (adj.)
major (adj.)	**shift** (v.)	
milestone (n.)	**sink in** (phr. v.)	

The discovery of vitamins in the early 20th century was a huge _____ in the history of nutritional science. People quickly accepted the idea that taking vitamin pills could _____ to a healthy lifestyle. It is now becoming clear, however, that this may not always be true. _____, research suggests that not all the effects of vitamins are positive. Although they are _____ very good for you, certain vitamins can be harmful in large quantities.

Reports about the problems related to vitamins may _____ from one vitamin to another, depending on the _____ of your information. It is now generally agreed, however, that people who take large amounts of vitamins A and D should _____ their habits. Too much of these vitamins can cause _____ health problems. Interestingly, the amount of vitamin sales over the past decade has been _____ and may

actually be increasing. While the belief in the positive effects of vitamins

happened quickly, the understanding that vitamins can be harmful still

needs to _____.
                    10

iQ ONLINE **C.** Go online for more practice with the vocabulary.

D. Answer these questions.

1. What can cause a groundswell of interest in a trend, according to
   Felicia Busch?

   _____

   _____

2. What kinds of milestones can begin a trend?

   _____

   _____

3. What factors affect beliefs and attitudes about nutrition and health?
   Give two examples.

   _____

   _____

   _____

4. Where do people get most of their information about health and nutrition?

   _____

5. What does Linda Gilbert say is the crucial factor that influences trends?

   _____

   _____

6. What trend are consumers currently interested in?

   _____

   _____

E. Read the statements about nutrition trends. Check (✓) the correct source for each statement.

	Felicia Busch	Linda Gilbert	FMI	IFIC
1. Food-related illnesses can influence people's opinions about nutrition.	☐	☐	☐	☐
2. People are less interested in nutrition now than they used to be.	☐	☐	☐	☐
3. To be influenced by a trend, you have to get the same information in several different ways.	☐	☐	☐	☐
4. Most people get their health information from magazines first.	☐	☐	☐	☐
5. Our ideas about nutrition can be influenced by what ordinary people say.	☐	☐	☐	☐
6. People were given too much information about fats all at once.	☐	☐	☐	☐
7. Different media often rely on each other for stories about nutrition.	☐	☐	☐	☐

F. Write *T* (true) or *F* (false) for each statement. Then correct each false statement to make it true.

_____ 1. Felicia Busch believes that there is only one kind of trend.

_____

_____ 2. One factor that affects public opinion is how we react to news stories and books.

_____

_____ 3. People turn to their health-care providers for most of their information about health and nutrition.

_____

_____ 4. From the mid-1980s through the mid-1990s, the percentage of consumers reporting that they were very concerned about the nutritional content of the food they ate fell slightly.

_____

_____ 5. According to IFIC, the topics of disease prevention and food-borne illnesses account for most of the media discussions about diet, nutrition, and food safety.

_____

G. **Answer these questions about statements in the article.**

1. Why do you think that "trends that arise from groundswells are more common than those that arise from major milestones"? (paragraph 2)

_____

_____

2. According to the article, people get more information about health and nutrition from books and magazines than from television. Give a possible explanation for this. (paragraph 4)

_____

_____

3. What does Felicia Busch mean when she says, "Reporters tend to 'feed' off each other"? (paragraph 6)

_____

_____

4. What does Felicia Busch mean by "science is an ongoing process"? (paragraph 8)

_____

_____

5. Why do you think that "for most of us, watching trends is easier than predicting them"? (paragraph 11)

_____

_____

Q? WRITE WHAT YOU THINK

A. Discuss the questions in a group. Look back at your Quick Write on page 133 as you think about what you learned.

1. Think about the sources of nutritional information mentioned in Reading 2. Which sources do you trust the most? Why?

2. How do you think trends in nutrition are similar to or different from trends in other areas you know about, such as technology or fashion?

B. Think about the unit video, Reading 1, and Reading 2 as you discuss the questions. Then choose one question and write a paragraph in response.

1. After reading the information about nutrition trends in Reading 2, do you think the author's aim in Reading 1 to challenge the scientific approach to eating is likely to be successful? Why or why not?

2. How are the purposes of Reading 1 and Reading 2 different? Which do you think is more objective? Explain your reasons.

3. What do you think Michael Pollan would say about genetically modified food? Why?

Vocabulary Skill   Cause and effect collocations

Many different collocations with prepositions are used to express cause and effect. Recognizing these phrases will help you understand how these ideas are related.

Some collocations are used when the cause is the subject of the sentence.

> *bring about, contribute to, lead to, result in, be a factor/factors in, be responsible for*
>
> Limiting your intake of certain foods can **result in** a better diet and a healthier you.
>   cause   effect
>
> Scientific research often **contributes to** new nutrition trends.
>   cause   effect

Some collocations are used when the effect is the subject of the sentence.

> *arise from, develop from, stem from, be due to, be brought about by, be caused by*
>
> The first kind of trend **develops from** a groundswell of interest.
>   effect   cause
>
> The drop in concern about nutrition **is due to** public opinion about health advisors.
>   effect   cause

a traffic accident

A. In these sentences, the cause is the subject. Use a different collocation from the Vocabulary Skill box to complete each sentence. Use the correct tense.

1. Tiredness and stress _____are responsible for_____ many traffic accidents.

2. Greenhouse gases _____ global warming.

3. A good diet _____ excellent health.

4. Poverty _____ much of the crime in our society.

5. Eric's carelessness _____ his injury.

6. The poor economy _____ the failure of the company last year.

B. In these sentences, the effect is the subject. Use a different collocation from the Vocabulary Skill box to complete each sentence. Use the correct tense.

1. Sylvie's good health _____is due to_____ her excellent eating habits.

2. The hotel fire _____ an electrical problem.

3. My fight with my brother _____ a misunderstanding.

4. The high price of gas _____ a petroleum shortage.

5. Harry's love of history _____ a childhood trip to the museum.

6. The success of the book _____ the action-packed plot.

C. Work with a partner. Write six cause and effect sentences of your own: three with the cause as subject and three with the effect as subject. Use a different collocation in each sentence.

Cause as subject

1. _____

_____

2. _____

_____

3. _____

_____

Effect as subject

1. _____

_____

2. _____

_____

3. _____

_____

iQ ONLINE **D.** Go online for more practice with cause and effect collocations.

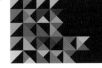

WRITING

UNIT OBJECTIVE ▶▶▶▶ At the end of this unit, you will write a cause and effect essay about the positive or negative effects of science on the food we eat. This essay will include specific information from the readings, the unit video, and your own ideas.

Writing Skill | Writing a cause and effect essay

A **cause and effect essay** examines the **reasons (causes)** an event, situation, or action occurs or the **results (effects)** of an event, situation, or action. There are many ways to structure a cause and effect essay.

One effect with several causes

balanced diet

plenty of exercise ⟶ **good health**

enough sleep

One cause with several effects

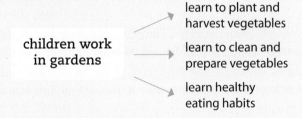

children work in gardens

learn to plant and harvest vegetables

learn to clean and prepare vegetables

learn healthy eating habits

Organization

- The introduction describes the event, situation, or action that you are examining. It includes the thesis statement. The thesis states the cause(s) and effect(s) you will examine or gives your opinion.
- Each body paragraph examines a cause or effect that you have chosen and provides supporting information, such as facts, examples, and descriptions. A strong body paragraph contains one main point and at least two pieces of information to support it.
- The conclusion summarizes the cause(s) and effect(s) discussed. It may also predict what will happen in the future or give advice.

A. **WRITING MODEL** Read the model cause and effect essay. Then answer the questions below.

Why Do Weight-Loss Diets Fail?

The popularity of diet crazes over the last 30 years shows that many of us think we are overweight. It also suggests that we want to do something about it. Diet books with the latest scientific advice become bestsellers, and yet we continue to gain weight. Who's responsible? It's easy to blame scientific experts, but in my view, the problem is often with us, the dieters. We can't lose weight because of the way we think about food.

If we cannot follow a plan every day, no diet book can help. Many dieters change from one type of diet to another, so they never allow their bodies to get into a healthy rhythm. Others start out strongly on a program and lose a few pounds. Then, when their weight stays the same for a few weeks, they become discouraged and lose their self-control. If the weight doesn't go away quickly, they give up.

But the number on the scale is not our only challenge. Modern life is so fast and stressful that many diets are ruined by "comfort eating." When we feel down, we want a slice of cheesecake or a chocolate brownie with ice cream to make us feel better. We use food as an escape. On the other hand, some of us use food as a reward. If we've done something well, we think we "deserve it."

We also need to pay attention to the food we eat. We should read food labels carefully and remember that we are often misled by them. Although a food package may say "low-fat," manufacturers sometimes replace the fat with carbohydrates, sugar, and other fattening substances. In addition, they may not take out much of the fat. Low-fat ice cream can have 70% of the fat of regular ice cream, so a scoop and a half of low-fat ice cream is more fattening than one scoop of regular.

These are just a few of the reasons why our diets fail, but they all arise from our state of mind and our ability to pay attention. The next time you reach for the cookie jar, remember: control your mind and you can control your body! The most important factor in losing weight is in our heads.

1. Does the essay focus on the causes of an issue or the effects of an issue?

   _____

2. What kind of information is used to support the thesis statement?

   _____

3. Why does the author think weight-loss diets fail?

   _____

B. Complete the outline of the essay on page 144. You do not have to use the writer's exact words.

the essay on page 144

I. Thesis statement: _____

_____

II. Cause 1: _People don't follow the plan._____

   A. Support 1: _____

   B. Support 2: _____

III. Cause 2: _____

   A. Support 1: _____

   B. Support 2: _We use food as a reward._____

IV. Cause 3: _____

   A. Support 1: _Low-fat foods may contain other fattening substances.___

   B. Support 2: _____

V. Concluding advice: _____

_____

C. Write three causes and three effects for each topic below. Use your own ideas. Then determine whether the causes or the effects would make a better essay for each topic.

_____ ⟶

_____ ⟶ **good nutrition** ⟶ _____

_____ ⟶   ⟶ _____

  ⟶ _____

_____ ⟶

_____ ⟶ **safe food** ⟶ _____

_____ ⟶   ⟶ _____

  ⟶ _____

```
_____                           _____
                    ⟶
                            enough food
_____    ⟶        for all      ⟶   _____

_____    ⟶                      ⟶   _____
```

D. **WRITING MODEL** Read the model cause and effect essay. Then answer the questions on page 147.

From Science to Common Sense

It is easy to say "less science, more common sense," but it is good to remember that our common sense is based on science. "What everyone knows" at one time was not common knowledge, and it was science that brought these ideas to light. Specifically, science has had huge effects on nutrition, as well as on the safety and quantity of available food.

Common sense says that we need a variety of foods for a healthy diet, but it was science that found the link between our diet and nutritional deficit diseases. We can eat citrus fruit for the vitamin C that our bodies need to fight the disease called scurvy. We know, too, because of the efforts of science, that too much sugar or salt can cause health problems, and we are constantly looking at our food for ways that diet can improve our health.

Food safety has been greatly increased by science. We know that bacteria and other microbes can get into our food and make us sick, but it took Louis Pasteur in 1859 to prove that microbes could come from the air, not arise spontaneously from food. The process that he developed, known as pasteurization, has prevented many cases of food-caused illness, and because of science, we know more techniques to protect ourselves—refrigeration, washing our hands, and covering food to keep flies off it. These techniques might not seem like science, but it is science that showed the link between these practices and prevention of food-related illness.

Having enough to eat has long been affected by science in many ways. Domesticating animals and plants, the beginning of agricultural science, started thousands of years ago and laid the foundations of having readily available food. Through the understanding of how to increase yields, discourage pests, and store food—all aspects of science—we have been able to provide enough food to feed our ever-growing population. In addition, science has increased our knowledge of mechanical forces so that we can transport food faster and for longer distances than ever before, thus increasing the variety and amount of available food.

Science has had an enormous effect on the food that we eat and in educating us about nutrition, keeping our food safe, and making it possible to have enough so that many people don't ever go hungry. We have not yet solved all of our food issues, but with science, we have a good chance of doing so.

1. Does the essay focus on causes or effects? _____

2. What kind of information is used to support the thesis statement?

   _____

3. What is a specific example that supports the thesis?

   _____

 E. Go online for more practice with writing a cause and effect essay.

Grammar   Agents with the passive voice

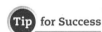 **for Success**

The passive is often used without an agent in order to sound objective, for example, in journalism. You may also choose the passive without an agent in order to avoid taking responsibility for an action or to avoid blaming another person.

In an active sentence, the subject is the **agent**—the person or thing that performs the action of the verb. In a passive sentence, the subject is the **receiver**—the person or thing that is affected by the action of the verb. The passive is formed with **be + past participle**. In a passive sentence, the agent is optional. If it is included, it follows the preposition *by*.

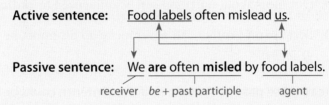

Active sentence: Food labels often mislead us.

Passive sentence: We **are** often **misled** by food labels.

    receiver   *be* + past participle   agent

Most passive sentences do not include the agent because it is obvious or unnecessary.

Fruits and vegetables **are** usually **picked** ~~by people~~ when they are freshest.
People **were encouraged** ~~by experts~~ to eliminate eggs from their diets.

The passive is used with *by* + an agent to:

• complete the meaning of a sentence

Many new trends **are promoted** by the media.
Many diets **are ruined** by "comfort eating."

• give new, important, or surprising information

The diet plan **was recommended** to me by my doctor.
The apples **are picked** early in July by machines.

A. Read these passive sentences. Check (✓) the sentence if the agent is necessary. If the agent is not necessary, cross it out.

☐ 1. I'm sorry, sir. All the cookies have been sold ~~by a salesclerk~~.

☐ 2. At the charity auction, everything will be sold by a famous chef.

☐ 3. We don't order pizza from that place anymore: it's always delivered cold by the delivery person.

☐ 4. That restaurant is far away. Their food is delivered by a man on a motorcycle.

☐ 5. Karen got sick at the restaurant and was examined by a medical student.

☐ 6. My friend is going to the doctor's office and will be examined by the doctor at 10:30 a.m.

☐ 7. The professor was honored by the university for her achievements.

☐ 8. The documentary was watched by a TV audience of millions.

☐ 9. Our ideas about nutrition can be influenced by ordinary people.

☐ 10. Because my brother can never make up his mind, he is easily influenced by people.

Tip for Success

Only include the agent when it is specific. You do not usually write *by someone, by people*, etc.

B. Read these passive sentences. If the sentence could be complete without an agent, add a period. If an agent is necessary to complete the meaning, add an appropriate agent.

1. That house is going to be repainted _____

2. In my favorite restaurant, all the food is prepared _____

3. My computer is being repaired _____

4. The accident victim was taken to the hospital _____

5. Many famous authors are influenced _____

6. I was trying to get to sleep, but I was disturbed _____

7. Everyone was shocked when the office was broken into _____

8. After the author's death, his last novel was finished _____

iQ ONLINE

C. Go online for more practice with agents with the passive voice.

D. Go online for the grammar expansion.

 In this assignment, you are going to write a cause and effect essay about the positive or negative effects of science on the food we eat. As you prepare your essay, think about the Unit Question, "Should science influence what we eat?" Use information from Reading 1, Reading 2, the unit video, and your work in this unit to support your essay. Refer to the Self-Assessment checklist on page 150.

 Go to the Online Writing Tutor for a writing model and alternate Unit Assignments.

PLAN AND WRITE

A. **BRAINSTORM** Follow these steps to help you organize your ideas.

1. Work with a partner. Brainstorm the positive and negative effects that science has had on food. Write them in the chart. Include ideas from the readings, the unit video, and your own ideas.

Effects of science on food	
Positive effects	**Negative effects**
Food is safer.	Too many choices in supermarkets can be confusing.

2. Compare the positive and negative effects. Decide whether you think science has had a positive or negative effect on the food we eat.

Writing **Tip**

Your essay must have unity, so choose only the effects that support your thesis statement.

B. **PLAN** Follow these steps to plan your essay.

1. Look at your ideas from Activity A. Decide whether the subject of your cause and effect essay is positive or negative effects.

2. Choose three main effects to write about from the chart in question 1 in Activity A.

 3. Go to the Online Resources to download and complete the outline for your cause and effect essay.

C. **WRITE** Use your **PLAN** notes to write your essay. Go to *IQ Online* to use the Online Writing Tutor.

1. Write your essay on the positive or negative effects of science on the food we eat. Be sure to include an introduction with a thesis statement, three body paragraphs, and a conclusion.

2. Look at the Self-Assessment checklist below to guide your writing.

REVISE AND EDIT

A. **PEER REVIEW** Read your partner's essay. Then go online and use the Peer Review worksheet. Discuss the review with your partner.

B. **REWRITE** Based on your partner's review, revise, and rewrite your essay.

C. **EDIT** Complete the Self-Assessment checklist as you prepare to write the final draft of your essay. Be prepared to hand in your work or discuss it in class.

SELF-ASSESSMENT		
Yes	No	
☐	☐	Does the essay clearly describe three effects of science on the food we eat?
☐	☐	Does the essay contain an introduction, three body paragraphs, and a conclusion?
☐	☐	Are passive verbs used correctly? Are agents included and omitted appropriately?
☐	☐	Does the essay use cause and effect collocations appropriately?
☐	☐	Does the essay include vocabulary from the unit?
☐	☐	Did you check the essay for punctuation, spelling, and grammar?

D. **REFLECT** Go to the Online Discussion Board to discuss these questions.

1. What is something new you learned in this unit?

2. Look back at the Unit Question—Should science influence what we eat? Is your answer different now than when you started the unit? If yes, how is it different? Why?

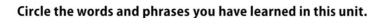

TRACK YOUR SUCCESS

Circle the words and phrases you have learned in this unit.

Nouns
access 🔑 AWL
approach 🔑 AWL
benefit 🔑 AWL
expert 🔑 AWL
finding
link 🔑 AWL
milestone
source 🔑 AWL

Verbs
arise (from) 🔑
challenge 🔑 AWL
contribute (to) 🔑 AWL
develop (from) 🔑
eliminate 🔑 AWL
encourage 🔑

lead (to) 🔑
modify AWL
participate 🔑 AWL
shift 🔑 AWL

Phrasal Verbs
bring about
result in
sink in
stem from

Adjectives
major 🔑 AWL
physical 🔑 AWL
practical 🔑
stable 🔑 AWL

Adverbs
currently 🔑
primarily 🔑 AWL

Phrases
be brought about by
be caused by
be due to
be a factor/
   factors in
be responsible for

🔑 Oxford 3000™ words
AWL Academic Word List

Check (✓) the skills you learned. If you need more work on a skill, refer to the page(s) in parentheses.

READING ☐	I can recognize a writer's bias. (p. 131)
VOCABULARY ☐	I can identify and use cause and effect collocations. (p. 140)
WRITING ☐	I can write a cause and effect essay. (p. 143)
GRAMMAR ☐	I can use agents appropriately with the passive voice. (p. 147)
UNIT OBJECTIVE ▶▶▶ ☐	I can gather information and ideas to write a cause and effect essay about the effects of science on the food we eat.

READING ▶ using an outline
VOCABULARY ▶ word forms
GRAMMAR ▶ reported speech with the present tense and shifting tenses
WRITING ▶ writing a summary

UNIT QUESTION

Does school prepare you for work?

A Discuss these questions with your classmates.

1. What skills and abilities do students learn in school that can help them in their careers?

2. What or who helps students prepare for adult life the most? School? Culture? Parents?

3. Look at the photo. What type of work are the people preparing to do? What skills are they learning?

B Listen to *The Q Classroom* online. Then answer these questions.

1. In Yuna's opinion, how does writing essays and studying algebra prepare you for work?

2. In what ways does Yuna say work is different from school? Do you think school is preparing you for work? Why or why not?

C Go to the Online Discussion Board to discuss the Unit Question with your classmates.

153

D Work with a partner. Look at the skills you need to succeed in school and at work. Discuss these questions.

1. Would you add anything to either list? Would you take anything away? Add your ideas or cross out the ones that you do not think are necessary.

2. Which of the skills you learn in school help you succeed at work? Try to match specific skills in each list.

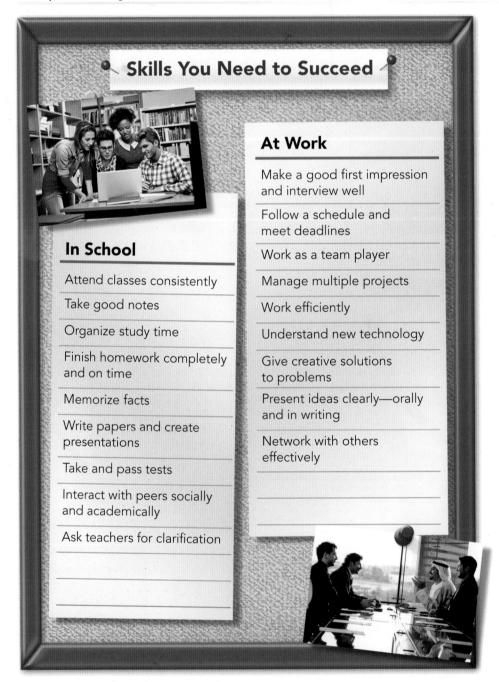

Skills You Need to Succeed

In School

Attend classes consistently

Take good notes

Organize study time

Finish homework completely and on time

Memorize facts

Write papers and create presentations

Take and pass tests

Interact with peers socially and academically

Ask teachers for clarification

At Work

Make a good first impression and interview well

Follow a schedule and meet deadlines

Work as a team player

Manage multiple projects

Work efficiently

Understand new technology

Give creative solutions to problems

Present ideas clearly—orally and in writing

Network with others effectively

E Join another pair. Discuss your answers to the questions in Activity D.

PREVIEW THE UNIT

READING 1 | From Student to Employee: A Difficult Transition

UNIT OBJECTIVE ▶▶▶ You are going to read a magazine article that examines the transition from student to employee. Use the article to gather information and ideas for your Unit Assignment.

PREVIEW THE READING

A. PREVIEW For many people, getting their first full-time job after graduation from school is an important turning point: It is the beginning of one's adult life. Read the title and look at the picture. What is the author's opinion about students getting their first job after graduation?

_____

_____

B. QUICK WRITE Can you think of reasons for the author's opinion about students getting their first job after graduation? Write for 5–10 minutes in response. Be sure to use this section for your Unit Assignment.

C. VOCABULARY Check (✓) the words you know. Then work with a partner to locate each word in the reading. Use clues to help define the words you don't know. Check your definitions in the dictionary.

adjust (v.) 🔑	encounter (v.) 🔑
ambiguous (adj.)	expertise (n.)
analyze (v.) 🔑	fixed (adj.) 🔑
anticipate (v.) 🔑	interpret (v.) 🔑
collaborative (adj.)	pattern (n.) 🔑
constant (adj.) 🔑	transition (n.) 🔑

🔑 Oxford 3000™ words

 D. Go online to listen and practice your pronunciation.

A. Read the article and gather information about whether or not school prepares you for work.

From Student to Employee: A Difficult Transition

by Mina Alonso

1   It is a chilly January morning on the campus of San Jose State University, and the start of a new term. Twenty-two-year-old Ryan Adams is walking with some friends to their first class. Ryan is beginning his final semester as a college student; at the end of May, he will graduate with a degree in finance[1]. Even though graduation is a few months away, Ryan is already working on a résumé and plans to start applying for jobs in April. He is both excited and a little nervous about making the **transition** from student to full-time employee. "I'm hoping to have a job by the summer," he explains. "You know, it'll be good to finally get out into the working world. On the other hand, it'll be the first real job I've ever had and that's a little scary."

2   By the time Ryan graduates, he will have spent four years in college and a total of sixteen years

Many recent graduates struggle in the workplace.

of his life in school. Like many students, Ryan believes that the time and money spent on his education will pay off[2]: he will eventually be able to get a good job and do well in the field he has chosen. And yet, in spite of all of the years spent in school preparing to enter the workplace, many recent graduates say that they struggle with the transition from classroom to career world and have difficulty **adjusting** to life on the job.

3   Writer and editor Joseph Lewis, who blogs for the website WorkAwesome.com, suggests one reason why this is the case. Lewis believes that most of our school experiences—from childhood through university—are fairly predictable, while life in the working world is far more **ambiguous**. In school, for example, the **pattern** stays more or less the same from year to year. All students have to take a **fixed** number of classes each year and in those classes they have to do certain things to succeed: study assigned material, do homework, and take and pass tests. In the workplace, however, **constant** change is the norm, and one has to adapt quickly. A project you are working on this month might suddenly change next month—or next week—and it's often hard to **anticipate** what you'll be doing six to twelve months from now. Life in the workplace can be uncertain in other ways as well. Lewis notes that in school, for example, you advance each year to the next grade "and that change carries with it a sense[3] of progress, a sense

---

[1] **finance:** the management and investing of money
[2] **pay off:** to bring good results

[3] **sense:** a feeling

of . . . growth and importance." In the workplace, however, "you have no idea when you might be promoted; it depends on the economy[4], on your coworkers, on your boss or clients, or a hundred other things you can't control."

4   Another problem that graduates entering the workforce **encounter** is that they are unprepared to think analytically. In school, many students— including those in college—spend a lot of time memorizing facts and repeating what they "learned" on tests. But in the workplace, notes the Career Services Network at Michigan State University, employees "are often expected to think critically and make decisions about their work, not just follow a supervisor's[5] instructions." An employee who is facing a problem at work, for example, needs to be able to identify different solutions, select the best course of action[6], and explain his choice to others. Less time needs to be spent in school on testing, says one recent report, and more on helping students to **analyze** and **interpret** information, solve problems, and communicate their ideas effectively—skills that will prepare them to succeed in today's workplace.

5   Finally, many recent graduates say that one of the biggest difficulties they face is adjusting to teamwork on the job. In some ways, school does prepare one for the **collaborative** nature of the workplace. Learners sit in classes every day with many other students. They must listen to others' opinions, participate at times in group discussions, and learn how to get along outside the classroom. Nevertheless, in school, a student normally works independently to complete most tasks (tests, homework, and projects) and receives a grade according to how well he or she has done. In the workplace, however, employees must regularly interact with others and are often dependent on their coworkers for their success. In other words, if an employee has to work with others to complete a given project, that employee's success not only depends on his hard work and **expertise**, but also on how well his colleagues perform. Knowing how to participate effectively in teamwork—and deal with problems when they arise—is extremely important, and yet, it is also something many students don't get enough practice with in a school setting.

6   How can we better prepare young adults for the workplace? Recent graduates, looking back on their educational experience, have some advice. Many think that all students should be required to do an internship[7] while they are in school. Volunteering part-time at a company, hospital, or government organization, for example, can help one gain experience and learn skills needed to succeed in the real world. Other graduates believe that teachers should include more teamwork as part of class activities; such tasks would familiarize students with the demands of collaborating with colleagues in the workplace. Still others feel there should be more focus on developing writing and public speaking skills— abilities many employees must regularly use on the job. Pairing this kind of practical work experience with classroom instruction, say the graduates, will help prepare students for the realities of the workplace and make the transition from school to career world less stressful.

---

[4] **economy:** the financial system of a given country or region
[5] **supervisor:** a boss or manager

[6] **course of action:** a plan
[7] **internship:** a job or training program, often done without pay, to gain practical work experience

B. VOCABULARY Here are some words from Reading 1. Read the sentences. Circle the answer that best matches the meaning of each bold word.

1. Making the **transition** from student to full-time employee won't be easy, but you'll do fine.
   a. effort   b. goal   c. change

2. After the long summer holiday, it's hard to **adjust** to working in an office again.
   a. apply   b. leave   c. adapt

3. His job responsibilities have always been **ambiguous**. No one is really sure what he does.
   a. certain   b. unclear   c. helpful

4. Most people's lives follow a typical **pattern**: they graduate from school, get a job, and eventually get their own apartment.
   a. belief   b. order   c. behavior

5. In this job, you'll work a **fixed** number of hours: 8 to 5:30, Monday to Friday.
   a. flexible   b. short   c. certain

6. It's hard to study with **constant** interruptions every five minutes.
   a. occasional   b. frequent   c. brief

7. I knew getting a job would be hard, but I didn't **anticipate** that it would take six months.
   a. wish   b. hope   c. expect

8. Jane is starting a new job, and she is worried that she will **encounter** many problems.
   a. experience   b. solve   c. define

9. Please **analyze** the information in the report carefully.
   a. skim   b. question   c. examine

10. How do you **interpret** the ending of that story? I didn't really understand it.
    a. explain   b. predict   c. tell

11. The project was a **collaborative** effort; we all worked on it together.
    a. shared   b. difficult   c. unlikely

12. His **expertise** is in international banking. He's been in the field for almost 25 years.
    a. unusual habit   b. special skill   c. favorite hobby

 C. Go online for more practice with the vocabulary.

D. Circle the correct answer.

1. Which statement best describes the problem discussed in the article?
   a. Many recent graduates are bored by the jobs available to them.
   b. It's difficult for many recent graduates to find good jobs.
   c. Many graduates aren't ready for today's workplace challenges.

2. What is mainly responsible for this problem?
   a. students' performance in school
   b. employers' hiring practices
   c. schools' methods of instruction

3. Look at paragraphs 3–5. A good subheading for this section of the article would be ___.
   a. Three Ways Educators and Employers Can Work Together
   b. Difficulties Graduates Experience in the Workplace
   c. The Workplace: Yesterday, Today, and Tomorrow

4. Paragraphs 3–5 describe how school experiences ___ life in the workplace.
   a. are different from
   b. help us with
   c. are similar to

5. According to the article, which skills are essential in today's workplace?
   a. being able to solve problems and contribute to a team
   b. remembering facts quickly and working well independently
   c. speaking a second language and being able to work long hours

6. The purpose of paragraph 6 is to ___ the problem discussed in the article.
   a. describe how graduates have overcome
   b. suggest ways of solving
   c. criticize society for contributing to

E. Answer these questions.

1. In paragraph 1, how does the writer introduce the topic? What do you think is the purpose of using a quote from a student?

   _____

   _____

2. Who is cited in paragraph 3? What problem does he discuss?

   _____

   _____

3. What network is cited in paragraph 4? What problem does the network raise?

_____

_____

_____

4. Who is cited in paragraph 6? Why are they cited?

_____

_____

WRITE WHAT YOU THINK

A. Discuss these questions in a group.

Critical Thinking **Tip**

For the Write What You Think questions, you give an opinion and **justify** your point of view with reasons. When you justify your opinion, you have to examine your reasoning and see if it is logical. This process allows you to improve your argumentation skills.

1. In paragraph 6 of Reading 1, there are several suggestions to help young adults adjust to life in the workplace. In your opinion, are the solutions useful? Which one do you think would help the most? Why?

2. What other skill(s) should schools focus on to prepare students for the workplace? Think of at least one idea and explain why you think this skill is important.

3. Rate your own school experience on a scale from 1 (poor) to 5 (excellent) in terms of how it prepared (or is preparing) you for the workplace. Give at least two reasons that explain your rating.

B. Choose one question and write a paragraph in response. Look back at your Quick Write on page 155 as you think about what you learned.

Reading Skill | Using an outline

An **outline** can help you understand how a text is organized. It shows the relationship between the main ideas and the specific information that supports them. There are many ways to organize an outline. One common way is to use Roman numerals (I, II, III) for the main ideas and letters (A, B, C) for the supporting points.

When you outline a text, you briefly summarize the ideas using some words from the text and some of your own words. You do not always need to write complete sentences.

A. Look back at Reading 1 on pages 156–157 and follow these steps.

1. Underline the thesis statement in the introduction (paragraphs 1–2).

2. In paragraph 3, underline the main idea and circle two supporting points.

3. Compare the sentences in the article with those in the outline below. Notice that the sentences in the outline are shorter but still focus on the key information.

Tip for Success

An outline of a reading can help you study for a test. You can look over the outline to find the main ideas and supporting points instead of rereading the whole text.

I. Introduction (paragraphs 1–2)

Thesis statement: Many recent graduates have difficulty adjusting to life on the job.

II. School experiences are fairly predictable; the working world is more ambiguous. (paragraph 3)

   A. In school, the pattern stays mostly the same; in the workplace, constant change is the norm.

   B. In school, you advance each year; in the workplace, you don't know when you might be promoted.

B. **Reread paragraphs 4–6 in Reading 1 and complete the outline for sections III, IV, and V below.**

III. Recent graduates are not prepared to think analytically.

   A. In school, _____.

   B. In the workplace, _____.

   C. Schools should spend less time on _____.

   D. Schools should spend more time on _____

   _____.

IV. Many recent graduates have difficulty _____.

   A. _____

   _____

   B. _____

   _____

V. _____

   _____

   A. _____

   B. _____

   C. There should be more focus on developing writing and public speaking skills.

C. Use your outline from Activity B and the reading to complete the chart comparing school and the workplace.

School	Workplace
predictable	
	constant change
	don't know when you'll be promoted
memorize facts and take tests	
	interact with others and dependent on coworkers
receive grades on individual work	

 D. Go online for more practice using an outline.

E. Go online to read *Work That Gets You Hired* and check your comprehension.

READING 2 | Making My First Post-College Career Decision

 You are going to read a blog post by a graduating student who is considering his work options. Use the blog post to gather information and ideas for your Unit Assignment.

PREVIEW THE READING

A. PREVIEW Choosing a job is one of the most important decisions a student makes after graduation. Read the title and subtitle, and skim the first paragraph. Answer these questions.

1. What two career options is the student trying to decide between?

_____

2. Which one do you think he's going to choose?

_____

B. QUICK WRITE Consider your answer to question 2 in Activity A. Why do you think the student will make that career choice? Write for 5–10 minutes in response. Be sure to use this section for your Unit Assignment.

C. **VOCABULARY** Check (✓) the words you know. Use a dictionary to define any new or unknown words. Then discuss how the words will relate to the unit with a partner.

acquire *(v.)* 🔑	enable *(v.)* 🔑	institution *(n.)* 🔑	reluctant *(adj.)*
approach *(v.)* 🔑	incentive *(n.)*	particular *(adj.)* 🔑	utilize *(v.)*
contact *(v.)* 🔑	income *(n.)* 🔑	permanent *(adj.)* 🔑	

🔑 Oxford 3000™ words

D. Go online to listen and practice your pronunciation.

WORK WITH THE READING

A. Read the blog post and gather information about whether or not school prepares you for work.

Making My First Post-College Career Decision

Going Corporate[1]

TUESDAY, APRIL 7   COMMENTS 16

1   As college graduation **approaches** and I prepare to enter the working world, I've had a hard time deciding what I should do with my life. On the one hand, I wonder: am I an entrepreneur—the sort of innovative person who could start and grow my own business? Then at other times I think: would it be better to accept a position in a large corporation and climb the ranks[2]? As I get ready to make the transition from student to full-time employee, I find myself thinking about these questions quite often. The good news is, I think I've finally got some answers.

From Internship to Full-Time Job

2   I've always been interested in accounting and technology, and for the past year, I've been interning at a large telecommunications

---

[1] **going corporate:** planning to join a large company as an employee
[2] **climb the ranks:** to move upward in a company through promotions

company. It's been a great way for me to get some work experience and to see if this **particular** field is right for me. My internship has shown me that telecommunications isn't really the kind of work that I want to do long-term. Nevertheless, I've learned a lot about communicating, collaborating, and dealing with office politics[3] in the workplace. I know that I'll be able to use these skills in whatever job I do.

3   When I began my final year in college last fall, I started perusing the job postings, looking for a full-time (paying) position in accounting. At the time, I noticed job ads for all of the public accounting firms, and though I thought they were interesting, I ignored them. I assumed they were for the December graduates[4]. Was I ever mistaken! It turns out that they were postings for regular May graduates like me! When I realized my error, I quickly put together a résumé and **contacted** professors for recommendations. I eventually interviewed with several companies, and within a week I'd gotten a job. I felt relieved; I had taken care of my future. It was November, and I wouldn't even be starting until the following July.

Learning Is Key

4   Though I interviewed with different companies, I decided to accept a position with a large accounting firm, primarily because I'd already interned in the corporate world[5] and wanted to gain more experience working for a large **institution**. Also, compared with the telecommunications company I'd been at, accounting firms' employees tend to work fewer hours for more pay.

5   Why did I feel the need to get a job so quickly? Maybe I was anxious about earning an **income** and supporting myself after graduation, but I prefer to think I accepted the position because of what I could learn. At this point in my life, I believe that working for a large accounting firm will **enable** me to meet different people and **utilize** the skills I've **acquired** in school and during my internship. I also think it will provide me with the experience I need to grow in this field. However, once the job becomes predictable—once I stop learning and being challenged—then there won't be any **incentive** for me to continue with this company. At that point, I'll have to make some decisions about what I want to do next.

Creating Opportunities

6   Ultimately, I see myself doing one of two things in life: becoming an executive[6] somewhere or starting something successful on my own. Do I have lofty[7] goals? Sure I do. Do I know how, when, or where I will achieve them? Not at all. For this reason, I'd rather start out at a big company and see where it leads me. Eventually, I will either develop something on my own or continue to learn and do well as an employee. In any case, I know that I'll be given many new opportunities in my job with the accounting firm, and I'll do my best to take advantage of those.

7   With all that said, I'm only 20 years old: I have time to make decisions. At this point, I'm **reluctant** to make a **permanent** career choice, and in reality, I may never make such a choice. In the end, I might become a corporate executive somewhere *and* start my own company. Whatever happens, I'm sure I'll do fine. Anyway, it's impossible to predict the future, and so for now, I just want to see how it goes with my first job out of college.

---

[3] **office politics:** competition among people in the workplace
[4] **December graduates:** In the U.S., most students graduate in May or June, but some finish early or take an extra term and graduate in December.
[5] **the corporate world:** related to working for a large company
[6] **executive:** a senior manager in a company
[7] **lofty:** large and important

In Unit 5, you
learned how to
use collocations
with prepositions
to express cause
and effect. Use
collocations from
Unit 5 to write
sentences with the
following words
from Activity B:
incentive and *income*.

B. **VOCABULARY** Complete the sentences with the vocabulary from Reading 2.

acquire *(v.)*	**incentive** *(n.)*	**permanent** *(adj.)*
approach *(v.)*	**income** *(n.)*	**reluctant** *(adj.)*
contact *(v.)*	**institution** *(n.)*	**utilize** *(v.)*
enable *(v.)*	**particular** *(adj.)*	

1. She spends almost a third of her monthly _____ on clothes for work.

2. We'll get a $1,000 bonus if we finish the project early. That's a(n) _____ to work harder!

3. The best way to _____ Mr. Perez is by email. He checks his messages often.

4. Getting a college degree will _____ you to get a better job.

5. Tom wants to major in business, but he doesn't know what _____ type of business he is most interested in.

6. Even though Laura is unhappy, she's _____ to quit her current job until she gets a new one.

7. Don't use that pen on the whiteboard. The ink is _____ and you won't be able to erase it.

8. Ann wants a job where she'll be able to _____ her Spanish language skills.

9. As I _____ my high school graduation, there is a part of me that isn't ready to finish school.

10. Simon works for a large financial _____ in London. The company has offices worldwide.

11. The training program helps people _____ new workplace skills and get better jobs.

 C. Go online for more practice with the vocabulary.

D. Each of these headings refers to the main idea of a paragraph in the blog. Write the correct paragraph number next to each heading. (There is one extra heading.)

___ a. A chance to grow and learn

___ b. Get that job!

___ c. Future career goals

___ d. What I like about accounting and technology

___ e. What being an intern taught me

___ f. No rush to decide

_1_ g. Graduation nerves: What do I do next?

___ h. Accounting: The right choice for me

E. Use the actions in the box to complete the author's timeline below. Then write a paragraph using the ideas from the timeline to show what happened and will happen to the author.

graduate from college	get a job	reconsider employment options
put together résumé	start a job	take advantage of opportunities in job
start interning		

April 7

F. Write *T* (true) or *F* (false) for each statement. Then correct each false statement to make it true.

___ 1. The blogger is interested in a career in telecommunications.

_____

___ 2. He feels that his experience as an intern was useful.

_____

_____ 3. He plans to start working full-time in December when he graduates.

_____

_____ 4. He believes that telecommunications firms pay higher salaries than accounting firms.

_____

_____ 5. When his job is no longer challenging, he'll probably quit it and look for a new one.

_____

_____ 6. He can imagine himself in a management position at some point in the future.

_____

_____ 7. Having a steady job is the writer's goal.

_____

_____ 8. He is optimistic about the future.

_____

G. **The blogger writes about having made several decisions. Using what he writes or implies, complete the chart with each choice he made and a reason for that choice.**

Decision	Choice	Reason
What kind of internship should he take?	telecommunications company	to see whether he liked the field and to get experience working in a large corporation
When should he apply for a full-time job?		
What kind of job should he accept?		
What will he do when his new job becomes predictable?		
When will he start his own company?		

WRITE WHAT YOU THINK

A. Discuss the questions in a group. Look back at your Quick Write on page 162 as you think about what you learned.

1. What do you think of the career choices the blogger in Reading 2 has made so far and his plans for the future? Respond to his entry and tell him your opinion.

2. The blogger in Reading 2 describes his career goals. What are yours? Talk about at least one; explain what your goal is and how and when you plan to achieve it.

B. Before you watch the video, discuss the questions in a group.

1. What skills do people need to become entrepreneurs and create their own jobs?

2. Why might young people want to become entrepreneurs rather than work for a company?

3. Does school prepare students to become entrepreneurs?

C. Go online to watch the video about entrepreneurs who create new jobs. Then check your comprehension.

> **aspiring** *(adj.)* wanting to start the career or activity that is mentioned
>
> **creating your own destiny** *(phr.)* finding an original way to do something
>
> **pool** *(v.)* to combine resources
>
> **renegade** *(n.)* a person who lives outside of a group or society he or she used to belong to
>
> **turnout** *(n.)* the number of people who attend a particular event

VIDEO VOCABULARY

D. Think about the unit video, Reading 1, and Reading 2 as you discuss the questions. Then choose one question and write a paragraph in response.

1. Do you think it is important for a person to get a full-time job immediately after finishing school?

2. The blogger in Reading 2 feels no pressure to choose a permanent job. Considering the ideas presented in Reading 1, what do you think are some of the advantages and disadvantages of this attitude?

analyze

analyst

Learning all forms of a word and how they are used helps you build your vocabulary. This skill will also give you more flexibility in your writing and speaking.

Notice how different forms of the same word are used in different contexts.

> **analyze (v.)** *to examine the nature or structure of something, especially by separating it into its parts*
> Please **analyze** the information in the report closely.
>
> **analyst (n.)** *a person who examines facts in order to give an opinion about them*
> Martin is a financial **analyst** for a large corporation.
>
> **analytical (adj.)** *using a logical method in order to understand something*
> The course helps students to develop **analytical** skills.
>
> **analytically (adv.)** *doing something by using a logical method*
> Many recent graduates are unprepared to think **analytically**.

Dictionaries will list all the word forms and their definitions. When you look up a word, you will usually need to read several entries to find all the word forms.

All dictionary definitions are from the *Oxford Advanced American Dictionary for learners of English* © Oxford University Press 2011.

Tip for Success

When you learn the meaning and spelling changes for different word forms, also pay attention to how the pronunciation is different (e.g., *acquire/acquisition*).

A. These words come from Reading 1 and Reading 2. Complete the chart. Use your dictionary to help you. (An *X* indicates that a word form doesn't exist or you don't need to know it at this time.)

	Verb	Noun	Adjective	Adverb
1.	acquire	*acquisition*	X	X
2.		adjustment		X
3.	X		ambiguous	
4.	anticipate		anticipated	X
5.		collaboration		
6.	X	constant		
7.		interpretation	interpretive	X
8.	X	particulars		
9.	X	permanence		
10.	X		reluctant	

B. Complete each pair of sentences with the correct forms of a word from the chart in Activity A.

1. a. Starting my job was a big _____, but I'm finally used to it.

   b. Your office chair can go higher or lower. The seat is _____.

2. a. Abdullah works in sales and is _____ on the phone with clients.

   b. New employees need _____ instruction. Learning about a new job takes time.

3. a. Are you only visiting, or have you moved here _____?

   b. When I started working here, I was part-time. Now I'm a _____ employee.

4. a. May was _____ to ask her teacher for help, but she finally did.

   b. Adam asked his boss for a raise, and she _____ agreed.

5. a. Her answer was _____. What exactly did she mean?

   b. The message is worded _____. I'm not sure what it means.

6. a. The staff will _____ on the new marketing plan.

   b. There needs to be close _____ between teachers and parents for students to do well in school.

7. a. The match between the two soccer teams was the most _____ sporting event of the year.

   b. When they posted the job, they didn't _____ that they would get over 1,000 replies.

8. a. Let's talk generally about our business trip now. We can discuss the _____ (where we'll stay, what we'll do, etc.) later.

   b. Keep your schedule open tomorrow for the boss's visit—_____ the hours from 10 to noon.

C. Choose two words from the chart in Activity A. Write one sentence for each form of the word. Then share your sentences with a partner.

D. Go online for more practice with word forms.

WRITING

UNIT OBJECTIVE ▶▶▶▶ At the end of this unit, you will write a summary of Reading 1. This summary will include specific information from the reading stated in your own words.

| **Grammar** | **Reported speech with the present tense and shifting tenses** |

You can use **reported speech** to report what someone says, writes, or thinks. In academic writing, it is common to report information with the present tense when the information involves current opinions or ongoing situations.

Reported statements with *that* clauses

- Identify the person who made the statement using a present tense reporting clause.

- Put the information that you are reporting in a *that* clause. (The word *that* is often omitted.)

> **Original:**   Jim Sweeny: You should make a list of questions.
> **Reported:**   Jim Sweeny **says** (that) students should make a list of questions.*
>   ‾‾‾‾‾‾‾‾‾‾‾‾‾‾‾   ‾‾‾‾‾‾‾‾‾‾‾‾‾‾‾‾‾‾‾‾‾‾‾‾‾
>   reporting clause   noun clause

You can also report statements with verbs like *tell* or *explain*, or verbs that express thoughts or feelings such as *feel*, *think*, and *believe*. Notice that *tell* is followed by a noun or pronoun.

> Jim Sweeny **tells students** (that) they should make a list of questions.
> Jim Sweeny **thinks** (that) students should make a list of questions.

Reported questions with *wh-* clauses

You usually use a *wh-* clause to report a question. Although these clauses begin with question words (*who*, *what*, *where*, *when*, *why*, *how*), they use statement word order.

> **Original:**   Many students: What should you wear to an interview?
> **Reported:**   Many students **wonder** what *they should wear* to an interview*.
>   ‾‾‾‾‾‾‾‾‾‾‾‾‾‾‾‾‾‾‾‾‾‾   ‾‾‾‾‾‾‾‾‾‾‾‾‾‾‾‾‾‾‾‾‾‾‾‾‾‾‾
>   reporting clause   noun clause

*In reported speech, pronouns and possessives often have to change to keep the original meaning.
You should make a list of questions. → The article says (that) **students** should make a list of questions.

You can also report that someone *answered* a question about something. In this case, the *wh-* clause doesn't report exactly what someone said, but says what question was answered. Reporting verbs such as *explain*, *describe*, and *tell* are common.

> **Original answer:** News article: You should wear a suit to an interview**.
>
> **Reported answer:** The article **explains** <u>what you should wear to an interview</u>.
>
> The article **tells you** <u>what you should wear to an interview</u>.

Reported speech with shifting tenses

When a past tense reporting verb is used, there is often a shift in tense in the verb(s) in the noun clause.

Some common shifts are present to past tense, present perfect (progressive) and past tense to past perfect (progressive), and *will* to *would*.

> **Original:** As I **prepare** to enter the working world, I**'ve had** a hard time deciding what to do.
>
> **Reported:** He said that as he **prepared** to enter the working world, he**'d had** a hard time deciding what to do.
>
> **Original:** I **started** perusing the job postings.
>
> **Reported:** He reported that he **had started** perusing the job postings.
>
> **Original:** I **will develop** something on my own or continue to learn and do well as an employee.
>
> **Reported:** He added that he **would develop** something on his own or continue to learn and do well as an employee.

**Answers the question *What should you wear to an interview?*

Tip for Success

A reporting clause can contain a general subject, such as *many people say* or *some people think*.

A. Check (✓) the sentences that use reported speech. Then circle the reporting clause and underline the noun clause in the sentences you checked.

☐ 1. In spite of all the years spent in school preparing to enter the workplace, many recent graduates say that they have difficulty adjusting to life on the job.

☐ 2. Joseph Lewis notes that in school you advance each year, but at work the same isn't true.

☐ 3. In the workplace, employees must regularly interact with others and are often dependent on their coworkers for their success.

☐ 4. Many people wonder how we can better prepare young adults for the workplace.

☐ 5. One recent report tells educators that less time should be spent on testing in school.

☐ 6. In the article, some recent graduates explain what current students can do to prepare.

☐ 7. Volunteering part-time at a company, hospital, or government organization can help one gain experience and learn skills needed to succeed in the real world.

☐ 8. Other graduates feel there should be more focus on developing writing and public speaking skills.

B. Circle the answer that best completes each statement.

1. Michael is always studying. I wonder ___.
   a. what his major is   b. what is his major   c. what major he is

2. My brother says ___ to major in journalism.
   a. that he was wanting   b. that wants   c. he wants

3. The article ___ students how to dress for a job interview.
   a. tells that   b. tells   c. tells to

4. Take this quiz. It will tell you ___ for you.
   a. which best job is   b. which is best job   c. which job is best

5. A lot of students believe ___ include more teamwork activities in class.
   a. teachers they   b. that teachers   c. teachers that
      should   should   should

6. The website explains ___ apply for an internship at the company.
   a. how   b. you how   c. how you

C. Read each sentence. Report the information using the verb in parentheses and a noun clause. Change pronouns where appropriate.

1. Jim Sweeny to students: There are things you can do to prepare for an interview. (tell)

   Jim Sweeny tells students (that) there are things they can do

   to prepare for an interview.

2. News article: Many recent graduates aren't ready for the workplace. (say)

   _____

   _____

3. Many students: Learning a foreign language is challenging. (believe)

   _____

   _____

4. Tara: How can I get a good job? (wonder)

_____

5. Many students: What should we do after graduation? (want to know)

_____

6. The school handbook: Students must take four years of English and three years of math to graduate. (tell)

_____

_____

D. Read each sentence. Report the information using the verb in parentheses and a noun clause. Shift the tense of the underlined verbs and change pronouns where appropriate.

1. As I <u>get</u> ready to make the transition to full-time employee, I <u>find</u> myself thinking about these questions. (say)

He said that as he got ready to make the transition to full-time

employee, he found himself thinking about these questions.

2. I'<u>ve been interning</u> at a large telecommunications company. (report)

_____

3. I <u>started</u> perusing the job postings, looking for a full-time position in accounting. (explain)

_____

_____

4. I <u>decided</u> to accept a position with a large accounting firm. (tell his readers)

_____

_____

5. I <u>know</u> I'<u>ll</u> be given many new opportunities in my job with an accounting firm. (add)

_____

_____

6. Why <u>do</u> I <u>have</u> lofty goals? (ask)

_____

7. How, when, or where <u>will</u> I achieve them? (wonder)

_____

8. Whatever <u>happens</u>, I'<u>m</u> sure I'<u>ll</u> do fine. (conclude)

_____

E. Go online for more practice with reported speech with the present tense and shifting tenses.

F. Go online for the grammar expansion.

Writing Skill   Writing a summary

Writing

To prepare to write a summary, you may want to outline a text as you read. See the Reading Skill box on page 160 for instructions on outlining as a reading strategy.

A **summary** is a shorter version of the original text. When you write a summary, you tell the reader the main ideas using some words from the text and some of your own words.

Before you write a summary

1. Read the entire text and ask yourself what the author's **purpose** is.

2. Reread the introductory paragraph(s) and find the **thesis statement**.

3. Reread the rest of the text. In each paragraph, highlight, underline, or circle the **main idea** and **key points**. You can also annotate the important information.

When you write a summary

1. Begin by stating the **title** of the text, the **author's full name** (if it's given), and his or her **purpose** for writing.

2. Use the text you highlighted or annotated to explain the author's **thesis** and **main ideas**.

3. Follow these guidelines.

   • Keep the summary short (about one-third to one-fourth as long as the original).
   • Include only the original text's main ideas. Do not include details, examples, information that is not in the original, or your own opinion.
   • Write the summary mostly in your own words, but do not change the author's ideas. This is called **paraphrasing**.

A. Read the article about preparing for a job interview. Follow steps 1–3 in *Before you write a summary* in the Writing Skill box. Then answer the questions below.

Preparing for Your First Job Interview
by Jim Sweeny

You've just graduated from school. Now comes the scary part: interviewing for your first job. For many recent graduates, this is an anxiety-provoking time. However, there are some simple ways to prepare for this challenging experience.

First, you should make a list of the questions you might be asked. In many job interviews, you have to answer questions about your academic experience and how it has prepared you for the job. For example, you might be asked to discuss how your participation in student government or sports has given you experience working on a team. You will, of course, also be asked how your experience and talents fit with the company's goals.

Once you've got your questions, you should then think about possible answers and practice responding to them. Employers will expect you to talk in detail about your experience and use examples. Make sure that your answers describe particular situations you faced, the actions you took, and the results you achieved. Once you've got your responses, try practicing on your friends or family members. This will make you feel comfortable speaking in front of a person.

Finally, don't get discouraged if you aren't hired the first, second, or third time you interview. Think of every interview as practice for the most important one: the interview that will get you a job.

1. What is the author's purpose for writing the text?
   a. He's describing his first job interview experience.
   b. He's comparing and contrasting two interviewing styles.
   c. He's explaining how to get ready for a job interview.

2. What is the thesis statement? Underline it.

3. What two main ideas did you mark that support the thesis statement?

4. In the last paragraph, how does the author conclude the article?
   a. He restates the main points.
   b. He makes a final suggestion.
   c. He makes a prediction about the future.

B. **WRITING MODEL** Read the model summaries of the article on page 176. Complete the checklist below. Then answer the questions on page 178.

Summary 1

In the essay "Preparing for Your First Job Interview," author Jim Sweeny gives advice to recent graduates who are interviewing for their first job. Specifically, he says that there are simple things they can do to prepare for the interview. First, Sweeny tells students that they should make a list of questions they might be asked. These questions are usually about how a person's school experience relates to the job. Then Sweeny says that students should prepare answers to the questions and practice responding to them, and he explains a way to do this. In conclusion, he tells students not to get discouraged by the interviewing process.

Summary 2

In this essay, the author gives advice to recent graduates who are interviewing for their first job. He says that looking for a first job is stressful, but there are ways to prepare for an interview. Sweeny says that students should be prepared to answer questions about their school experience and how it relates to the job they are applying for. In fact, the questions I was asked at my first interview were about my school activities. In conclusion, he tells students not to get discouraged by the interviewing process.

The summary . . .	Summary 1	Summary 2
1. states the original text's title.	☐	☐
2. states the author's full name (if given).	☐	☐
3. states the author's purpose for writing.	☐	☐
4. identifies the thesis statement.	☐	☐
5. identifies all of the text's main ideas.	☐	☐
6. does not include details, examples, information not in the text, or the writer's opinion.	☐	☐
7. is mostly written in the student's own words.	☐	☐
8. is clear and easy to follow.	☐	☐

1. Which summary is better? _____

2. Why? _____

   _____

3. What three things can be done to the poor summary to improve it?

   _____

   _____

   _____

C. **WRITING MODEL** Read the model summary of Reading 2. Then follow the steps below.

In the blog entry "Making My First Post-College Career Decision," a graduating student discussed his transition from student to employee. The student explained what career path he had chosen and why. He said he'd interned in a large telecommunications company and gained workplace experience but had learned it wasn't the kind of work he wanted to do. In his senior year, he interviewed for jobs in accounting and accepted one in a large accounting firm. Many graduating students don't find a job that easily. He asked why he'd needed to get a job so quickly and answered that he believed he'd accepted the job so he could utilize the skills he had acquired in school and in his internship and get experience in the field. Employees in accounting firms work fewer hours. He added, however, that when he stopped learning and being challenged in the job, he would need to make another decision. He saw himself becoming an executive or starting his own business. He wondered if he had lofty goals and said he did. It doesn't seem likely he'll succeed. He concluded that he would take advantage of the opportunities his new accounting job provided but that he was young and had time to make decisions about his future. He believed he would do fine and was ready for the transition.

---

1. Underline the purpose twice.

2. Put the thesis statement in brackets.

3. Circle the reporting verbs.

4. Underline the shifts in tense.

5. Cross out three sentences that don't belong: one detail, one idea not in the original text, and one opinion.

D. Complete the checklist below for the summary in Activity C.

The summary . . .	
1. states the original text's title.	☐
2. states the author's full name (if given).	☐
3. states the author's purpose for writing.	☐
4. identifies the thesis statement.	☐
5. identifies all of the text's main ideas.	☐
6. does not include details, examples, information not in the text, or the writer's opinion.	☐
7. is mostly written in the student's own words.	☐
8. is clear and easy to follow.	☐

 E. Go online for more practice with writing a summary.

 Write a summary

 In this assignment, you are going to write a summary of Reading 1. As you prepare your summary, think about the Unit Question, "Does school prepare you for work?" Use information from Reading 1 and your work in this unit to support your summary. Refer to the Self-Assessment checklist on page 180.

Go to the Online Writing Tutor for a writing model and alternate Unit Assignments.

PLAN AND WRITE

A. **BRAINSTORM** Follow these steps to help you organize your ideas.

1. Reread Reading 1 on pages 156–157. Look at any annotating or highlighting that you did. Cross out details, examples, information not in the reading, or any text that expresses your own opinion.

2. Review the outline you completed on page 161. Decide if you need to add or change anything to make it more accurate.

Writing **Tip**

Use the full name of the author and anyone mentioned in the text the first time you cite the person. After that, use the person's last name.

B. **PLAN** **Follow these steps to plan your summary.**

1. Identify the title of the text and the author's full name (if given).

2. Identify the author's purpose.

3. Rewrite the thesis statement using your own words.

4. Identify the main ideas. Rewrite them using mostly your own words.

5. Using mostly your own words, state how the author concludes the article.

 6. Go to the Online Resources to download and complete the outline for your summary.

 C. **WRITE** **Use your** **PLAN** **notes to write your summary. Go to *iQ Online* to use the Online Writing Tutor.**

1. Write your summary of Reading 1. Remember to summarize important points by paraphrasing the author's purpose, thesis statement, main ideas, and conclusions. Use reported speech to report the ideas of the author and others.

2. Look at the Self-Assessment checklist below to guide your writing.

REVISE AND EDIT

 A. **PEER REVIEW** **Read your partner's summary. Then go online and use the Peer Review worksheet. Discuss the review with your partner.**

B. **REWRITE** **Based on your partner's review, revise, and rewrite your summary.**

C. **EDIT** **Complete the Self-Assessment checklist as you prepare to write the final draft of your summary. Be prepared to hand in your work or discuss it in class.**

SELF-ASSESSMENT		
Yes	No	
☐	☐	Does the summary state the text's title, author's name, and author's purpose?
☐	☐	Does the summary clearly identify the thesis statement and all the main ideas?
☐	☐	Does it include only the main ideas and important information from the text?
☐	☐	Is it mostly written in your own words?
☐	☐	Is reported speech used correctly?
☐	☐	Does the summary include vocabulary from the unit?
☐	☐	Did you check the summary for punctuation, spelling, and grammar?

D. **REFLECT** Go to the Online Discussion Board to discuss these questions.

1. What is something new you learned in this unit?

2. Look back at the Unit Question—Does school prepare you for work? Is your answer different now than when you started the unit? If yes, how is it different? Why?

TRACK YOUR SUCCESS

Circle the words you have learned in this unit.

Nouns	Verbs	Adjectives
expertise AWL	acquire 🔑 AWL	ambiguous AWL
incentive AWL	adjust 🔑 AWL	collaborative
income 🔑 AWL	analyze 🔑 AWL	constant 🔑 AWL
institution 🔑 AWL	anticipate 🔑 AWL	fixed 🔑
pattern 🔑	approach 🔑 AWL	particular 🔑
transition 🔑 AWL	contact 🔑 AWL	permanent 🔑
	enable 🔑 AWL	reluctant AWL
	encounter 🔑 AWL	
	interpret 🔑 AWL	
	utilize AWL	

🔑 Oxford 3000™ words

AWL Academic Word List

Check (✓) the skills you learned. If you need more work on a skill, refer to the page(s) in parentheses.

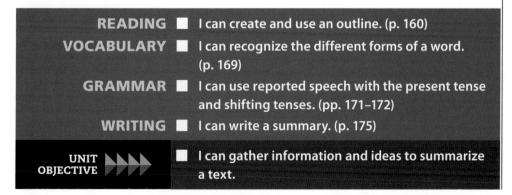

READING ☐	I can create and use an outline. (p. 160)
VOCABULARY ☐	I can recognize the different forms of a word. (p. 169)
GRAMMAR ☐	I can use reported speech with the present tense and shifting tenses. (pp. 171–172)
WRITING ☐	I can write a summary. (p. 175)
UNIT OBJECTIVE ▶▶▶▶ ☐	I can gather information and ideas to summarize a text.

READING	▶	understanding the purpose of quoted speech
VOCABULARY	▶	word roots
WRITING	▶	writing an opinion essay
GRAMMAR	▶	adverb phrases of reason

Anthropology

UNIT QUESTION

Is discovery always a good thing?

A Discuss these questions with your classmates.

1. What discoveries have you heard about in recent years? Which discovery did you find the most exciting?

2. Do you think money should be spent on exploration, or is it better spent on other things?

3. Look at the photo. What can be discovered by deep-sea exploration? Do you think it is important to make new discoveries?

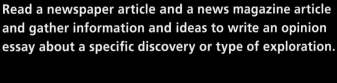

UNIT
OBJECTIVE ▶▶▶▶ Read a newspaper article and a news magazine article and gather information and ideas to write an opinion essay about a specific discovery or type of exploration.

🔊 **B Listen to *The Q Classroom* online. Then answer these questions.**

1. Sophy and Yuna disagree about the Unit Question. What opinions do they express? What's your opinion?

2. Marcus doesn't think we should spend money on discovery in space or the deep ocean. What does he think we should spend money on? What's your opinion?

 C Go online to watch the video about the culture of the Adi tribe in the Himalayan hills. Then check your comprehension.

fallow *(adj.)* not used for growing crops, especially so the quality of land will improve

indigenous *(adj.)* belonging to a particular place rather than coming to it from somewhere else

millet *(n.)* a type of plant that grows in hot countries and produces very small seeds used to make flour

overcome *(adj.)* stopped or conquered by someone or something

scavenge *(v.)* to search through waste for things that can be used or eaten

VIDEO VOCABULARY

 D Go to the Online Discussion Board to discuss the Unit Question with your classmates.

183

E Read about these four people who are exploring new places and ideas.

ARCTIC EXPLORATION

Nabil Al Busaidi is an Omani adventurer who has gone to both the North Pole and Antarctica. He is visiting schools to tell about his adventures and to provide inspiration for young people.

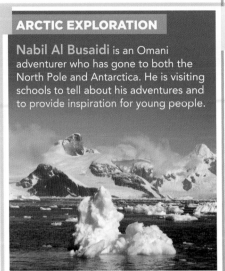

ARCHEOLOGICAL EXPLORATION

"Zeray" Alemseged (pronounced *AL-mess-ged*) discovered the oldest known skeleton of a human: a person he named *Selam*. The skeleton is 3.3 million years old. He is continuing his study of Selam to learn more about human history.

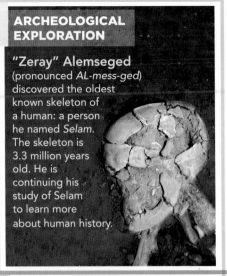

SPACE EXPLORATION

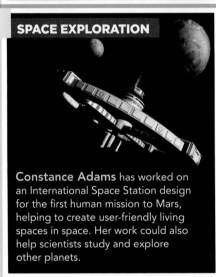

Constance Adams has worked on an International Space Station design for the first human mission to Mars, helping to create user-friendly living spaces in space. Her work could also help scientists study and explore other planets.

UNDERWATER EXPLORATION

Robert Ballard is best known for his discovery of the wreck of the Titanic. He helps to design machines for deep-sea exploration and has developed an educational program about the oceans used by millions of students.

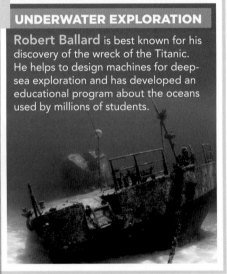

F Work in a group. Imagine you are members of the Future Explorer's Foundation (FEF). Every year FEF awards $500,000 to an explorer who has done original work. Discuss these questions and choose the winner from the descriptions above. Your decision must be unanimous.

1. Does the explorer's work help a lot of people? If so, who does it help?

2. Does the work help us to better understand our planet?

3. Will this work help future generations? In what way?

4. How will $500,000 help the explorer continue his or her work?

G Tell the class who your group selected and why.

READING

READING 1 | A Tribe Is Discovered

You are going to read an article from *The Scotsman* newspaper about a tribe of people living in the Amazon rainforest. Use the article to gather information and ideas for your Unit Assignment.

PREVIEW THE READING

A. **PREVIEW** Read the title and look at the picture. The article reports on the tribe's first contact with the civilized world. List three ways the tribe's way of life might differ from that of modern civilizations.

_____

_____

_____

B. **QUICK WRITE** How do you think the tribe reacted to the appearance of strangers in their world? Write for 5–10 minutes in response. Be sure to use this section for your Unit Assignment.

C. **VOCABULARY** Check (✓) the words you know. Use a dictionary to define any new or unknown words. Then discuss how the words will relate to the unit with a partner.

adopt *(v.)* 🔑	fatal *(adj.)*
cite *(v.)*	genuinely *(adv.)* 🔑
confirm *(v.)* 🔑	hostile *(adj.)*
conflict *(n.)* 🔑	inevitable *(adj.)* 🔑
deter *(v.)*	moral *(adj.)* 🔑
dilemma *(n.)*	motive *(n.)*

🔑 Oxford 3000™ words

D. Go online to listen and practice your pronunciation.

A. Read the article and gather information about whether discovery is always a good thing.

A Tribe Is Discovered

the Amazonian rainforest

1   It's like a scene from a novel—but this time it's for real. Photographed from a passing airplane, colorful figures can be seen in a clearing[1] in the Amazonian rainforest. Two men with bows and arrows stand ready to fire at the overhead threat. They are painted bright orange with paint made from an Amazonian tree. Just feet behind them, a figure painted black also stares up into the sky.

2   Beyond them, the entire village is coming to life. Other tribesmen emerge from traditional thatched longhouses and prepare to fight, while young children run for safety. As the small aircraft continues to circle above, images of the village are recorded and the tribe's existence is **confirmed** to the outside world.

3   The group lives in six huts in the Acre region of the Brazilian rainforest on the Brazil-Peru border and have had no known contact with the "civilized" world. The body language of the Acre tribe suggests that they have a way of life worth defending. From the images on the Internet last week, all of them—adults and children alike—look fit and healthy. They have none of the material possessions of the developed world, but they appear to be content without them.

4   "We did the overflight to show their houses, to show they are there, to show they exist," said José Carlos dos Reis Meirelles Júnior, an uncontacted tribes[2] expert who works for the Brazilian government's Indian affairs department. "This is very important because there are some who doubt their existence."

5   However, since the pictures have been published and because more people are now aware of the village's existence, a debate has begun about new risks and dangers to the tribe. How long will it be before wealthy adventurers and tourists go in search of a unique Amazonian experience? How long will it be before illegal loggers attempt to clear them off their land to cut down valuable lumber[3]?

6   Their discovery poses[4] a **moral dilemma** for the authorities. Should the Acre tribe be left alone to continue their contented lifestyle for as long as they can? Or should contact be forced by well-intentioned scientists to prepare the uncontacted tribe for its **inevitable** first encounter with the twenty-first century?

7   Dr. Nicole Bourque, a Glasgow University anthropologist who has studied Amazonian cultures, says that views are divided even among experts. "Some will say leave them untouched. Others, probably the majority, will say more contact is inevitable. So the best thing you can hope for is 'managed contact,' where you send an

[1] **clearing:** an open space in a forest where there are no trees
[2] **uncontacted tribes:** groups of people who live without significant contact with modern civilization
[3] **lumber:** wood from trees used for construction
[4] **poses:** creates a problem that has to be dealt with

appropriate person to prepare the tribe for what might happen. At least then the first outsiders they meet are decent people."

8   It is impossible to calculate how many tribes of uncontacted people survive in the world's jungles. The best guess of experts is that around 100 small groups remain, mostly in the Amazonian rainforest—an area the size of Western Europe. Other isolated[5] groups are also believed to exist in remote areas of heavily forested islands, such as Papua New Guinea.

9   How many of these tribes are **genuinely** unaware of the modern world is also unknown. What is certain, though, is that contact almost always ends in disaster. A decade ago, "first contact" was made with the Murunahua (pronounced *moor-uh-now-uh*) group that was living in an area in the Peruvian jungle. About 100-strong, they were surviving well until illegal loggers came in search of mahogany, a highly valued wood. David Hill, a researcher for Survival International, a global charity that campaigns for the rights of threatened indigenous peoples, has seen the consequences.

10   "They were forcibly contacted by illegal loggers, who shoot to kill. Since then, 50% of them have died. Some were shot, but most died from diseases that were introduced to them." Simple viruses such as the flu, which Westerners have natural defenses against, can prove **fatal** to tribes that have always lived in isolation.

11   Last year, Hill traveled to Peru to interview the remaining members of the tribe. One survivor, Jorge, told him: "When the loggers made contact with us, we came out of the rainforest. That was when the disease began. Half of us died. My aunt died; my nephew died. Half of my people died."

12   The group now lives in a more conventional[6] village and has **adopted** Western-style clothing and a money-based economy. However, other Murunahua groups still exist and still live in traditional communities deep in the forest. They don't seem to want to be found. "What has happened," says Hill, "is they have moved even deeper into the forest."

13   Hill is delighted that last week's image of the Acre tribe made global headlines. "It puts pressure on governments to stop the logging," he said. "I have no doubt that the aim of the flight was right. It was designed to discover where the uncontacted tribes are living, how many of them there are, and how they are living. If you don't know where they are, then you can't protect them as well."

14   However, he firmly recommends leaving the Acre tribe on its own. "We would warn strongly against further contact," Hill said, **citing** the proven threat of disease.

15   One practical way of protecting the tribes is to limit the activities of the loggers; the Brazilian government has already closed down 28 illegal sawmills in Acre state. Another is to **deter** curious tourists. Most people are discouraged by the difficulty of reaching an area like this. However, in places like the highlands of West Papua, travelers can already pay 8,000 dollars to be led into the jungles for "first contact experiences."

16   Dr. Bourque is saddened by this. "You get the curiosity factor, and you want your picture taken with a tribesman so you can tell your friends at home or post it on your blog. People don't think about the long-term impact on these communities."

17   However, she believes that contact with friendly outsiders is preferable to **conflict** with possibly **hostile** commercial interests. She thinks the time may be close when uncontacted groups have to be gently brought into the modern age.

18   "It would be better if first contact came from the appropriate people with the right **motives** and the right medical support, who could prepare them for the future and what might happen."

---

[5] **isolated:** having little contact with other people

[6] **conventional:** considered normal or acceptable by society

a peregrine falcon

Vocabulary Skill Review

In Unit 6, you learned to recognize different word forms to expand your vocabulary. Use a dictionary to find different forms of the vocabulary words *adopt, confirm, conflict,* and *moral.*

B. VOCABULARY Here are some words from Reading 1. Read the excerpt below. Then write each bold word next to the correct definition. You may need to change verbs to their base form and nouns to the singular form.

In the middle of the 20th century, the number of peregrine falcons in North America started falling. People noticed that there were fewer birds, but they didn't know why. Eventually, scientists **confirmed** that the cause was the pesticide DDT, which was **fatal** to these birds. It seemed **inevitable** that they would die out completely if something was not done.

Therefore, scientists collected young birds and raised them away from danger. This practice produced a **dilemma** for some bird-lovers: If they found a peregrine falcon nest, should they inform the scientists or not?

Clearly, the scientists were **genuinely** trying to help the peregrine falcons by taking them out of a **hostile** environment. Their **motives** were clear: If the program was successful, there would be more wild falcons. However, people worried that if the falcons were removed from their nests, they wouldn't live very long. They feared that if scientists found out about the falcon nests, they would disturb them and the falcons would die.

Some people responded to this **conflict** by informing scientists about the birds, while others felt the more **moral** action was to keep the information quiet. Fortunately, scientists were able to **cite** examples of successfully raising peregrine falcons and setting them free. Other peregrine falcons managed to survive without help. Now, peregrine falcons in North America are no longer in danger. In fact, some peregrine falcons have moved to cities. To **deter** office workers from getting too close to the birds, companies have **adopted** the practice of setting up video cameras that let people watch them safely.

1. _____ (*adj.*) cannot be avoided or prevented

2. _____ (*v.*) to discourage someone from doing something

3. _____ (*n.*) purpose or reason for doing something

4. _____ (*v.*) to mention something as a reason or example

5. _____ (*adj.*) involving right and wrong behavior

6. _____ (*n.*) a situation in which you have to make a very difficult choice

7. _____ (*adv.*) really; truly

8. _____ (*v.*) to start to use a particular method or show a particular attitude

9. _____ (*v.*) to show that something is definitely true or correct

10. _____ (*adj.*) causing or ending in death

11. _____ (adj.) very unfriendly; ready to argue or fight

12. _____ (n.) a situation that involves a serious disagreement

iQ ONLINE **C. Go online for more practice with the vocabulary.**

D. Answer these questions.

1. Who are the Acre people?

   _____

2. How do they live?

   _____

3. Why are they in the news?

   _____

4. Why did the author give the example of the Murunahua people?

   _____

   _____

5. What two actions has the Brazilian government taken to protect the Acre?

   _____

   _____

6. Who is Nicole Bourque?

   _____

7. Who is David Hill?

   _____

E. Circle the correct answer.

1. What was the Brazilian government's purpose in photographing the Acre tribe?
   a. They wanted to show how well they were taking care of the tribe.
   b. They wanted to encourage tourists to visit.
   c. They wanted to show that the tribe really existed.

2. Why were the tribesmen prepared to fight when they saw the plane?
   a. They are naturally hostile.
   b. They thought they were being attacked.
   c. They were tired of being disturbed.

3. What can be inferred about the tribe from the photographs on the Internet?
   a. They want material possessions.
   b. They suffer from many diseases.
   c. They are satisfied with their existence.

4. Tourists and loggers are two examples of people who ____.
   a. are a threat to the tribe
   b. can help the tribe
   c. should contact the tribe

5. What do the remaining uncontacted tribes have in common?
   a. They live in forests.
   b. They live on islands.
   c. They live in the Amazon.

6. The Murunahua people's troubles began because they ____.
   a. left the rainforest
   b. lived near valuable trees
   c. made the loggers angry

7. What happened to the Murunahua group after they were forcibly contacted?
   a. Half of them died, mostly from illness.
   b. Half of them got shot by the loggers, but they survived.
   c. Half of them met with David Hill.

8. While some Murunahua live in a conventional village, other groups ____.
   a. wear Western clothing and use money
   b. attacked the loggers
   c. moved farther into the forest

9. Why is David Hill delighted that the Acre tribe has been in the news?
   a. It means they will be well taken care of.
   b. It may influence the actions of the government.
   c. It will make it easier for people to find the tribe.

F. Write the name of the person or group next to the statement they might make.

the Acre	David Hill	government authority
logger	Nicole Bourque	tourist

_____ 1. We want all the people of Brazil to live well, including the Acre.

_____ 2. The government needs to make sure that the tribe is protected.

_____ 3. Hey, it's OK. I'm not sick or anything, and I won't hurt anybody.

_____ 4. All I want is the wood. They can have the rest of the forest.

_____ 5. Leave us alone.

_____ 6. We need to have medical personnel ready when we contact them.

G. **The article presents a problem and two possible solutions. Use information from the article to answer these questions.**

1. What is the problem, or moral dilemma, that the authorities face?

   _____

2. What is David Hill's recommendation?

   _____

3. What is Nicole Bourque's recommendation?

   _____

4. In the chart, list the main benefit and the main risk of David Hill's recommendation. Then do the same for Nicole Bourque's recommendation.

	Benefit	Risk
David Hill's recommendation		
Nicole Bourque's recommendation		

5. Discuss your answers to questions 1–4 with a partner.

 H. **Go online to read _New Discoveries about Diseases_ and check your comprehension.**

 # WRITE WHAT YOU THINK

A. Discuss these questions in a group.

1. What do you think the authorities should do about the Acre tribe—contact them or leave them alone?

2. If the members of the tribe were introduced to the modern world, what would be the best way to help them make this transition?

3. What is your opinion of the type of tourism mentioned in Reading 1? Should travelers be allowed to visit tribes like the Acre for their own entertainment?

B. Choose one question and write a paragraph in response. Look back at your Quick Write on page 185 as you think about what you learned.

Reading Skill Understanding the purpose of quoted speech

When reading a text, it is important to understand the purpose of a quotation. Quotations may be used to state **facts** or give **opinions**. Facts are statements that can be proved or disproved. They may, for example, describe actions or give explanations. In contrast, opinions offer personal preferences or judgments. They can illustrate different sides of an argument.

> **Fact:**   "They were forcibly contacted by illegal loggers, who shoot to kill. Since then, 50% of them have died."
>
> **Opinion:** "We would warn strongly against further contact."

 **for Success**

Don't assume that an article expresses the writer's opinion. Journalists may quote many other people's opinions without expressing their own.

A. Scan Reading 1 on pages 186–187 and find the quotations from Nicole Bourque and David Hill. Label them *NB* for Nicole Bourque or *DH* for David Hill.

B. Bourque's and Hill's comments sum up two different sides of the moral dilemma. Which of the two experts is in favor of more contact with the tribe?

_____

C. Read these quotations from Reading 1. Write *F* (fact) or *O* (opinion).

____ 1. "We did the overflight to show their houses, to show they are there, to show they exist. This is very important because there are some who doubt their existence."

____ 2. "So the best thing you can hope for is 'managed contact,' where you send an appropriate person to prepare the tribe for what might happen."

____ 3. "When the loggers made contact with us, we came out of the rainforest. That was when the disease began. Half of us died."

____ 4. "What has happened is they have moved even deeper into the forest."

____ 5. "I have no doubt that the aim of the flight was right."

____ 6. "It [the overflight] was designed to discover where the uncontacted tribes are living, how many of them there are, and how they are."

_____ 7. "You get the curiosity factor, and you want your picture taken with a tribesman so you can tell your friends at home or post it on your blog."

_____ 8. "It would be better if first contact came from the appropriate people with the right motives and the right medical support, who could prepare them for the future and what might happen."

 D. Go online for more practice understanding the purpose of quoted speech.

READING 2 | Alaska's Pebble Mine: Minerals vs. Nature

 You are going to read an article from the news magazine *The Atlantic* about the proposed Pebble Mine in Alaska's Bristol Bay region. There is a controversy about whether extracting minerals will destroy the natural beauty and resources of the area. Use the article to gather information and ideas for your Unit Assignment.

PREVIEW THE READING

A. **PREVIEW** Read the title and first paragraph. Why do you think some people do not want the Pebble Mine project? Why do you think other people are in favor of it? Discuss your opinion with your classmates.

B. **QUICK WRITE** Is the discovery and extraction of minerals a good thing? Write for 5–10 minutes in response. Be sure to use this section for your Unit Assignment.

C. **VOCABULARY** Check (✓) the words you know. Then work with a partner to locate each word in the reading. Use clues to help define the words you don't know. Check your definitions in the dictionary.

abundant *(adj.)*	intervene *(v.)*
alliance *(n.)*	overwhelmingly *(adv.)*
ample *(adj.)*	preliminary *(adj.)*
controversial *(adj.)*	significant *(adj.)* 🔑
dread *(v.)*	sustainable *(adj.)*
extensive *(adj.)* 🔑	unduly *(adv.)*

🔑 Oxford 3000™ words

 D. Go online to listen and practice your pronunciation.

WORK WITH THE READING

)) **A.** Read the article and gather information about whether discovery is always a good thing.

Alaska's Pebble Mine: Minerals vs. Nature

1 Alaska's Bristol Bay region is located on the Bering Sea in the state's southwest corner. It is rich with large reserves of natural resources. One of those resources, the world's largest sockeye-salmon fishery, generates an estimated $1.5 billion annually. The thousands of acres of surrounding wetlands, ponds, and lakes are treasured because there isn't much untouched land left in America. Bristol Bay is also home to a large population of Alaska Natives, whose cultures and lifestyles revolve around the region's "wildness" and especially its salmon. Those are the living, breathing resources of Bristol Bay. And then there are the inorganic resources—oil and gas and mineral deposits. These are not yet fully explored, but they represent much more wealth than Alaska is receiving now.

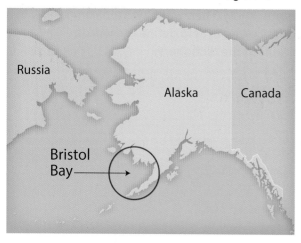

2 A deposit of gold, molybdenum[1], and copper has been discovered in Bristol Bay. In fact, it is the largest known untapped copper deposit in the world. It's known as the Pebble prospect. A Canadian company called Northern Dynasty Minerals started exploring the area in 2000. The corporation's plans to build the "Pebble Mine" have yet to progress much beyond the idea stage.

3 The Pebble Mine hasn't been built yet because the process of getting state and federal permits for a project of this size is long. The project is also highly **controversial**. The mine pits[2] two of Alaska's biggest industries, fishing and mining, against each other in a classic resource war. Both are extractive[3], but only fishing is **sustainable**. Weighing gold against salmon is weighing money against nature.

4 According to some, deciding whether to mine ought to be left to Alaskans. They will feel the effects either way. The Pebble Partnership promises to create jobs and bring in revenue. The state residents should know best whether this would do more long-term good than the protection of salmon stocks and preservation of untouched land. Polls have shown that the majority of Alaskans oppose the mine.

---

[1] **molybdenum:** a silver-grey metal that breaks easily
[2] **pit . . . against:** to test someone in a struggle against someone else

[3] **extractive:** relating to the process of removing or obtaining something, especially minerals

5   However, in 2010, concerned Alaskans decided that the federal government needed to **intervene**. An unlikely **alliance** of commercial fishermen, native tribes, and concerned citizens joined together. They decided that their best hope for stopping the Pebble Mine was to get the federal government to step in. The alliance petitioned the U.S. Environmental Protection Agency (EPA) to conduct a **preliminary** investigation. It would look at the potential ecological impact of a large-scale mining operation in Bristol Bay. The agency could shut down the Pebble Mine project by determining that it would have "unacceptable" negative effects on the Bristol Bay watershed[4].

6   In the spring of 2013, the EPA released a draft of its watershed assessment. It indicated that the mine would have an **overwhelmingly** negative impact on the Bristol Bay watershed. EPA Administrator Gina McCarthy said in a statement, "**Extensive** scientific study has given us **ample** reason to believe that the Pebble Mine would likely have **significant** and negative impacts on the Bristol Bay watershed and its **abundant** salmon fisheries. This process is not something the agency does very often, but Bristol Bay is an extraordinary and unique resource."

7   It isn't surprising that companies have been fighting to mine the rich deposits of gold and copper in Bristol Bay for more than a decade. But the most recent development in the Pebble Mine story delivered a small shock. On February 28, 2014 the agency did what environmentalists hoped and what the Pebble Partnership **dreaded** it would. It temporarily prevented the U.S. Army Corps of Engineers from issuing any mining permits in Bristol Bay. That effectively halts the development process. However, this action is not a final decision.

the Bristol Bay shore near Naknek, Alaska

8   Northern Dynasty CEO Tom Collier said his company is not going to give up on its plan. According to the Associated Press, Collier said the EPA's actions to date "have gone well outside of its normal practice, have been biased throughout, and have been **unduly** influenced by environmental advocacy organizations." He also said that he remains "confident" about the future of the mine, and that his company will continue to try and gain the EPA's approval to move forward. If anything, this is the beginning, not the end, of the Pebble Mine controversy.

9   According to nature writer and longtime Alaska resident Bill Sherwonit, "Ultimately, for Alaskans, the issue will boil down to this: Do the benefits of tapping into one of the planet's richest mineral lodes outweigh the risks to one of the world's last, great fisheries?"

---

[4] **watershed:** the region or area drained by a river, stream, etc.

B. **VOCABULARY** Complete the sentences with the vocabulary from Reading 2.

abundant *(adj.)*	dread *(v.)*	preliminary *(adj.)*
alliance *(n.)*	extensive *(adj.)*	significant *(adj.)*
ample *(adj.)*	intervene *(v.)*	sustainable *(adj.)*
controversial *(adj.)*	overwhelmingly *(adv.)*	unduly *(adv.)*

1. The two groups formed a(n) _____ to fight against building a new highway.

2. This is a very _____ topic, and it's unlikely they can come to an agreement about what to do.

3. The discovery will be _____ to the scientific community.

4. They were asked to _____ in the conflict to prevent matters from getting worse.

5. The levels of pollution in the area are _____ high. It's now difficult to see clearly through all the smog.

6. That type of farming destroys the land, so it is not _____.

7. We don't make much money, but it is _____ because it covers our expenses.

8. There was _____ evidence to confirm that he had discovered a new source of energy.

9. The news they received was _____ bad.

10. Because I didn't study for the test, I _____ finding out my score.

11. The damage from the fire was _____, covering a large area of the forest.

12. The _____ results from the first study show that the mine will damage the area.

 C. Go online for more practice with the vocabulary.

D. Circle the answer that best completes each statement.

1. The purpose of the article is ___.
   a. to argue for building the Pebble Mine
   b. to encourage people to visit Bristol Bay
   c. to explain the controversy about extracting minerals in Bristol Bay

2. Paragraphs 4 and 5 are about ___.
   a. why the Pebble Mine should not be built in Bristol Bay
   b. who should decide about allowing mining of the resources in Bristol Bay
   c. what the results of a study of the Bristol Bay watershed are

3. The EPA study is discussed in paragraphs 6 and 7 to ___.
   a. inform the reader about the results of the study
   b. bias the reader against building the mine
   c. explain the reason for doing a study

4. In paragraph 8, the CEO of Northern Dynasty Minerals ___.
   a. expresses facts about the future of the mine
   b. gives his opinion of the future of the mine
   c. explains why he doesn't like the EPA

5. In paragraph 9, longtime Alaska resident Bill Sherwonit is quoted to ___.
   a. convince the reader that mining in Bristol Bay is a bad idea
   b. pose a factual question about the future of Bristol Bay
   c. give an opinion that Alaskans will have to make a hard decision

E. Read each statement. Write *Y* (yes) if it can be inferred from the reading or *N* (no) if it is not a correct inference. Write the paragraph number where you found information to support your answer.

___ 1. Bristol Bay is important to the people of Alaska. (para. ___)

___ 2. Native people in Bristol Bay live in modern cities. (para. ___)

___ 3. The alliance doesn't want the mine to be built. (para. ___)

___ 4. The groups in the alliance have common interests and goals. (para. ___)

___ 5. The EPA study found a slight negative impact on the watershed in Bristol Bay. (para. ___)

___ 6. The company that wants to build the mine agrees that the EPA should have expressed an opinion. (para. ___)

_____ 7. Environmentalists are happy with the results of the study. (para. _____)

_____ 8. The controversy will be resolved soon. (para. _____)

F. Answer these questions.

1. What are the resources of Bristol Bay? _____

    _____

    _____

2. Which resources are sustainable? _____

    _____

3. When did Northern Dynasty start exploring Bristol Bay?

    _____

4. Why hasn't the Pebble Mine been built? _____

    _____

5. What are the positive aspects of building the Pebble Mine?

    _____

6. What are the negative aspects of building the Pebble Mine?

    _____

7. Who asked the federal government to intervene? _____

    _____

    _____

8. What did they ask for? _____

    _____

9. What were the findings of the study conducted by the EPA?

    _____

    _____

10. What happened in February 2014 as a result of the study?

    _____

11. What will the company trying to build the Pebble Mine do about the results?

    _____

WRITE WHAT YOU THINK

A. Discuss the questions in a group. Look back at your Quick Write on page 193 as you think about what you learned.

Critical Thinking **Tip**

Question 2 in Activity B asks you to support your ideas with information from the texts and from your own knowledge. When you put information from different sources together, you are **synthesizing**. Synthesizing is a necessary skill for academic writing.

1. The article explains the controversy about mining in Bristol Bay. Do you think the article is biased toward one side? If so, which side and why?

2. Who should decide whether to build the mine, the Alaskan (local) people or the U.S. government?

3. Should the Pebble Mine be built? Why or why not?

B. Think about the unit video, Reading 1, and Reading 2 as you discuss the questions. Then choose one question and write a paragraph in response.

1. Consider this statement: "All the major discoveries on Earth have already been made—new discoveries just fill in the details." How true do you think the statement is?

2. Are we right to keep investigating the few wild places left on Earth in the name of discovery? Explain your ideas with support from the readings and any knowledge you have of similar situations.

Vocabulary Skill | Word roots

Many words, particularly in academic English, come from Latin roots. A **root** is the part of a word that contains the basic meaning. Roots can be combined with prefixes and suffixes to form words and word families. The Latin root *-dict-*, for example, means *say* or *speak*. It is used to form words such as:

> *contradict (v.)* to say that something that someone else has said is wrong
> I'm tired of Roger. He keeps **contradicting** everything I say.
>
> *diction (n.)* the way that someone says words
> That newsreader needs to improve his **diction**. I can't understand a word on his new program.
>
> *predict (v.)* to say something will happen in the future
> It is difficult to **predict** the weather.

Knowing the basic meaning of common roots, prefixes, and suffixes will help you understand the meaning of many unfamiliar words.

All dictionary definitions are from the *Oxford Advanced American Dictionary for learners of English* © Oxford University Press 2011.

A. Work with a partner. Study the word roots and examples in the chart below. Add two other examples from the box. Then circle the correct basic meaning. Use your dictionary if necessary.

antibiotics	genus	portable	unconscious
biography	inscribe	reverse	versatile
conscious	inspect	speculate	video
generate	manuscript	transport	vision

Word root	Basic meaning	Examples	Other examples
1. -bio-	(life) / death	**bio**logy, **bio**diversity	antibiotics biography
2. -gen-	kill / produce	**gen**etics, indi**gen**ous	
3. -port-	carry / drop	sup**port**, re**port**	
4. -sci-	forget / know	**sci**ence, **sci**entist	
5. -scrib-, -script-	hear / write	de**scrib**e, de**script**ion	
6. -spec-, -spect-	look / say	**spec**imen, **spec**ies	
7. -vers-	run / turn	con**vers**ion	
8. -vid-, -vis-	listen / see	e**vid**ence, **vis**it	

B. Choose five words from Activity A that are less familiar to you. Write sentences that illustrate their meanings.

1. _Because she had an infection, she had to take antibiotics._

2. _____

3. _____

4. _____

5. _____

6. _____

 C. Go online for more practice with word roots.

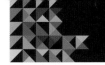

WRITING

At the end of this unit, you will write an opinion essay about a specific discovery or type of exploration. This essay will include specific information from the readings, the unit video, and your own ideas.

Writing Skill Writing an opinion essay

Writing **Tip**

In an opinion essay, avoid generalizations and other unsupported statements. They weaken your position because they are often easy to challenge.

The purpose of writing an **opinion essay** is to give a personal response to a topic. The essay expresses how you feel about an issue. It may try to convince your readers that your view of a topic is the correct one, or one that they should take seriously.

An effective opinion essay should follow these guidelines.

- In your introduction, express your opinion clearly in a thesis statement.
- In your body paragraphs, provide specific reasons for your opinion— one main reason in each body paragraph. Support your reasons with facts, examples, and logical arguments.
- In your conclusion, summarize your opinion.

A. **WRITING MODEL** Read the model opinion essay. Underline the thesis statement and circle the three main reasons for the author's opinion.

Is Deep-Sea Exploration Worth the Money?

In difficult economic times, the amount of money spent on exploration and discovery is always reduced. This has happened several times over the last 50 years with both space and deep-sea exploration. People are generally more enthusiastic about space, but I feel the oceans hold the solutions to some of the biggest problems of the twenty-first century. We must continue to invest in exploration of the deep sea so that we can take advantage of its benefits.

The deep sea contains resources that could bring improvements in the field of medicine. Antibiotics are becoming less effective in the treatment of illnesses, and scientists think that plant life in the deep oceans may provide a solution. They hope to develop new medicines that will make it possible to fight disease for years to come. Some substances produced from deep-sea species are already being used in improved medical testing procedures. Recognizing the importance of this research, the 2008 Nobel Committee awarded the Nobel Prize for Chemistry to scientists in this area.

At a time when existing forms of fuel are limited, the deep ocean could provide new sources of fuel. For more than 50 years, oil companies have been drilling in areas like the North Sea. Realizing that these offshore resources will not last forever, oil companies are now considering other sources, including the huge amounts of oil beneath the ocean bed. However, extracting it safely will require major advancements in technology. Another possible deep-sea fuel source is methane. Having

discovered that methane exists on the ocean floor in the form of ice crystals, scientists believe this could be a fuel source for the future.

Finally, using the deep sea for the disposal of nuclear waste is a controversial issue that needs to be explored further. Some organizations have proposed dropping nuclear waste into the deepest parts of the ocean and sealing it into the ocean floor. Many scientists claim that this process would involve less danger to the environment than current storage methods. While I find this idea disturbing, I accept that most people do not want to live near nuclear waste, so I think the proposal needs to be investigated.

These are just three of the many ways in which learning about the deep ocean may change our lives for the better. In my view, such advances in our knowledge justify the expense of carrying out deep-sea research. The demand for land is only continuing to grow. The time has come when the 70 percent of our planet covered by water is just too big to ignore.

Tip for Success

Remember: When you summarize, you combine or shorten language using some words from the text and some of your own words.

B. Complete the outline of the essay by briefly summarizing the information you have read.

I. Thesis statement: _____

_____

II. Reason 1: _The deep sea could bring improvements in medicine._

A. Support 1: _____

B. Support 2: _Scientists who research this area won a Nobel Prize._

III. Reason 2: _____

A. Support 1: _____

B. Support 2: _____

IV. Reason 3: _____

    A. Support 1: _____

    B. Support 2: _Deep-ocean disposal could be safer than current methods._

V. Concluding idea: _____

_____

C. Choose three topics from the box. Then write your opinion and three reasons to support your opinion.

archeological exploration	minerals
Arctic exploration	new place
finding an urban park	new species of animal
genetically modified food	space exploration

Example:

Opinion: _Finding a park or garden within a city is an important discovery._

Reason 1: _Being in a park is good for my health._

Reason 2: _A park extends my living space._

Reason 3: _Being in a park gives me choices._

1. Opinion: _____

    Reason 1: _____

    Reason 2: _____

    Reason 3: _____

2. Opinion: _____

    Reason 1: _____

    Reason 2: _____

    Reason 3: _____

3. Opinion: _____

    Reason 1: _____

    Reason 2: _____

    Reason 3: _____

D. WRITING MODEL Read the model opinion essay. Then answer the questions that follow.

Exploring the Concrete Jungle

"Concrete jungle" is a common expression used to speak about cities, especially those in the United States that do not have much "green space." Finding a public park or garden in the midst of all the concrete can be a truly wonderful discovery.

I feel better when I can spend time outdoors around trees and grass, not to mention birds and butterflies. The presence of other living things is calming and revitalizing, and I can clear my mind of all the stress of the day. In fact, the University of Exeter Medical School has shown that there is an increase in mental health for people who move to greener cities. In addition, just getting to a park makes me get up and get moving, so I get some exercise even before I arrive at my destination. Once at the park, I usually keep moving, whether at a brisk walk or a leisurely stroll, so I continue to benefit physically.

A second reason for searching out a park is that it extends my living space. I live in a small apartment with very little room. I can use a park for activities that I cannot do at home, such as exercising and walking. At home, I am likely to knock something off a table or hit my foot on a piece of furniture. Another extension of my living space comes from my very limited ability to keep plants alive. By visiting a public garden, I can enjoy flowers and plants without worrying about overwatering them or not having enough sunlight for them.

Furthermore, I have choices in a park. I can stay by myself, strike up a conversation with someone, or engage in a game of soccer, depending on what I want to do that day. I have no obligation to buy something, as I do in a coffee shop or café, and no pressure to spend money, like I have in a shopping mall. While some parks are closed at night, others are not, so I can enjoy what they have to offer at many times of the day or night.

I am lucky to live in a city that has a lot of public parks, which improve my health, extend my living space, and give me choices. Because I appreciate having plants, animals, and other people around me, I look for green areas wherever I go. How about you? Have you discovered any parks or gardens around you?

---

1. What is the thesis statement? Underline it, and circle the reasons that support it.

2. For each reason, give two supporting details from the essay.

   Reason 1: _____

   _____

Reason 2: _____

_____

Reason 3: _____

_____

 E. Go online for more practice with opinion essays.

Grammar   Adverb phrases of reason

Adverb clauses of reason give information about why an action occurs. They usually begin with a subordinator such as *because* or *since*. When the subjects of both clauses are the same, an adverb clause can often be reduced (shortened) to an **adverb phrase**.

To reduce an adverb clause with a simple verb, omit the subject and change the verb to the present participle (verb + -*ing*).

Adverb clause: <u>Since they realize</u> that offshore resources will not last **forever**, oil companies are now considering other sources.
Because they recognized the importance of this research, the Nobel Committee awarded the Nobel Prize for Chemistry to scientists in this area.

Adverb phrase: <u>Realizing</u> that offshore resources will not last forever, oil companies are now considering other sources.
<u>Recognizing</u> the importance of this research, the Nobel Committee awarded the Nobel Prize for Chemistry to scientists in this area.

To reduce an adverb clause with a perfect verb, use *having* + the past participle of the verb.

Adverb clause: <u>Because they had discovered</u> that methane exists on the **ocean floor**, scientists believed this could be a fuel source for the future.

Adverb phrase: <u>Having discovered</u> that methane exists on the ocean floor, scientists believed this could be a fuel source for the future.

Adverb phrases of reason almost always come before the main clause.

 **for Success**

Using adverb phrases can help you express complex ideas in fewer words. Vary your writing by using both adverb clauses and adverb phrases.

A. Reduce each adverb clause in bold to an adverb phrase.

1. **Because they want to develop the area,** energy companies came to Bristol Bay.

    Wanting to develop the area, _____

2. **Since they have lived there for centuries,** the Alaska Natives do not want Bristol Bay to be damaged.

_____

3. **Because he understands the danger of disease,** David Hill warns against further contact with the tribe.

_____

4. **Because they realized that people doubted the tribe's existence,** the Brazilian government organized a flight to photograph them.

_____

5. **Since she has accepted that more contact with the tribes people is inevitable,** Nicole Bourque thinks scientists should be the first people to visit them.

_____

B. Write the full adverb clause form of each adverb phrase. Look at the main clause to help you choose the correct verb form: present, past, or perfect.

1. Understanding the threat to the tribes people, the government is limiting access to the area where they live.

   Because they understand the threat to the tribes people, _____

2. Recognizing the importance of the discovery, newspapers published the story immediately.

_____

3. Having heard about the discovery of a new tribe, the journalists flew to the area.

_____

4. Hoping to stop the Pebble Mine, an alliance of commercial fishermen, native tribes, and concerned citizens asked the government to get involved.

_____

5. Having determined that the mine would have a negative impact, the EPA temporarily stopped Northern Dynasty Minerals from building it.

_____

 C. Go online for more practice with adverb phrases of reason.

D. Go online for the grammar expansion.

 In this assignment, you are going to write an opinion essay about a specific discovery or type of exploration. As you prepare your essay, think about the Unit Question, "Is discovery always a good thing?" Use information from Reading 1, Reading 2, the unit video, and your work in this unit to support your essay. Refer to the Self-Assessment checklist on page 208.

iQ ONLINE   Go to the Online Writing Tutor for a writing model and alternate Unit Assignments.

PLAN AND WRITE

A. **BRAINSTORM**   Follow these steps to help you organize your ideas.

1. Think of specific discoveries that you read about in this unit, other discoveries that interest you, or different types of exploration in general (such as space exploration or archeological exploration).

2. Work with a partner. Choose three discoveries or types of exploration and write them in the chart. Brainstorm the positive and negative aspects of each and add your ideas.

Discoveries or types of exploration	Positive aspects	Negative aspects
1.		
2.		
3.		

3. Compare the positive and negative aspects of each discovery or type of exploration. Choose one and decide whether you think it is a good thing or a bad thing.

B. **PLAN** Follow these steps to plan your essay.

1. Write a thesis statement that clearly expresses your opinion about whether the discovery or type of exploration is a good thing or a bad thing.

2. Choose your best ideas from Activity A. Include three specific reasons and two or three pieces of supporting information for each reason.

 3. Go to the Online Resources to download and complete the outline for your opinion essay.

 C. **WRITE** Use your **PLAN** notes to write your essay. Go to *iQ Online* to use the Online Writing Tutor.

1. Write your opinion essay. Remember to write an introduction with a thesis statement expressing your opinion, body paragraphs providing specific reasons, and a conclusion summarizing your opinion.

2. Look at the Self-Assessment checklist below to guide your writing.

REVISE AND EDIT

 A. **PEER REVIEW** Read your partner's essay. Then go online and use the Peer Review worksheet. Discuss the review with your partner.

B. **REWRITE** Based on your partner's review, revise, and rewrite your essay.

C. **EDIT** Complete the Self-Assessment checklist as you prepare to write the final draft of your essay. Be prepared to hand in your work or discuss it in class.

SELF-ASSESSMENT		
Yes	No	
☐	☐	Does the essay clearly express how you feel about the topic?
☐	☐	Are the reasons supported with facts, examples, and logical arguments?
☐	☐	If adverb phrases of reason are included, are they used correctly?
☐	☐	Does the essay include vocabulary from the unit?
☐	☐	Did you check the essay for punctuation, spelling, and grammar?

 D. **REFLECT** Go to the Online Discussion Board to discuss these questions.

1. What is something new you learned in this unit?

2. Look back at the Unit Question—Is discovery always a good thing? Is your answer different now than when you started the unit? If yes, how is it different? Why?

TRACK YOUR SUCCESS

Circle the words you have learned in this unit.

Nouns
alliance
conflict 🔑 AWL
dilemma
motive AWL

Verbs
adopt 🔑
cite AWL
confirm 🔑 AWL
deter
dread
intervene AWL

Adjectives
abundant
ample
controversial AWL
extensive 🔑
fatal
hostile
inevitable 🔑 AWL
moral 🔑
preliminary AWL
significant 🔑 AWL
sustainable AWL

Adverbs
genuinely 🔑
overwhelmingly
unduly

Roots
-bio-
-dict-
-gen-
-port-
-sci-
-scrib-
-script-
-spec-
-spect-
-vers-
-vid-
-vis-

🔑 Oxford 3000™ words
AWL Academic Word List

Check (✓) the skills you learned. If you need more work on a skill, refer to the page(s) in parentheses.

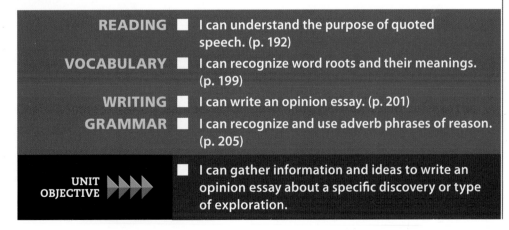

READING ☐	I can understand the purpose of quoted speech. (p. 192)
VOCABULARY ☐	I can recognize word roots and their meanings. (p. 199)
WRITING ☐	I can write an opinion essay. (p. 201)
GRAMMAR ☐	I can recognize and use adverb phrases of reason. (p. 205)
UNIT OBJECTIVE ▶▶▶▶ ☐	I can gather information and ideas to write an opinion essay about a specific discovery or type of exploration.

READING	▷	identifying counterarguments and refutations
VOCABULARY	▷	collocations with prepositions
WRITING	▷	writing a persuasive essay
GRAMMAR	▷	adverb clauses of concession

UNIT QUESTION

Why is it important to play?

A Discuss these questions with your classmates.

1. What were your favorite games as a child? Give examples and explain why you liked them.

2. Do you think adults need time to play? What is playtime for an adult?

3. Look at the photo. Is it important for adults to play? How are these adults having fun?

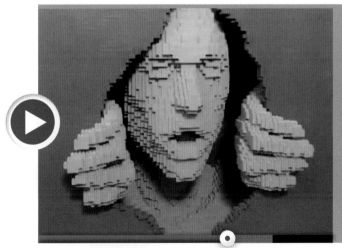

 B Listen to *The Q Classroom* online. Then answer these questions.

1. What are the reasons for playing according to the students? In your opinion, what is the best reason given for playing? Why?

2. All of the opinions are positive. Are there any negatives to playing?

 C Go online to watch the video about Legos for adult enthusiasts. Then check your comprehension.

breaking out *(phr.)* escaping a place or situation

nerdiness *(n.)* a characteristic of a person who is bored or uncomfortable in social situations or unfashionable

neurotic *(adj.)* not behaving in a reasonable, calm way because you are worried about something

palpable *(adj.)* something easily noticed by the mind or senses

VIDEO VOCABULARY

 D Go to the Online Discussion Board to discuss the Unit Question with your classmates.

211

E Many different kinds of people have spoken about work and play.
Read the quotations below and discuss these questions with a partner.

1. What does each quotation mean?

2. Do you agree with the quotation? Why or why not?

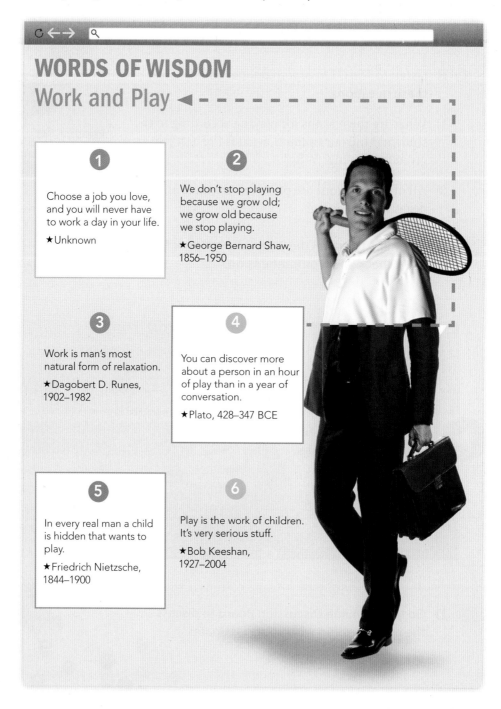

WORDS OF WISDOM
Work and Play ◄ - - - - - - - - - - - - - -

1

Choose a job you love, and you will never have to work a day in your life.

★Unknown

2

We don't stop playing because we grow old; we grow old because we stop playing.

★George Bernard Shaw, 1856–1950

3

Work is man's most natural form of relaxation.

★Dagobert D. Runes, 1902–1982

4

You can discover more about a person in an hour of play than in a year of conversation.

★Plato, 428–347 BCE

5

In every real man a child is hidden that wants to play.

★Friedrich Nietzsche, 1844–1900

6

Play is the work of children. It's very serious stuff.

★Bob Keeshan, 1927–2004

F Choose your favorite quotation in Activity E. Share it with your partner. Explain your choice.

 You are going to read an excerpt from a book by Stuart Brown, MD, an expert in the field of child psychology. Use the excerpt to gather information and ideas for your Unit Assignment.

PREVIEW THE READING

Stuart Brown, MD

A. `PREVIEW` The excerpt discusses what makes play essential in our lives, not only for children but for adults as well. Read the title and look at the picture. How do you think play can be beneficial in these areas?

education   health   relationships   work and business

B. `QUICK WRITE` Pick one of the four areas listed in Activity A. How do you think play can be beneficial in that area? Write for 5–10 minutes in response. Be sure to use this section for your Unit Assignment.

C. `VOCABULARY` Check (✓) the words you know. Use a dictionary to define any new or unknown words. Then discuss how the words will relate to the unit with a partner.

beneficial *(adj.)*	**innovative** *(adj.)*
catalyst *(n.)*	**mundane** *(adj.)*
conflicted *(adj.)*	**rigid** *(adj.)*
give in to *(phr. v.)*	**skeptic** *(n.)*
grim *(adj.)*	**strive** *(v.)*
incorporate *(v.)*	**therapy** *(n.)*

iQ `ONLINE` **D.** Go online to listen and practice your pronunciation.

WORK WITH THE READING

🔊 **A.** Read the book excerpt and gather information about the importance of play.

The Promise of Play

1 I have spent a career studying play, communicating the science of play to the public, and working for Fortune 500 companies[1] on how to **incorporate** it into business. I have used play **therapies** to help people who are clinically depressed. I frequently talk with groups of parents who inevitably are concerned and **conflicted** about what constitutes[2] healthy play for their kids. I have gathered and analyzed thousands of case studies that I call play histories. I have found that remembering what play is all about and making it part of our daily lives are probably the most important factors in being a fulfilled[3] human being. The ability to play is not only critical to being happy, but also to sustaining social relationships and being a creative, **innovative** person.

2 If that seems to be a big claim, consider what the world would be like without play. It's not just an absence of games or sports. Life without play is a life without books, without movies, art, music, jokes, dramatic stories. Imagine a world with no flirting, no daydreaming, no comedy, no irony[4]. Such a world would be a pretty **grim** place to live. In a broad sense, play is what lifts people out of the **mundane**. I sometimes compare play to oxygen—it's all around us, yet goes mostly unnoticed or unappreciated until it is missing.

3 But what happens to play in our lives? Nearly every one of us starts out playing quite naturally. As children, we don't need instruction in how to play. We just find what we enjoy and do it. Whatever "rules" there are to play, we learn from our playmates. And from our play we learn how the world works and how friends interact. By playing, we learn about the mystery and excitement that the world can hold in a tree house, an old tire swing, or a box of crayons.

4 At some point as we get older, however, we are made to feel guilty about playing. We are told that it is unproductive, a waste of time, even sinful[5]. The play that remains is, like league sports, mostly very organized, **rigid**, and competitive. We **strive** to always be productive, and if an activity doesn't teach us a skill, make us money, or get us on the boss's

playing in the office

---

[1] **Fortune 500 companies:** the top 500 U.S. companies, according to *Fortune* magazine
[2] **constitutes:** is equal to; is considered to be
[3] **fulfilled:** happy or satisfied

[4] **irony:** an amusing or strange aspect of a situation that is different from what you expect
[5] **sinful:** wrong or evil

good side, then we feel we should not be doing it. Sometimes the sheer demands of daily living seem to rob us of the ability to play.

5   The **skeptics** among the audiences I talk to will say, "Well, duh. Of course you will be happy if you play all the time. But for those of us who aren't rich, or retired, or both, there's simply no time for play." Or they might say that if they truly

gave in to the desire to experience the joy of free play, they would never get anything done.

6   This is not the case. We don't need to play all the time to be fulfilled. The truth is that in most cases play is a **catalyst**. The **beneficial** effects of getting just a little true play can spread through our lives, actually making us more productive and happier in everything we do.

Vocabulary Skill Review

In Unit 7, you used word roots to understand the meaning of unfamiliar words. What are the word roots in the vocabulary words *conflicted, incorporate, innovative,* and *mundane*? Use a dictionary to find at least one other word with each root.

B. **VOCABULARY** Here are some words from Reading 1. Read the sentences. Then write each bold word next to the correct definition on page 216. You may need to change nouns to the singular form.

1. Teachers of young children **incorporate** a lot of play activities into their lessons.

2. After his skiing accident, Miguel needed months of **therapy** before he could walk again.

3. Many women feel **conflicted** about the decision to stop working after they have children. They want to be at home, but they also love their jobs.

4. The company's old business models aren't effective anymore. They need new, creative employees to develop **innovative** strategies.

5. Last night's news was particularly **grim**. It was filled with stories of disasters and crime.

6. I want a job that is unpredictable, challenging, and fun. I don't want to sit in an office all day doing **mundane** tasks.

7. There aren't **rigid** guidelines about how long a baby should nap. Parents need to be flexible with their children.

8. Adults **strive** to be successful in their careers and daily lives. Play activities are a welcome relief from that effort.

9. The government announced a new program to build playgrounds and parks. However, **skeptics** say the program is likely to fail.

10. I try to be responsible and work hard, but occasionally I **give in to** my desire to be irresponsible.

11. The World Cup was a major **catalyst** for my current enthusiasm for soccer.

12. Many people think that video games are harmful to children, but some studies show that they can be **beneficial** in developing certain mental skills.

▶▶▶▶ | Reading and Writing   **215**

a. _____ (n.) a person or thing that causes a change

b. _____ (adj.) having a helpful or useful effect

c. _____ (adj.) unpleasant and depressing

d. _____ (phr. v.) to stop fighting against something

e. _____ (v.) to include something as a part of something else

f. _____ (v.) to try very hard to achieve something

g. _____ (adj.) dull; not interesting or exciting

h. _____ (n.) a treatment for a physical or mental problem

i. _____ (adj.) confused about what to do because you have strong opposing feelings

j. _____ (n.) a person who doubts that something is true

k. _____ (adj.) using new ideas or ways of doing something

l. _____ (adj.) following an exact process

iQ ONLINE **C.** Go online for more practice with the vocabulary.

D. Check (✓) the statements that the author would agree with.
- ☐ 1. Play is not only necessary, but it can be useful in many areas.
- ☐ 2. The value of play is not recognized by many people.
- ☐ 3. The ability to play is something that we have to learn.
- ☐ 4. As children, play helps us understand the world we live in.
- ☐ 5. Unproductive play is a waste of time.
- ☐ 6. People who aren't rich don't have the time to play.
- ☐ 7. Even a small amount of play can benefit adults.

E. Answer these questions.

1. What types of people, groups, or organizations has the author worked with?

_____

2. What benefits can play add to our lives? Give three examples.

_____

_____

3. What would be missing from life without play? Give three examples.

_____

4. What do children learn from play? Give two examples.

_____

5. Why don't people play enough when they get older? Give two reasons.

_____

_____

F. **Circle the answer that best completes each statement.**

1. The author includes the types of people, groups, and organizations he has worked with ____.
   a. to show that he is an expert
   b. to make himself sound important
   c. to give examples of people who want to play

2. Parents are concerned and conflicted about healthy play for their kids because ____.
   a. they think play is a waste of time
   b. there are many different opinions about children and play
   c. they didn't play as children and don't know how to play

3. The author considers jokes and stories to be forms of play because ____.
   a. they are innovative and creative
   b. they have rigid rules that have to be followed
   c. they are all around us

4. The statement "Whatever 'rules' there are to play, we learn from our playmates" suggests that ____.
   a. there are many rules that children have to learn in order to play
   b. adults never help children play
   c. children make up their own rules for their games

5. The author suggests that ____.
   a. play doesn't have to accomplish anything
   b. play should have a purpose, such as getting exercise
   c. play for adults should be organized and competitive

6. The author states that we don't have to play all the time to be fulfilled. This is because ____.
   a. no one has the time to play that much
   b. daily living robs us of the ability to play
   c. play is just the beginning of being happy

7. The author probably ____.

    a. plays a competitive sport

    b. plays a little bit every day

    c. watches other people play but doesn't play himself

G. In paragraph 2, Dr. Brown lists books, jokes, and stories as forms of play. Look at the list in the box. With a partner, discuss whether you think each activity can be considered play. Give reasons for your answers.

cooking a meal	reading a novel	watching TV
doing math problems	swimming in a race	writing an email
hiking up a mountain	talking with friends	

H. Go online to read *Office Toys—Productivity Boost or Distraction*? and check your comprehension.

WRITE WHAT YOU THINK

A. Discuss these questions in a group.

1. Is play a catalyst in your life? What activities do you think of as play, and how do they improve your life?

2. Do you agree with the author of Reading 1 that "play is what lifts people out of the mundane"? Explain the reasons for your opinion and give examples to support it.

B. Choose one question and write a paragraph in response. Look back at your Quick Write on page 213 as you think about what you learned.

Reading Skill	Identifying counterarguments and refutations

When you are reading a text, it is important to distinguish the author's opinion from any counterarguments. A **counterargument** is an idea that opposes the author's point of view. It is often introduced by a clause that identifies the source or a clause with a general subject, such as *many experts say* or *some people think*.

Counterargument: <u>The skeptics among the audiences that I talk to say</u>, "Well, duh. Of course you will be happy if you play all the time." . . . <u>Or they might say that</u> if they truly gave in to the desire to experience the joy of free play, they would never get anything done.

A counterargument is generally followed by a **refutation** from the author. A refutation tries to show that the counterargument is weak or incorrect. The refutation is often introduced by an expression that shows disagreement, such as *on the contrary* or *but in fact*.

> **Refutation:**   <u>This is not the case</u>. We don't need to play all the time to be fulfilled. <u>The truth is that</u> in most cases play is a catalyst.

Tip for Success

If you can clearly identify arguments, counterarguments, and refutations, you can better evaluate the author's ideas.

A. Match the counterarguments with the correct refutations. Then underline the clauses and expressions that introduce them.

Counterarguments

1. <u>Some people say that</u> there is no time for play, __f__

2. Some people argue that the office is the wrong place for play. ____

3. There are those who question whether play is a suitable activity for adults. ____

4. Some think that the best games for children have very clear rules. ____

5. Many claim that children can't learn effectively without adult supervision. ____

6. Some experts believe that children have too much free time, ____

Refutations

a. That is not the case. Children actually learn more by creating their own rules.

b. but, in fact, they need this time for creative play and rest.

c. The truth is, however, that employees work more creatively when they are relaxed.

d. In reality, children are very effective at organizing themselves.

e. On the contrary, studies have shown that play can make adults more productive.

f. <u>but the fact is that</u> even a small amount of play is helpful.

 B. Go online for more practice identifying counterarguments and refutations.

READING 2 | Child's Play: It's Not Just for Fun

 **UNIT OBJECTIVE** ▶▶▶ You are going to read an article from a business journal that looks at a type of children's play called *pretend play*. Use the article to gather information and ideas for your Unit Assignment.

PREVIEW THE READING

A. **PREVIEW** The article discusses what children learn from pretend play and questions whether children today have enough opportunities to engage in it. An example of pretend play is when children imagine they are people in a store.

Check (✓) the sentences that you think describe pretend play.

- ☐ The children decide what will happen.
- ☐ It's directed by an adult.
- ☐ It's a quick activity.
- ☐ It's a long activity.
- ☐ It helps children learn to concentrate.
- ☐ It requires imagination.

B. **QUICK WRITE** Is pretend play as a child important? Write for 5–10 minutes in response. Be sure to use this section for your Unit Assignment.

C. **VOCABULARY** Check (✓) the words you know. Then work with a partner to locate each word in the reading. Use clues to help define the words you don't know. Check your definitions in the dictionary.

complex *(adj.)* 🔑	**predetermined** *(adj.)*
conduct *(v.)* 🔑	**regulate** *(v.)*
consequently *(adv.)*	**structured** *(adj.)* 🔑
evident *(adj.)*	**subtle** *(adj.)*
impulsively *(adv.)*	**vital** *(adj.)* 🔑
inhibit *(v.)*	

🔑 Oxford 3000™ words

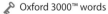

 D. Go online to listen and practice your pronunciation.

WORK WITH THE READING

🔊 **A. Read the article and gather information about the importance of play.**

Child's Play: It's Not Just for Fun

1   Joshua, Alicia, and Scott, five-year-old students in a kindergarten[1] in New York, have decided to "play store." At first one might wonder if this is a good use of their time in school. What value is there in pretending to be in a store? As the game progresses, however, it becomes obvious that playing store is, in fact, a very **complex** activity. In order to play store, Joshua, Alicia, and Scott have to decide on their roles—who will be the storekeeper, who will be the customer, and what role the third child will have. As they play, they must invent and act out scenes and respond to a changing narrative. When problems come up, the children must solve them in order to keep the game going. Through all this, their teacher occasionally steps in to assist them, but he never directs them or takes over their role-playing. While watching the game unfold[2], it becomes clear why many researchers say that pretend play is a critical part of a child's development.

2   In its most basic form, pretend play happens when a young child imagines that one thing is something else; say, a stick is a sword or a banana is a telephone. More complex pretend play, sometimes called *complex imaginative play* or *dramatic play*, involves specific roles and longer make-believe scenes. This is the type of play that Joshua, Alicia, and Scott were engaged in. Clearly, children are building both language skills and social skills while they are involved in complex pretend play: they learn to make compromises and take turns (e.g., "This time you can be the customer and next time I'll be the customer"), they learn to listen carefully to others and cooperate, and they practice problem solving. But children participating in complex pretend play are also developing skills on a much more **subtle** level.

3   In the field of early education, neuroscientist Adele Diamond and psychologist Deborah Leong have been instrumental[3] in promoting the importance of pretend play. According to these two scientists, when children engage in pretend play, they are developing the ability to self-**regulate**. Children who can self-regulate are able to control their emotions and their behavior, and they can resist acting **impulsively**. These children have learned to focus their attention and concentrate on one thing. They can avoid being distracted, and they can make thoughtful choices and decisions. These skills will be **vital** for their academic success in later years.

4   To demonstrate how pretend play nurtures self-regulation, researchers asked a group of four-year-old children to stand still for as long as possible. Most of the children couldn't stand still for more than a minute. However, when the same children were pretending they were

---

[1] **kindergarten:** a school or class for children between the ages of four and six

[2] **unfold:** to develop
[3] **instrumental:** very important

guards at a factory, they were able to stand still for more than four minutes. By pretend playing, these children increased the amount of time they could control their behavior.

5   Pretend play may help young children learn to self-regulate for one interesting reason. During pretend play, children talk aloud to themselves in a special way. Rather than describing what they have done, they tell themselves what they are going to do and how they are going to do it. In other words, they are actively planning and controlling their actions and behavior. This self-regulating talk, sometimes called *private speech*, helps children direct their thinking. Private speech is very common in the pretend play of children. As play becomes more **structured** and less imaginative, however, children use less private speech.

6   Unfortunately, much of the play that young children engage in today is not imaginative play, and **consequently**, it does not allow them to practice self-regulation. When children are playing organized sports, for example, they are being regulated by adults rather than by themselves. They have no chance to practice controlling their own behavior and impulses. Toys, television, and video games also **inhibit** imaginative play because they have **predetermined** scripts; they tell children what to do and how to do it. There is also much less time available for pretend play in kindergarten classes in the United States today. In one recent survey, 254 kindergarten teachers in New York and Los Angeles stated that children in their classes spent less than 30 minutes a day engaging in any kind of play.

7   According to Deborah Leong, "Kids aren't developing the self-regulation skills that they used to." This is **evident** when one compares children's behavior in the past to behavior today. In an experiment **conducted** in 1940, researchers asked children ages three, five, and seven to stand still. The three-year-old children weren't able to stand still at all. The five-year-old children were able to stand still for about three minutes, and the seven-year-old children were able to stand still for as long as the researchers wanted. When this same experiment was repeated recently, neither the three-year-old children nor the five-year-old children were able to stand still at all. The seven-year-old children were barely able to stand still for three minutes. For many educators, the inability of children today to control their behavior is a serious concern.

8   If pretend play truly helps children build social and language skills and learn to self-regulate, then clearly this type of play should be an important part of a child's early education. Educators and parents who think that playing during school hours is a waste of time need to look more carefully at the research. They need to understand that without opportunities for pretend play, children will not develop important behavioral and thinking skills. Play, they would see, isn't just all for fun.

B. **VOCABULARY** Complete the sentences with the vocabulary from Reading 2.

complex *(adj.)*	evident *(adj.)*	predetermined *(adj.)*	subtle *(adj.)*
conduct *(v.)*	impulsively *(adv.)*	regulate *(v.)*	vital *(adj.)*
consequently *(adv.)*	inhibit *(v.)*	structured *(adj.)*	

1. It is important to rest and relax before an exam. Too much stress

can _____ your ability to perform well.

student registration

2. Students must register for classes at their _____ times. Please check the website to find out the time that has been assigned to you.

3. It was _____ from the bruise on the boy's face that he had been hurt.

4. Many Internet services offer tools for parents to _____ what their children can see.

5. The boy got angry and _____ threw the toy across the room. Now he's sorry he did it.

6. The child wasn't listening, so I tried a more _____ approach. I asked her to play with me.

7. Nowadays, teachers spend more time teaching basic skills, and _____, young children have less time to play.

8. Psychology researchers _____ experiments to test their ideas about human behavior.

9. Soccer and tennis are _____ activities; they have very clear rules for players.

10. The ability to play is _____ for human beings. It helps us be happy and innovative.

11. You may think children's games are simple, but they are actually quite _____ and have many rules.

iQ ONLINE **C. Go online for more practice with the vocabulary.**

D. Check (✓) the main idea of the article.

☐ 1. Without the ability to self-regulate, children cannot control their emotions or behavior.

☐ 2. Young children need opportunities for pretend play because it helps them build language and social skills and learn to self-regulate.

☐ 3. All types of play are important for the development of social, language, and thinking skills in young children.

E. Complete the chart with the main idea of each paragraph.

Para.	Topic	Main idea
1	introduction	Pretend play is an important activity for a child's development.
2	the benefits of pretend play	
3	pretend play and the ability to self-regulate	
4	children's ability to control their behavior	
5	why private speech helps children learn to self-regulate	Private speech helps children learn to self-regulate because they talk about what they are going to do and how.
6	ways children play today	
7	behavior of children today versus in the past	
8	conclusion	

F. The author cites research studies to support his ideas about pretend play. Answer the questions about those studies. For questions 1–9, write the paragraph number where you found the answer.

1. What are the names of the scientists who have been instrumental in promoting the importance of pretend play? (para. ____)

   _____

2. What fields of study are they in? (para. ____)

   _____

3. What did researchers ask a group of four-year-old children to do? (para. ____)

   _____

4. How were the children able to increase the time they were able to stand still to four minutes? (para. ____)

   _____

5. How many kindergarten teachers were surveyed? (para. ___)

_____

6. How much time did they report that children in their classes spent

playing? (para. ___) _____

7. What evidence does the author provide to support Deborah Leong's

statement that children aren't developing the self-regulation skills that

they used to? (para. ___)

_____

8. When was the first study conducted? (para. ___) _____

9. How old were the children in the two studies? (para. ___)

_____

10. How long was each group of children able to stand still? Complete the chart.

Age	Past	Recent
3	not able to stand still	
5		
7		

G. Write a detail or example from the reading to support each statement.

1. Children learn important social and language skills when they engage in
   pretend play.

_____

2. Children who can self-regulate can control their behavior.

_____

3. Children are learning to self-regulate when they engage in pretend play.

_____

4. Many types of play don't allow children to practice controlling their
   own behavior.

_____

5. Children today can't control their behavior as well as children in the past.

_____

WRITE WHAT YOU THINK

A. Discuss the questions in a group. Look back at your Quick Write on page 220 as you think about what you learned.

page 220

Critical Thinking Tip

Question 2 in Activity A asks you to imagine, or **hypothesize**, what the author might say. Hypothesizing is what scientists do when they take all the information they know and try to come up with new ideas or explanations.

1. What effects might the inability to self-regulate have on children later in life? Give specific examples to support your answer.

2. Some educators believe that children have enough time to play at home, so they don't need to spend time in school playing. How might the author of Reading 2 respond to this belief?

B. Think about the unit video, Reading 1, and Reading 2 as you discuss the questions. Then choose one question and write a paragraph in response.

1. In Reading 1, Stuart Brown stresses the value of play throughout our lives. Do you think the type of play mentioned in Reading 2 is also important to adults? Why or why not?

2. In schools in many countries, children are spending more and more time studying and less time playing. Is this healthy or unhealthy in your opinion? Why?

Vocabulary Skill | Collocations with prepositions

There are several common collocation patterns with prepositions that are important to recognize and learn.

Verb + preposition

By playing, we **learn about** the mystery and excitement that the world can hold.

Verb + object + preposition

The demands of daily living seem to **rob** us **of** the ability to play.

Adjective + preposition

At some point as we get older, we are made to feel **guilty about** playing.
Children are building both language skills and social skills while they are **involved in** complex pretend play.

Noun + preposition

The beneficial **effects of** getting just a little true play can spread through our lives.

Many verbs, adjectives, and nouns are followed by only one preposition. Others can be followed by various prepositions with different uses or meanings.

Tip for Success

When you write down a new word while reading, check the word to see if there is a preposition you should also write down. Dictionaries often list common collocations.

A. Read the paragraphs and the sentences that follow. Complete the collocations with the correct prepositions.

I have spent a career studying play, communicating the science of play to the public, and working for Fortune 500 companies on how to incorporate it into business. I have used play therapies to help people who are clinically depressed. I frequently talk with groups of parents who inevitably are concerned about what represents healthy play for their kids.

1. Deborah lost three games, but she didn't seem very **concerned** _____ it.

2. Keeping their children amused **represents** a challenge _____ some parents.

3. Many teachers try to **incorporate** play activities _____ their schedules.

4. My brother is **working** _____ a local businessman _____ new designs for children's playground equipment.

When children engage in pretend play, they are developing the ability to self-regulate. Children who can self-regulate are able to control their emotions and their behavior, and they can resist acting impulsively. These children have learned to focus their attention and concentrate on one thing. They can avoid being distracted, and they can make thoughtful choices and decisions. These skills will be vital for their academic success in later years.

5. John thinks the local play group has improved his son's **ability** _____ compromise.

6. Fun time is **vital** _____ parent-child relationships.

7. Vera has been having trouble **concentrating** _____ her homework.

8. Children need the opportunity to **engage** _____ fun activities with adults.

B. Write five sentences using collocations from Activity A.

1. _____

2. _____

3. _____

4. _____

5. _____

  C. Go online for more practice with collocations with prepositions.

WRITING

UNIT OBJECTIVE ▶▶▶▶ At the end of this unit, you will write a persuasive essay that explains how video games are helpful or harmful to children. This essay will include specific information from the readings, the unit video, and your own ideas.

Writing Skill   Writing a persuasive essay

In a **persuasive essay**, the writer presents an issue, takes a position on the issue, and develops an argument to convince the reader that this position is correct. Persuasive essays often require research: you must collect evidence that relates to the topic, such as facts, statistics, and quotations from expert sources.

Consider this question: *Is play essential to a child's healthy development?* As the writer, you can argue that play is essential or that play is not essential. Either way, your position should be expressed clearly in a thesis statement in your introduction.

Then you must persuade the reader that this position is right. Your body paragraphs should:

- clearly present the main arguments that support your thesis statement
- include facts, evidence, and examples that support each main argument
- present one or more counterarguments to show that you have considered opposing opinions
- acknowledge counterargument(s) where appropriate and respond to them with refutations

Finally, your conclusion should summarize all the arguments you have stated. It may also give a warning, prediction, or suggestion about what should happen next.

See the Reading Skill on pages 218–219 for information on counterarguments and refutations.

A. **WRITING MODEL** Read the model persuasive essay. Circle the thesis statement. Underline the main ideas in paragraphs 2, 3, and 4.

Are Competitive Games Harmful to Children?

1   There is a cry of rage, and a tennis racket crashes to the ground. Jake, age 7, has just lost another match and is now in tears beside the court. His sister Sally, just one year older, looks at her mother and rolls her eyes: it is hard to enjoy winning when this keeps happening.

It is not an unusual situation, and it is one reason why many people argue that competition is bad for children. However, the truth is that competitive games are valuable preparation for adult life.

2   Games with winners and losers give children the chance to experience life's ups and downs. Take Jake, for example: even though he is unhappy now, he will probably be smiling and laughing with his sister in a few minutes, just like the last time this happened. Gradually, he will learn that the world does not end when you lose a game. Eventually, he may even be able to lose with a smile on his face. This is an important lesson. Not everything in life goes the way you would like, and it is important to know how to handle disappointment when it occurs.

3   Children who participate in competitive games develop qualities that will allow them to succeed in the complex world of adult life. For example, one of the missions of the Youth Olympic Games is to inspire young people to adopt the Olympic values, which include striving, determination, and optimism. Competition

creates the desire to do better. Children have to learn to succeed in a competitive atmosphere in order to take advantage of opportunities in the future. Although it is possible to win by chance occasionally, people who win and keep winning work very hard to achieve their success.

4   On the negative side, there are those who will say that competition actually encourages some bad values, which does happen. It is common to see sports competitions in which the desire to win has replaced the desire to have fun. You may even see very young children playing violently—like the sports stars they see on TV. While the bad behavior of young athletes is troubling, the problem is not the competition itself. In reality, the blame lies with the professional players who are bad role models for these children. In fact, a recent study of young athletes by the School of Physical Health Education at the University of Wyoming showed an improvement in mood after exercise; athletes were less depressed or tense.

5   Of course, there are parents who argue that children of Jake's age are too young to handle the pain of losing. But whether we like it or not, adult life is very competitive, and keeping children away from competition does them more harm than good. If children do not learn how to compete, they will be defeated by people who can. It is an unfortunate fact of life: whether ten or a hundred people want the same job, there can be only one winner. Wouldn't you want your child to be that person?

Writing **Tip**

The combination of counterargument and refutation is a powerful technique. It shows that you have considered other opinions and creates an opportunity to say what is wrong with them. This can be more persuasive than concentrating entirely on your own point of view.

B. Reread the essay on pages 228–229. Then circle the correct answer.

1. The thesis statement is ____.
   a. at the beginning of the introduction
   b. at the end of the introduction
   c. in the first body paragraph

2. The example of Jake in the introduction is ____.
   a. the author's view
   b. a counterargument
   c. background information

3. Consider this sentence from paragraph 2: "Games with winners and losers give children the chance to experience life's ups and downs." This is ____.
   a. the main idea of the paragraph
   b. a fact that supports the main idea
   c. a counterargument

4. Consider this sentence from paragraph 3: "Children have to learn to succeed in a competitive atmosphere in order to take advantage of opportunities in the future." This is ____.
   a. the thesis statement
   b. an example that supports a main idea
   c. a counterargument

5. Consider this sentence from paragraph 4: "In reality, the blame lies with the professional players who are bad role models for these children." This is ____.
   a. the main idea of the paragraph
   b. a counterargument
   c. a refutation

6. Which counterargument does the author recognize as true?
   a. Competition is bad for children.
   b. Children of Jake's age are too young to handle the pain of losing.
   c. Competition can encourage some bad values.

7. In the conclusion, the author does *not* ____.
   a. suggest what should happen next
   b. make a prediction
   c. give a warning

C. Read the thesis statement and first body paragraph of a persuasive essay. Write possible arguments, counterarguments, and refutations for the essay.

Thesis statement: Scheduling too many activities may be harmful for children because it doesn't allow enough time for creative free play and having every hour of every day filled can be stressful.

Body paragraph 1

Overscheduling of children's activities, leaving them little time for free play, may be harmful. Pediatricians and child psychologists agree that play, especially child-driven free play, is essential to children's development. However, many children today don't have enough time for sufficient free play. The reason is overscheduling of their activities. While parents often do this because they work and think they need activities for their children after school, children really need free time in their schedules just to play and create their own fun. Parents also believe that structured extracurricular activities like music and sports are necessary to prepare their children for when it comes time to go to college. Academics are given more time, even in kindergarten, for this reason.

Argument: Full schedules don't allow enough time for creative free play.

Counterargument: Many parents believe that their children need activities after school, especially structured activities like music and sports to prepare them for college.

Refutation: In fact, limiting extracurricular activities and allowing time for creative play may help children do better in the activities they do participate in, so they won't be any less prepared for college.

---

1. Argument: Pediatricians and child psychologists agree that play, especially child-driven free play, is essential to children's development.

   Counterargument: Some educators argue that children have more to learn in this complex world, so more time needs to be spent on academic subjects and less on play.

   Refutation: _____

2. Argument: Young children need time with no activities.

   Counterargument: _____

   Refutation: Doing nothing helps children learn to entertain themselves and not depend on others.

3. Argument: _____

   Counterargument: There are child psychologists who say it's not scheduling too many activities that's bad. The real problem is how much importance parents put on doing well in extracurricular activities, which causes children stress.

   Refutation: _____

4. Argument: _____

   Counterargument: _____

   Refutation: _____

D. **Write the arguments or counterarguments and refutations to these ideas from Reading 1 and Reading 2.**

1. Argument: Playing "store" is a good use of children's time.

   Counterargument: _____

   Refutation: _____

2. Argument: It is unfortunate that children play so many organized sports.

   Counterargument: _____

   Refutation: _____

3. Argument: Children need to use their imaginations when they play, not just follow a script.

   Counterargument: _____

   Refutation: _____

4. Argument: _____

   Counterargument: Others believe that employees should not play at work because they are getting paid to work, not to play.

   Refutation: _____

5. Argument: _____

   Counterargument: On the other hand, some people believe play should be about following rules, not creating them.

   Refutation: _____

 E. **Go online for more practice with persuasive essays.**

In an argument, you can use certain adverb clauses to acknowledge an idea and show that it is less important than the idea in the main clause. This is called **concession**. Concession clauses convey the idea "That's true, but . . ." Some subordinators that show concession are:

| although | even though | though | while | despite the fact that |

> **Although it is possible to win by chance occasionally,** people who win and keep winning work very hard to achieve their success.
> (Argument = If you want to win often, hard work is important.)
>
> **While the bad behavior of young athletes is troubling,** the problem is not the competition itself.
> (Argument = Competition does not cause bad behavior in players.)

Consider these two ideas about recess in school schedules.

Recess is important for children.   Recess reduces class time.

Depending on your point of view, one idea is your argument, and the other is the counterargument that you want to refute.

>   concession clause   main clause
> Even though it is important for children, recess reduces class time.
> (Argument = Recess **should** be shorter.)
>
>   concession clause   main clause
> Even though it reduces class time, recess is important for children.
> (Argument = Recess **should not** be shorter.)

Tip for Success

A concession clause often comes before a main clause. When this happens, a pronoun may come before the noun it refers to.

A. Use the subordinators in parentheses to combine the sentences. First, write a sentence that supports idea *a*. Then write a sentence that supports idea *b*. When combining sentences, replace the subject in one of the clauses with a pronoun.

1. a. Children need lots of active play.

    b. It is vital that children rest.

    (although) _Although it is vital that they rest, children need lots of active play._

    (while) _____

    _____

2. a. Competitive play is helpful for children.

b. Competitive play encourages bad behavior.

(even though) _____

_____

(despite the fact that) _____

_____

3. a. Losing a game is a horrible experience.

b. Losing a game can be a good lesson for children.

(while) _____

_____

(though) _____

_____

B. Complete the sentences with your own ideas. Then discuss your sentences with a partner. Identify the argument and counterargument in each sentence.

1. Even though sports are difficult for some children, _____

_____

_____.

2. Although _____

_____,

businesses should encourage more fun activities in the office.

3. Despite the fact that _____

_____,

writing programs should not be eliminated from schools.

4. Though people say they are too busy to relax, _____

_____

_____.

C. Go online for more practice with adverb clauses of concession.

D. Go online for the grammar expansion.

Write a persuasive essay

 In this assignment, you are going to write a persuasive essay about how video games are helpful or harmful to children. As you prepare your essay, think about the Unit Question, "Why is it important to play?" Use information from Reading 1, Reading 2, the unit video, and your work in this unit to support your essay. Refer to the Self-Assessment checklist on page 236.

iQ ONLINE   Go to the Online Writing Tutor for a writing model and alternate Unit Assignments.

PLAN AND WRITE

A. BRAINSTORM Follow these steps to help you organize your ideas.

1. Work in groups. Discuss the questions based on your experience.
   a. Why do children play video games?
   b. Where do they play them? At home? Somewhere else?
   c. Do children play video games alone or with others? Who?
   d. How often do they play, and how long do they spend playing video games?
   e. What are some different kinds of video games? Are some better for children than others?
   f. What skills can children learn from playing video games?

2. Complete the T-chart with your ideas.

Arguments for letting children play video games	Arguments against letting children play video games

B. PLAN Follow these steps to plan your essay.

1. Compare the arguments in question 2 in Activity A and decide if video games are good or bad for children. Then complete the chart on page 236. Choose three arguments to persuade your reader that video games either help or harm children. Think of possible counterarguments. Then respond to them with refutations.

Arguments for or against	Counterarguments	Refutations

Writing Tip

You may wish to research quotations to provide facts and opinions that support your ideas. It is important to give the sources for any ideas that you use in your own writing, whether you paraphrase or quote the original words.

2. Go to the Online Resources to download and complete the outline for your persuasive essay.

C. **WRITE** Use your **PLAN** notes to write your essay. Go to *iQ Online* to use the Online Writing Tutor.

1. Write your persuasive essay. Remember to use arguments, counterarguments, and refutations to persuade your audience.

2. Look at the Self-Assessment checklist below to guide your writing.

REVISE AND EDIT

A. **PEER REVIEW** Read your partner's essay. Then go online and use the Peer Review worksheet. Discuss the review with your partner.

B. **REWRITE** Based on your partner's review, revise, and rewrite your essay.

C. **EDIT** Complete the Self-Assessment checklist as you prepare to write the final draft of your essay. Be prepared to hand in your work or discuss it in class.

SELF-ASSESSMENT		
Yes	No	
☐	☐	Does the essay build a convincing argument using facts, evidence, and examples?
☐	☐	Are counterarguments and refutations introduced clearly?
☐	☐	Are adverb clauses of concession used appropriately?
☐	☐	Are collocations with prepositions used correctly?
☐	☐	Does the essay include vocabulary from the unit?
☐	☐	Did you check the essay for punctuation, spelling, and grammar?

D. **REFLECT** Go to the Online Discussion Board to discuss these questions.

1. What is something new you learned in this unit?

2. Look back at the Unit Question—Why is it important to play? Is your answer different now than when you started the unit? If yes, how is it different? Why?

TRACK YOUR SUCCESS

Circle the words and phrases you have learned in this unit.

Nouns
ability (to) 🔑
catalyst
effect (of) 🔑
skeptic
therapy

Verbs
concentrate (on) 🔑 AWL
conduct 🔑 AWL
incorporate (…into) AWL
inhibit AWL
learn (about) 🔑
regulate AWL
represent (…for) 🔑
strive
work (with) 🔑

Phrasal Verbs
engage in 🔑
give in to
rob…of

Adjectives
beneficial AWL
complex 🔑 AWL
concerned (about) 🔑
conflicted AWL
evident AWL
grim
guilty (about) 🔑
innovative AWL
involved (in) 🔑 AWL
mundane
predetermined

rigid AWL
structured 🔑 AWL
subtle
vital (for) 🔑

Adverbs
consequently AWL
impulsively

Subordinators
although 🔑
despite the fact
  that 🔑 AWL
even though
though 🔑
while 🔑

🔑 Oxford 3000™ words
AWL Academic Word List

Check (✓) the skills you learned. If you need more work on a skill, refer to the page(s) in parentheses.

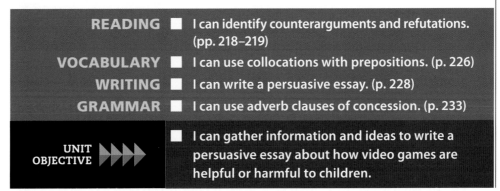

READING	☐ I can identify counterarguments and refutations. (pp. 218–219)
VOCABULARY	☐ I can use collocations with prepositions. (p. 226)
WRITING	☐ I can write a persuasive essay. (p. 228)
GRAMMAR	☐ I can use adverb clauses of concession. (p. 233)
UNIT OBJECTIVE ▶▶▶	☐ I can gather information and ideas to write a persuasive essay about how video games are helpful or harmful to children.

iQ ONLINE extends your learning beyond the classroom. This online content is specifically designed for you! *iQ Online* gives you flexible access to essential content.

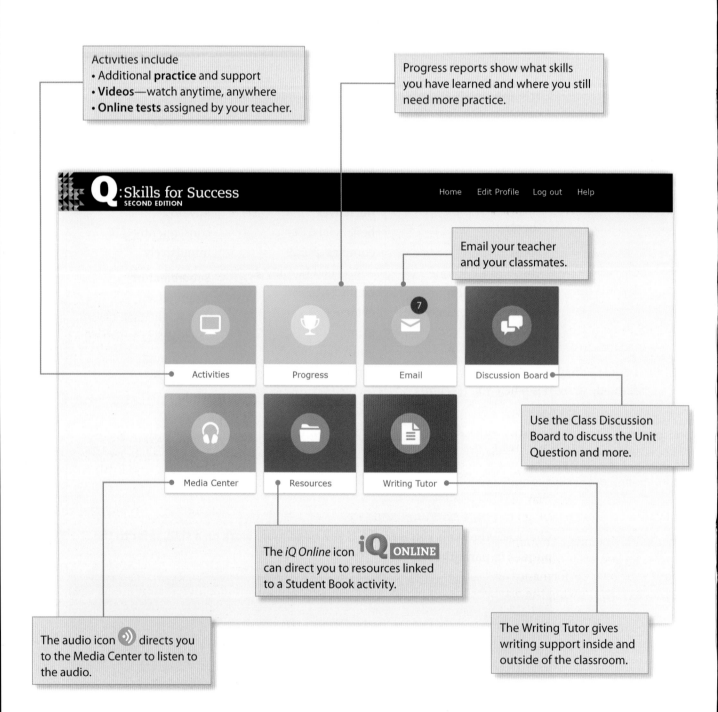

Activities include
- Additional **practice** and support
- **Videos**—watch anytime, anywhere
- **Online tests** assigned by your teacher.

Progress reports show what skills you have learned and where you still need more practice.

Email your teacher and your classmates.

Use the Class Discussion Board to discuss the Unit Question and more.

The *iQ Online* icon **iQ ONLINE** can direct you to resources linked to a Student Book activity.

The audio icon directs you to the Media Center to listen to the audio.

The Writing Tutor gives writing support inside and outside of the classroom.

Q:Skills for Success
SECOND EDITION

Home   Edit Profile   Log out   Help

Activities   Progress   Email   Discussion Board

Media Center   Resources   Writing Tutor

SEE THE INSIDE FRONT COVER FOR HOW TO REGISTER FOR *iQ ONLINE* FOR THE FIRST TIME.

Take Control of Your Learning

You have the choice of where and how you complete the activities. Access your activities and view your progress at any time.

Your teacher may

- assign *iQ Online* as homework,
- do the activities with you in class, or
- let you complete the activities at a pace that is right for you.

iQ Online makes it easy to access everything you need.

Set Clear Goals

STEP 1 If it is your first time, look through the site. See what learning opportunities are available.

STEP 2 The Student Book provides the framework and purpose for each online activity. Before going online, notice the goal of the exercises you are going to do.

STEP 3 Stay on top of your work, following the teacher's instructions.

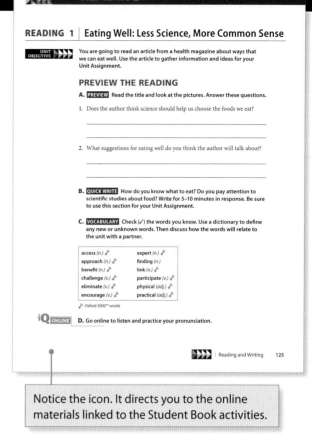

Notice the icon. It directs you to the online materials linked to the Student Book activities.

STEP 4 Use *iQ Online* for review. You can use the materials any time. It is easy for you to do follow-up activities when you have missed a class or want to review.

Manage Your Progress

The activities in *iQ Online* are designed for you to work independently. You can become a confident learner by monitoring your progress and reviewing the activities at your own pace. You may already be used to working online, but if you are not, go to your teacher for guidance.

Check 'View Reports' to monitor your progress. The reports let you track your own progress at a glance. Think about your own performance and set new goals that are right for you, following the teacher's instructions.

iQ Online is a research-based solution specifically designed for English language learners that extends learning beyond the classroom. I hope these steps help you make the most of this essential content.

Chantal Hemmi, EdD TEFL
Center for Language Education and Research
Sophia University, Japan

VOCABULARY LIST AND CEFR CORRELATION

🔑 The keywords of the **Oxford 3000™** have been carefully selected by a group of language experts and experienced teachers as the words which should receive priority in vocabulary study because of their importance and usefulness.

AWL **The Academic Word List** is the most principled and widely accepted list of academic words. Averil Coxhead gathered information from academic materials across the academic disciplines to create this word list.

The Common European Framework of Reference for Languages (CEFR) provides a basic description of what language learners have to do to use language effectively. The system contains 6 reference levels: **A1, A2, B1, B2, C1, C2**. CEFR leveling provided by the Word Family Framework, created by Richard West and published by the British Council. http://www.learnenglish.org.uk/wff/

UNIT 1

achievement (n.) 🔑 AWL, B1

acknowledged (for) (adj.) 🔑 AWL, C1

confront (v.) 🔑, B1

constrained (adj.) AWL, C1

criteria (n.) 🔑 AWL, A2

inclined (adj.) AWL, C1

inherently (adv.) AWL, C2

initiative (n.) 🔑 AWL, B2

pursue (v.) 🔑 AWL, A2

resolve (n.) 🔑 AWL, B2

version (n.) 🔑 AWL, B2

UNIT 2

concept (n.) 🔑 AWL, B2

distinguish (v.) 🔑, B2

evolve (v.) AWL, B1

feature (v.) 🔑 AWL, B2

focus on (phr. v.) 🔑 AWL, B2

in theory (idm.) 🔑 AWL, B2

individual (n.) 🔑 AWL, B1

investment (n.) 🔑 AWL, B2

liberate (v.) AWL, C1

mentally (adv.) 🔑 AWL, B2

minimize (v.) AWL, C1

negative (n.) 🔑 AWL, B2

neutral (adj.) AWL, B2

potential (adj.) 🔑 AWL, B2

priority (n.) 🔑 AWL, B2

promote (v.) 🔑 AWL, B2

remove (v.) 🔑 AWL, B2

residence (n.) AWL, B2

tend (v.) 🔑, B2

urban (adj.) 🔑, B2

visualize (v.) AWL, C2

UNIT 3

accurately (adv.) 🔑 AWL, B1

assumption (n.) AWL, B1

capture (v.) 🔑, B1

colleague (n.) 🔑 AWL, A2

consistent with (phr.) 🔑 AWL, B1

creative (adj.) 🔑 AWL, B1

equipped with (phr.) AWL, B2

exaggerate (v.) 🔑, C1

motivate (v.) AWL, B2

period (n.) 🔑 AWL, B1

rely on (phr. v.) 🔑 AWL, B2

select (v.) 🔑 AWL, B1

significance (n.) AWL, C1

suspect (v.) 🔑, B2

theoretically (adv.) AWL, C2

UNIT 4

advocate (v.) AWL, B2

alternative (n.) 🔑 AWL, B2

attain (v.) AWL, C1

complement (n.) AWL, C2

craft (n.) 🔑, B1

determination (n.) 🔑, B2

distinctive (adj.) AWL, B2

ensure (v.) 🔑 AWL, B2

essentially (adv.) 🔑, B2

exhibit (v.) 🔑 AWL, B2

imagery (n.) AWL, C2

maintain (v.) 🔑 AWL, B2

nerve (n.) 🔑, B1

recognize (v.) 🔑, B2

talent (n.) 🔑, B1

undertake (v.) AWL, B1

unique (adj.) 🔑 AWL, B2

UNIT 5

access (n.) 🔑 AWL, B1

approach (n.) 🔑 AWL, B2

benefit (n.) 🔑 AWL, B1

challenge (v.) 🔑 AWL, B2

contribute (v.) 🔑 AWL, B2

currently (adv.) 🔑, B2

eliminate (v.) 🔑 AWL, B1

encourage (v.) 🔑, B1

expert (n.) 🔑 AWL, B1

link (n.) 🔑 AWL, B2

major (adj.) 🔑 AWL, B2

modify (v.) AWL, C1

participate (v.) 🔑 AWL, B2

physical (adj.) 🔑 AWL, B2

practical (adj.) 🔑, B2

primarily (adv.) 🔑 AWL, B2

shift (v.) 🔑 AWL, B2

source (n.) 🔑 AWL, B2

stable (adj.) 🔑 AWL, B1

UNIT 6

acquire (v.) 🔑 AWL, B2

adjust (v.) 🔑 AWL, B2

ambiguous (adj.) AWL, C2

analyze (v.) 🔑 AWL, B2

anticipate (v.) 🔑 AWL, C1

approach (v.) 🔑 AWL, B1

constant (adj.) 🔑 AWL, B2

contact (v.) 🔑 AWL, A2

enable *(v.)* 🔑 AWL, B2
encounter *(v.)* 🔑 AWL, B2
expertise *(n.)* AWL, B2
fixed *(adj.)* 🔑, B2
incentive *(n.)* AWL, C2
income *(n.)* 🔑 AWL, B2
institution *(n.)* 🔑 AWL, B2
interpret *(v.)* 🔑 AWL, B2
particular *(adj.)* 🔑, B2
pattern *(n.)* 🔑, B2
permanent *(adj.)* 🔑, B1
reluctant *(adj.)* AWL, C1
transition *(n.)* 🔑 AWL, C1
utilize *(v.)* AWL, B2

UNIT 7

adopt *(v.)* 🔑, B2
cite *(v.)* AWL, B2
confirm *(v.)* 🔑 AWL, B2
conflict *(n.)* 🔑 AWL, B2
controversial *(adj.)* AWL, B2
extensive *(adj.)* 🔑, B2
genuinely *(adv.)* 🔑, B2
inevitable *(adj.)* 🔑 AWL, C1
intervene *(v.)* AWL, C2
moral *(adj.)* 🔑, B2
motive *(n.)* AWL, B2
preliminary *(adj.)* AWL, C1
significant *(adj.)* 🔑 AWL, B2
sustainable *(adj.)* AWL, C1

UNIT 8

beneficial *(adj.)* AWL, B2
complex *(adj.)* 🔑 AWL, B2
conduct *(v.)* 🔑 AWL, B2
conflicted *(adj.)* AWL, C1
consequently *(adv.)* AWL, B2
evident *(adj.)* AWL, B2
incorporate *(v.)* AWL, C2
inhibit *(v.)* AWL, C1
innovative *(adj.)* AWL, C1
regulate *(v.)* AWL, B2
rigid *(adj.)* AWL, B2
structured *(adj.)* 🔑 AWL, B2
vital *(adj.)* 🔑, B2

AUTHORS AND CONSULTANTS

Authors

Debra Daise taught ESL in Colorado for many years. She has served in a number of positions in Colorado TESOL and has long been interested in helping students develop a love of reading and writing.

Charl Norloff is currently teaching ESL methodology courses at the University of Colorado where she taught ESL for 30 years. Prior to that, she taught EFL in the Middle East. She has a special interest in teaching reading and writing to help students prepare for academic success.

Series Consultants

ONLINE INTEGRATION

Chantal Hemmi holds an Ed.D. TEFL and is a Japan-based teacher trainer and curriculum designer. Since leaving her position as Academic Director of the British Council in Tokyo, she has been teaching at the Center for Language Education and Research at Sophia University on an EAP/CLIL program offered for undergraduates. She delivers lectures and teacher trainings throughout Japan, Indonesia, and Malaysia.

COMMUNICATIVE GRAMMAR

Nancy Schoenfeld holds an M.A. in TESOL from Biola University in La Mirada, California, and has been an English language instructor since 2000. She has taught ESL in California and Hawaii, and EFL in Thailand and Kuwait. She has also trained teachers in the United States and Indonesia. Her interests include teaching vocabulary, extensive reading, and student motivation. She is currently an English Language Instructor at Kuwait University.

WRITING

Marguerite Ann Snow holds a Ph.D. in Applied Linguistics from UCLA. She teaches in the TESOL M.A. program in the Charter College of Education at California State University, Los Angeles. She was a Fulbright scholar in Hong Kong and Cyprus. In 2006, she received the President's Distinguished Professor award at Cal State, LA. She has trained EFL teachers in Algeria, Argentina, Brazil, Egypt, Libya, Morocco, Pakistan, Peru, Spain, and Turkey. She is the author/editor of publications in the areas of integrated content, English for academic purposes, and standards for English teaching and learning. She recently served as a co-editor of *Teaching English as a Second or Foreign Language* (4th ed.).

VOCABULARY

Cheryl Boyd Zimmerman is a Professor at California State University, Fullerton. She specializes in second-language vocabulary acquisition, an area in which she is widely published. She teaches graduate courses on second-language acquisition, culture, vocabulary, and the fundamentals of TESOL and is a frequent invited speaker on topics related to vocabulary teaching and learning. She is the author of *Word Knowledge: A Vocabulary Teacher's Handbook* and Series Director of *Inside Reading, Inside Writing,* and *Inside Listening and Speaking,* all published by Oxford University Press.

ASSESSMENT

Lawrence J. Zwier holds an M.A. in TESL from the University of Minnesota. He is currently the Associate Director for Curriculum Development at the English Language Center at Michigan State University in East Lansing. He has taught ESL/EFL in the United States, Saudi Arabia, Malaysia, Japan, and Singapore.